Private and Public on Social Network Sites

European University Studies

Europäische Hochschulschriften

Publications Universitaires Européennes

Series XL Communication

Reihe XL Kommunikationswissenschaft und Publizistik

Série XL Media et Journalisme, Communications

Volume/Band **109**

Jingwei Wu

Private and Public on Social Network Sites

Differences and Similarities between Germany and China in a Globalized World

PL ACADEMIC RESEARCH

Bibliografische Information der Deutschen Nationalbibliothek
The Deutsche Nationalbibliothek lists this publication in the Deutsche Nationalbibliografie; detailed bibliographic data is available in the internet at http://dnb.d-nb.de.

Zugl.: Berlin, Freie Univ., Diss., 2016

D 188
ISSN 0176-3725
ISBN 978-3-631-68103-9 (Print)
E-ISBN 978-3-653-07222-8 (E-PDF)
E-ISBN 978-3-631-70730-2 (EPUB)
E-ISBN 978-3-631-70731-9 (MOBI)
DOI 10.3726/b11197

PL Academic Research is an Imprint of Peter Lang GmbH.
Peter Lang – Frankfurt am Main · Bern · Bruxelles · New York · Oxford · Warszawa · Wien

This publication has been peer reviewed.

www.peterlang.com

Abstract

As people across the world increasingly reveal private information and political opinions on SNSs, the boundary between "the private" and "the public" becomes blurred while different understandings of this boundary across countries begin to exhibit some similarities. Based on these phenomena, this dissertation aims to answer the following questions: 1) where is the boundary between "the private" and "the public" on SNSs? 2) Is there a difference or a similarity in the boundary between "the private" and "the public" on SNSs across different countries? By reviewing different notions of "the private" and "the public" using different social approaches and procedures, I select the framework of sociability to investigate the distinction between private and public. Research using this theoretical framework is conducted by online surveys and interviews with selected SNSs users in Germany and China. My study points out that the clear boundary of "the private" and "the public" on SNSs is a result of acts of disclosure and/or withdrawal of personal information and political opinions. Globalization and mediatization, to a certain extent, contribute to similarities among different countries but do not erase the differences in their respective boundaries.

Zusammenfassung

In einer Zeit, in der Menschen weltweit eine Vielzahl privater Informationen und politischer Meinungen in sozialen Online-Netzwerken, so genannten Social Network Sites (SNSs), äußern und freigeben, scheint es, dass die Grenzen zwischen privatem und öffentlichem Leben verschwimmen. Außerdem sind Ähnlichkeiten in der Definition dieser Grenzen in unterschiedlichen Kulturen zu erkennen. Aufgrund der genannten Phänomene konzentriert sich das Promotionsprojekt auf folgende zentrale Forschungsfragen: 1. Wo liegt die Grenze zwischen Privatem und Öffentlichem in Bezug auf SNSs? 2. Gibt es Unterschiede oder Gemeinsamkeiten in der Abgrenzung zwischen Privatem und Öffentlichem im Rahmen eines interkulturellen Hintergrunds? Durch Prüfung von Privatheit und Öffentlichkeit unter Berücksichtigung verschiedener sozialer Aspekte und Verfahren werden die Rahmenbedingungen für Geselligkeit ermittelt und so die Unterschiede zwischen Privatheit und Öffentlichkeit analysiert. Dieser theoretische Rahmen wird auch durch Umfragen und Interviews mit SNSs-Nutzern in Deutschland und China gestützt. Meine Studie weist darauf hin, dass eine klare Grenze als Ergebnis der kontrollierten Verteilung persönlicher Daten und politischer Meinungen tatsächlich auch in SNSs existiert. Menschen aus unterschiedlichen Ländern definieren die Grenze zwischen Privatem und Öffentlichem unterschiedlich, auch wenn durch Globalisierung und Mediatisierung einige Ähnlichkeiten entstehen können.

Acknowledgments

This dissertation is not only my hard work, it is also an achievement filled with encouragement, support, love and appreciation. Five years ago, I embarked on an arduous climb up a steep and challenging mountain that was my doctoral research. It was the most demanding period of my academic life, but I was extremely lucky to have all of the following people who have held my hand throughout the entire journey:

Firstly, I would like to thank primary supervisor, Prof. Dr. Klaus Beck. He is the reason I came to Berlin for my doctoral studies. Every word he spoke to me brimmed with encouragement. When I was struggling to make ends meet concurrently with trying to complete my dissertation, his encouragement provided me with endless strength. His works in the field of Computer Mediated Communication, Communication Theory and Communication Sociology offered a lot of inspiration for my dissertation. His patient guidance, detailed comments and goodwill are very much appreciated. I am also grateful to Prof. Dr. Martin Emmer, my secondary supervisor, for tolerating my strange writing style, patiently helping me refine my ideas, offering fresh suggestions, and directing my theoretical concepts to operationalized surveys.

Next, I am also grateful to the professors and colleagues at New York University (NYU), where I was fortunate enough to be invited by Prof. Rodney Benson for an academic exchange program. There, he provided me with a lot of useful literature and suggestions. His courses on communication theory are some of the best theoretical courses I have ever attended. Prof. Helen Nissenbaum and my colleagues of the Privacy Research Group at NYU also helped me a lot with the designing of the questionnaire. I'm especially grateful to Danah Boyd, with whom I was lucky enough to engage in a short conversation, as she taught me more than I ever could learn by myself about research in the area of Privacy. Also, I thank Lily H. Chumley for having helped in the location of a suitable theoretical framework for this dissertation.

During my Ph.D. study, I was extremely lucky to have financial support from the Deutscher Akademischer Austausch Dienst (DAAD), FAZIT Stiftung for international conferences, as well as the Excellent Ph.D. Student Award from the Chinese Scholarship Council. Thanks to their support, I could concentrate on my research.

I would also like to thank my other professors, colleagues and friends. Prof. Dr. Barbara Pfetsch offered a helpful perspective in the analysis of diversities and similarities in a globalized world. Her courses on Political Communication also provided the basic theories for my dissertation. Fabian Klein, Vincenzo Di Giuseppe, Simon Berghofer and Dirk von Schneidemesser provided a lot of helpful comments and suggestions. Zhiwei Xu assisted in the conducting of the surveys in Beijing. Hai Liang helped in my data analysis. Additionally, Wendy Ashleigh Teo offered her professional skills in editing. I am especially thankful for all her efforts and patience in improving the quality of my dissertation.

I would like to sincerely express my appreciation for Prof. Dr. Alexander Görke, Prof. Dr. Carola Richter and Dr. Leyla Dogruel. As a committee, their support, guidance, and advice are invaluable.

My greatest debt is to my parents – Jinxing Wu and Likun Zhang, as well as my husband – Han Wang. Their emotional and financial support made this dissertation possible. This dissertation is dedicated to them.

I really appreciate all the people who have helped and encouraged me. They are like a beacon of light in my life, guiding my way along this academic journey.

Charlottenburg, Berlin JINGWEI WU
May 2016

Contents

I. Introduction

1.1 The Problem

With the diffusion of new communication technology, scholars claimed that the division between the private and public spheres is becoming blurred (Meyrowitz 1985, p. 71, Habermas 1991a, p. 141–158, Thompson 1995, p. 64). The global widespread of Internet and Communication Technology (ICTs) has changed the social structure, communication channels and personal relationships, and called considerable attention to the distinction between "the private" and "the public". Meanwhile, people around the world seem to become increasingly similar, rather than different, in regards to the usage of ICTs, a phenomenon that may result in the emergence of a global internet culture. The utilization of the Internet gives rise to the spread of "world-system status, privatization, democracy and cosmopolitanism" so that democracy is promulgated far and wide (Guillén and Suárez 2005, p. 45). Internet users also share similarities in their attitudes to online freedom of speech, privacy protection, trust and information security (Bellman, Johnson et al. 2004, p. 3, Dutta, Dutton et al. 2011, p. 6).

Although they hail from different countries, majority of the Internet users support the idea of online privacy. This trend indicates that levels of apprehensiveness are becoming more homogenous across the world, even in countries where no previous tradition of privacy existed, such as China. Accordingly, concerns over privacy increase with the modernization of Chinese society, the development of Chinese market economy and the changing social relations (Yuan, Feng et al. 2013, p. 1027–1029). Users across several countries, not only in China, feel that people should be able to freely express their opinions on the Internet (Dutta, Dutton et al. 2011, p. 12). The emerging Internet and ICTs seem to provide an effective domain for information exchanges, opinion expression and political deliberation process, which may benefit democracy ultimately. With a wide accessibility, the Internet facilitates better political participation and discussion, particularly for the resource-poor groups in civil society. Although members of these groups lack the ease of accessibility to traditional mass media and consequently, find it difficult to get involved in the public sphere, there are alternative platforms that create opportunities for political or civic participation on the Internet accessible to them. Not to mention in the last decade, we have witnessed the emergence of "Grassroots". Vast arrays of civic forums, through which views are exchanged and deliberated freely among citizens, provide platforms for individuals to express their opinions. The BBC World Service poll conducted across

26 countries in 2010 revealed that 78% adults felt that they enjoyed more freedom thanks to the Internet (BBC 2010, p. 1).

In practice, recent years have seen the emerging Social Network Sites (SNSs) gaining great popularity and amassing numerous users across the world while changing their communication networks at the same time. According to Ellison and Boyd (2013, p. 151)'s widely used definition:

> *"A social network site is a networked communication platform in which participants 1) have uniquely identifiable profiles that consist of user-supplied content, content provided by other users, and/or system-provided data; 2) can publicly articulate connections that can be viewed and traversed by others; and 3) can consume, produce, and/or interact with streams of user generated content provided by their connections on the site. The list of other users with whom a connection is shared is not limited to connections like friend (Facebook, MySpace) or relative (Geni), but also includes connections like follower (Twitter), professional (LinkedIn) or subscriber (YouTube)."*

SNSs are products of a marriage between ICTs and online networks. Some characteristics of Computer Mediated Communication (CMC) exert considerable effects on the disclosure behavior of people, such as the reduced nonverbal cues, the management of presentation and the pace to react and anonymity (McKenna and Bargh 2000, p. 60–62, Schouten, Valkenburg et al. 2009). CMC is different from Face-to-Face communication (FtFC) in that the former helps to reduce the handicaps of interaction, visual anonymity and uncertainty, and gives rise to sharing more private information (Joinson 2001, p. 188–189, Tidwell and Walther 2002, p. 332); whereas the latter may cause more risks to disclosure due to the uniqueness and ease of recognition of personal identity. Therefore, the inclination of disclosure behavior is a special but important phenomenon for the online interaction. In addition to the aforementioned characteristics of CMC, the most prominent attribute of SNSs is the networked communication. Users are connected via other nodes, so that ego-centered communicational networks are constructed. They get involved in these social networks which connect with huge number of other users. Generally, users are required to fill out some basic personal information, such as name, birthdate and gender, which is a kind of expression behavior. The interaction within these networks, therefore, can be increased, while disclosed information can be defused more widely due to the networked effect. As such, SNSs open a new communication channel with this networking function, one that is totally different from other ICTs platforms. Everyone in these networks needs to create a personal profile in order to connect with others. When they share their daily life, photos or feelings on profiles, this information is diffused through the various networks.

An increasing worldwide phenomenon indicates that people consume more social networks than any other category of sites. Rough figures claim that one fifth of a day is taken to play PCs while 30% of day is contributed to the mobile phones (Nielson 2012, p. 4). Users of SNSs often demonstrate a desire to present themselves, express feelings and develop relationships, while also seeking to erase feelings of loneliness (Morahan-Martin and Schumacher 2003, p. 665). According to Booth (2000, p. 1–2), some lonely individuals make use of the Internet to reduce stress and alleviative the negative feelings caused by loneliness. ICTs enable normal users to reveal and spread private information, even as the "illusion of privacy" created by the technology itself contributes to boundary problems (Barnes 2006, p. 12). The collection of personal information for commercial and business purposes further problematizes the boundary problem by raising the privacy question. In recent years, more companies have been dabbling in the advertising and marketing aspects of SNSs, especially taking advantage of the ease with which they can reach out to specific groups within a wider audience. As a result, these companies tend to direct the bulk of their advertising costs towards this avenue. On the contrary, users claimed that their profiles on social media, such as Facebook and Instagram, are part of a private domain purely for communication purposes with friends and families, and they do not want to be reached by any commercial organizations.

Habermas (1991a, p. 141–158) explains that the structural evolution that has occurred, and is occurring, within the public sphere is a result of the emergence of different forms of media and social changes introduced by new means of communication technology. Print media, radio, television have changed the public sphere profoundly such that now, the Internet expands the perimeters of the public domain and makes an obvious contribution to the public sphere by providing more platforms to express political opinions, and consequently, facilitating possible political participation while increasing political voices. Expression under a pseudo-anonymous name makes communication freer and more open. New types of communication technology, however, have created a new boundary between "the private" and "the public" (Papacharissi 2002, p. 22, Poor 2005). SNSs, as social domains, display both private (such as the development of private relationships) and public characteristics (such as the provision of discussion platforms) that lead to what Burkell, Fortier et al. (2013, p. 1) reveal to be the "loci of public display rather than private revelation". Collaboratively with interview results, they argue that the structure of an online profile is based on the idea of enabling 'everyone' to see them, although the intended audience is restricted by virtue of the users' desires. This openness of SNSs is inconsistent with the claim that social media is a private space (see studies from Ben-Ze'ev (2004, p. 96–104) and Livingstone (2006, p. 138–140), etc.); instead, it appears that participants view and treat online social networks as a public space.

Although the question of a clear distinction between "the private" and "the public" on social platforms have dominated many research exercises within the academic arena in recent years, most of the available studies focus primarily on themes of either "online privacy" or "SNSs as a public sphere" to evoke public discussion and opinion deliberation. The issues of combinative and overlapping private and public spaces have hitherto been ignored. It is hence my contention that SNSs can be considered as both private and public spaces, with a primary function of sharing personal information and distributing political discussion. My claim is corroborated by the high percentage of users who choose to selectively disclose information to a few people instead of the mass public. This presents an overlap of both domains that problematizes the demarcation of a truly private or truly public space. Therefore, SNSs can be also seen as a private space. Self-disclosure of personal information and voluntary expression of personal political opinions are two key branches of information that flow out of the private space into a public one. As such, SNSs should be considered a conflation of both private and public spaces and ought not be studied separately.

Various studies have argued that the division between what is private and what is public is becoming blurred as a consequence of new media technology (Meyrowitz 1985, p. 71, Thompson 1995, p. 120–125). However, Habermas (2004, p. 1) denies the idea of blurred boundary, and supports that "the private" and "the public" "complement each other". It can be quite difficult to explain the distinction of what constitutes "the private" and "the public", or to implement a clear dividing line between them in a networked society, particularly when technology complicates people's ability to control accessibility and visibility. What remains an open question is the location of a boundary between "the private" and "the public" in a networked society. By extension, we have to question *how* people can work with the current divider. Both are questions of utmost importance in regards to communication on SNSs – a cyber environment where networked communication and information-sharing take place.

Besides the problem of a clear demarcation between "the private" and "the public" in cyberspace, the worldwide emergence of SNSs has also raised questions about how this boundary differs or remains similar across countries. Among individuals and organizations that try to abuse private data, the issue of a boundary has generated some harms to the society, social relationships and even human lives (Thompson 2011, p. 64). Globalization, especially, creates more similarities among different countries across the world. This is then reflected in the cyberspace as a *seemingly* similar boundary that divides "the private" and "the public". More importantly, these international flows of media and technology innovations are seen as "powerful agents of change" (Rantanen 2005, p. 74). As ICTs become integrated into the everyday life, it influences a growing number of nations and promotes a global, rather than national, perspective in its exploration of how SNSs users manage the boundary between "the private" and "the public". Additionally, ICTs play essential roles in the understanding of how media technology influences concepts and behaviors in different social and cultural contexts. While little is known about how people in different countries define "the private" and "the public" on SNSs, we cannot assume that globalization will result in the homogenization or heterogenization of world cultures, which will further influence the social behaviors related to private and public distinctions.

In a quest for a satisfying answer, my research compares the boundary between "the private" and "the public" in Germany and China through an analysis of various historical, cultural, and social concepts of "private" and "public" definitions. This transnational comparison aims to examine the ways in which SNSs influence different socio-national concepts of "the public" and "the private". Whereas ideas of "the private" and "the public" are based on social development in Western countries, there is almost no tradition of privacy or of public opinions in China. Although, it must be acknowledged that conceptualizations of what is "private" and what is "public" have arisen with structural changes of social relations, that is itself a result of a rapid transition of contemporary China into a market economy. This allows the growing legitimization of the individual in social practices and the consequential individualization of Chinese society, giving rise especially to the Chinese privacy concerns. Also, platforms to express opinion have been innovated with the change in communication technology. Eastern countries of collectivistic culture do not have any modern notions of a "public" or "private" territory, and are in the works of processing a transformation of social structures and personal relationships. Therefore, it is necessary to conduct a transnational comparison order examine how Western norms of privacy protection and freedom of speech influence Eastern countries with respect to globalization, modernization, individualization and mediatization.

Some initial data collected from online questionnaires and interviews help to explore how SNSs users manage the content and extent of their self-disclosure and political expression. Two models are constructed to examine motivations of users who reveal or conceal information. By comparing the boundary between "the private" and "the public" in Germany with that in China, a transnational study offers more detailed differences and similarities in a globalized world.

1.2 Organization of Dissertation

This dissertation discusses the boundary between "the private" and "the public" on SNSs and culturally contextualizes the different interpretations and implementations of a boundary. Chapter II gives an historical overview of the private and public life of the Western society, and categorizes the information into five different frameworks that serve to distinguish "the private" and from "the public". Next, we will review all the frameworks and select one that is suitable for application in the context of SNSs. According to our theoretical framework, we will then decide on a definition for "the private" and "the public", and establish the boundary that divides them.

Chapter III analyzes the private and public characters of SNSs, and concludes that the construction of a boundary between "the private" and "the public" is a consequence of the transfer of information from the private to public space in the forms of self-disclosure and political expression. Based on Social Exchange Theory (SET), Social Penetration Theory (SPT) and Communication Privacy Management Theory (CPMT), we explore the mechanism of boundary management and the factors that influence the revealing or the concealing of private information.

Chapter IV introduces the historical notions of "the private" and "the public" in Germany and China, and analyses how these two countries differ in terms of economic development, media freedom and system, as well as culture. However, the phenomenon of globalization causes what were once contrasting cultures to become more or less similar cross the world. The Germans and the Chinese are classic examples of this similarity. Both societies are supposedly extraordinarily impacted by globalization, individualization and new communication technology, so much that they risk losing their uniqueness and begin to exhibit similar notions of "the private" and "the public" on SNSs. After analyzing the problems of cultural value that are presented by Hofstede (1980, p. 65–72, 1997, p. 129–130, 2001, p. 209–214), I will introduce Elias's (2010, p. 1–8) distinctions of *Kultur* and *Civilization,* and situate the boundary between "the private" and "the public" on SNSs in a cross-cultural context to analyze the differences and similarities between Germany and China.

In Chapter V, I will utilize two models in my examination of the motivations behind users' acts of self-disclosure and political expression, both of which lead to an information transfer from a private to a public space on SNSs. By the end of this chapter, I raise these questions: Are there differences/similarities in the ways a German user and a Chinese user perceive the boundary separating "the private" from "the public"? What are these differences/similarities?

The first five chapters provide the literature for this dissertation. Following, in chapter VI, I will deal with research methods and explain why I chose to use an online quantitative questionnaire and conduct qualitative interview to explore the boundary. I also delineate the processes of data collection, interviews and measurements of variables. Data quality will be evaluated and a representation of my samples will be discussed at the end of this chapter. Chapter VII sums up the findings of my work and chapter VIII provides a summary of the entire dissertation, as well as offers some suggestions for possible future research.

II. Conceptual Framework for Studying the Boundary Between "the Private" and "the Public"

How can "the private" and "the public" be defined? This abstract question has been repeatedly discussed throughout Western history in numerous disciplines such as Philosophy, Sociology, and Law and Media studies; but the answers are various and multiple. For the sake of this dissertation, I shall examine several common ways of defining "the private" and "the public" and set up five different frameworks in which these polarities can be more or less distinguished, with respect to the Western society. Preceding my discussion, notions of "the private" and "the public" in different time periods will be delineated in order to register the changes of the divisive boundary as facilitated by the increasing influence of new communications technology. Following, relationships between new communications technology and multiple definitions of "the private" and "the public" will be drawn, which I will use to formulate five frameworks to attempt to negotiate a distinction between both realms. Next, I will apply the sociability framework in a comprehensive investigation of what it means to be "private" and "public", and use the findings to conclude that the distinction between "the private" and "the public" is informed by socially appropriate behavior within situational context. In accordance with this framework, the boundary between "the private" and "the public" on SNSs is decided based on the target communication partner.

2.1 A Historical Overview of the Definitions of "the Private" and "the Public"

The essentials of private and public lives vary in different time periods. The conventional foundation of "the private" and "the public" can be traced back to ancient Greece. Over 3000 years ago, the market place (*agora*) in each city (*polis*) was a space of public life (*bios politikos*) for the Ancient Greek citizens. Public life at that time "was constituted in discussion (*lexis*)", and included forms of "consultation" and jurisdiction, and "common action (*praxis*)"; on the contrary, private life (*okios*) was attached to households (Habermas 1991a, p. 3–4). Arendt (1958, p. 22–50) supports this notion when she mentions that the distinctive feature of the ancient Greek private realm was its inhabitation quality, otherwise known as the domestic sphere in which people "lived together" and were "driven by common wants and needs". This realm of life that provided nourishment and reproduced human life was characterized by labor and work. Household consequently played an important role in the private life of the ancient Greek citizens. Correspondingly, the public realm was characterized by political action and speech. The succeeding ancient Roman empire shared this definition and conceptualized "the public" as public discussions, affairs and democracy, while associating "the private" with home and domestic affairs (Habermas 1991a, p. 3–4, DeCew 1997, p. 10).

A modern conceptualization of private/public private distinctions began in the 17th century and has been deeply influenced by the Nature Law Theory[1]. "The public" was related to the state, the government and the society, while "the private" referred to private property. The Nature Law Theory suggests that the aspects under the "personal control" of the citizen qualify as "private" whereas the aspects charged by the state is the "public" (Gobetti 1997, p. 107–110, Papacharissi 2010, p. 29). As such, households and personal relationships belong to "the private". Besides, citizens participate in political discussion and policy making, deal with state affairs in the public space, and both activities are considered public. The notion of "private property" has been introduced in the 18th century to describe matters that "heads of the households negotiate with the institution of political authority through the social contract" (Gobetti 1997, p. 110). In 1823, John Locke (1821, p. 115–125) further developed the Nature Law Theory and made a clear distinction between private and public by extending the notion of property to include thoughts: intellectual output, writing and even the imagination of people could be produced. On the other hand, things that were acquired through a person's "physical labor" were considered private properties. The word "public" at that time connoted another meaning for its society. In order to distinguish "the private" and "the public" more clearly, John Stuart Mill (2008, p. 279–288) defines these two realms as the public/private dichotomy: "the private" refers to personal affairs that are less related to the society and beyond social interference; whereas "the public" refers to social responsibilities and social conduct, namely,

1 The Nature Law Theory has its origins in the works of Aristotle. It's a system of natural laws that "guides political and legal authority and sets the moral standards for human conduct". There are two forms of Nature Law Theory. The first is known as "Classical Nature Law Theory", which is "based on Aristotle's teleological ethics and Stoicism", and was later influenced by Christian Philosophy. It deals with the distinction of nature and convention and is believed to be associated with concepts of justice. The other form is called the "Modern Nature Law Theory", which is developed by Grotius, Locke and Rousseau. It argues that nature laws grant natural rights, including rights to freedom, life and equality to each individual. Bunnin, N. and J. Yu (2008). The Blackwell dictionary of western philosophy. Malden, Oxford and Carlton, Blackwell Publishing.

actions that are restrained by society. With the change in social structure, the notions of private and public transformed and people witnessed a transformation of "the public" from the 17th and 18th centuries onwards. This change has been described as "the rise of the social" by Arendt (1958, p. 38–49). As the power of social groups and classes increased in the society, activities which took place in a domestic setting were shifted to the external. In the same period, the association of "the public" with "state property" extended to include not only individual property but also that of the magistrate (Schiewe 2003, p. 34).

By the end of the 19th century, the concept of "the public" had tentatively stabilized. The public sphere of the bourgeois, as described by Habermas (1991a, p. 181–195), revealed a special intersection between state, market and family in civil society during the 18th and 19th centuries. He ascribed this phenomenon to the essential role of emerging print media and its influences on the activities of the bourgeoisie. "The public" at this time was identical to "the public" of ancient Greek sense, and was synonymous with the "people (Bevölkerung)", which referred to not only the subject and the producer of public opinions, but also an opposition to the institution with which it worked together (Schiewe 2003, p. 30–59). Since then, the public sphere has been created in and out of civil society. The market and economic became the dominants of the private sphere.

The notions of "the private" and "the public" are also transformed as the innovation of media technology changes social structure and creates more possibilities for access to the private space. Media contributed to people's ability in terms of storing and transferring information speedily and precisely, to "make the largest units as manageable as smaller ones" (McLuhan 1994, p. 311). When communicating through telephone, radio, television, or computer, all the different locations seem to lose their distinctive features and blend into one gigantic cyberspace in which one and all are the same. Consequently, cultures and countries become more similar and people lose the sanctity of their private lives that has, prior to telecommunication, been inaccessible to the public (Fisher 1992, p. 11). Telecommunication, in the form of the telephone, connects the home with the exterior world and enables others outside this domestic realm to find out about household events. Television, or so-called electronic media, combines formerly private and public places and presents activities that were afore considered "backstage" to the public (Meyrowitz 1985, p. 93). The impact of electronic media thus confuses the broad understanding of what constitutes "the private" and "the public". As telecommunication gadgets such as radios and television sets become increasingly affordable, people begin to install them inside their bedrooms. As such, the broadcasts of public affairs and live events (i.e. president election debated) – that have prior been confined to the public domains before telecommunication mediums became accessible across all social classes – lost their public element and took on a more confused nature as a public program encroached within a private viewing domain. Consider this: broadcasted/televised programs usually feature many public figures who are unlikely to be acquainted with members of the audience in real life and who participate in discussions pertaining to social and public affairs. In terms of contents, such programs are unquestionably public events. However, a large percentage of the audience view these live telecasts from the comfort of their bedrooms, making this a private viewing. In this sense, the public and private natures of the live telecasts collide, exemplified by a public event carrying over into a private space via an electronic conduit. This collision makes it problematic to determine the nature of an event for the people experiencing it. In other words, the extension of public events into a private space leads to an experiential phenomenon termed "no sense of place", so that people find it difficult to distinguish between private and public places.

The electronic and digital media, especially, brings a new kind of transformation to the public sphere. Traditionally, a public sphere is constructed on mass media platforms where public affairs are deliberated. However, the Internet enables people to publish everything without economic and technical barriers, and consequently threatens the "gate keeper" selection process of journalists (Beck 2006, p. 223). Journalists lost the authority to select news according to its values and to choose the means of information dissemination. Instead, every person can replace the media and become a source of information or even the means of information propagation. Therefore, the definition of "the public" evolved to include this accessibility to the reception and production of news. In this way, the world becomes unified as a communication room in which a global public is created. From this perspective, access to the Internet becomes the condition for a new-age dissemination of public-information and communication as the communications network has the ability to overcome space, time and material, entities that were once essential to people (Schiewe 2003, p. 159). The ensuing convoluted nature of this new public sphere brought about by media transformation can never be understood (Thompson 2011, p. 58–59). A befitting model, therefore, should be formulated to explain the transformation of the public sphere in a digital era. To clearly understand what is meant by "the private" and "the public", we need to go further into several theoretical frameworks that offer possible distinctions between the two.

2.2 Theoretical Frameworks of the Boundary between "Private" and "Public"

As mentioned previously, several concepts of private and public distinction were developed within historical Western societies. In contrast, some Eastern parts of the world, for instance China, did not subscribe to the concepts of "the private" and "the public" and as such, demonstrated no clear understanding of either, much less saw the need of a divisive boundary between both. The Chinese neither understood nor practiced privacy as personality rights. Only after the 20th century did this change. Ideas of privacy and publicity emerged in accordance with processes of modernization and globalization. As the discussion of "the private" and "the public" in this chapter is focused on western conceptions, I will explain more on Chinese cultural and social background in Chapter IV. Based on the summaries of Weintraub (1997, p. 8–34), Papacharissi (2010, p. 31–34) and Gal (2002, p. 80–86), I present a few proposed theoretical frameworks to assist my investigation of the boundary between "the private" and "the public" after the 20th century below.

The *Liberal-Economic Framework* is based on a neo-classical economic theory that associates "the private" and "the private" with two sub-categories respectively known as the "non-governmental" and the "governmental" (Weintraub 1997, p. 7, Papacharissi 2010, p. 31). The market, generally in "non-governmental" forms of companies and commercial organizations, constitutes the private domain in this framework; on the contrary, the state/government, which plays a governmental role in modern society, constitutes the public domain. The market and state/government have been interdependent since the beginning of modern society. As such, this framework underscores the relationship between them, which in turn decides the national policies and political systems. As discussed above, the market became associated with the notion of "the private" in the 18th century. "The private" emphasizes on the ability of self-regulation, free market, based on competition and efficacy. Behaviors in the markets are the results of rational choices that an individual makes, which tries to achieve the greatest benefits using the lowest costs. Sometimes, though, the market itself cannot work perfectly with and by itself. In the modern society, the state or the government serves the purpose of governance or rule a certain economic behavior in order to avoid market failure. As such, on the public policy front, the distance between these two sections is oppositional and irreconcilable. Therefore, to understand "the private" and "the public" using the *Liberal-Economic Framework* "involved a preoccupation with the question of jurisdiction, especially with the demarcation of the sphere of the 'public' authority of the state from the sphere of formally voluntary relations between "private" individuals" (Weintraub 1997, p. 7–8). That is to say, the governor needs to strike a balance between the relationships of individuals and organizations, and correspondingly, between the individuals and the state.

The *Republican/Classical Framework* classifies political action under "the public" and the domains of "family and home" under "the private"(Weintraub 1997, p. 11–13, Papacharissi 2010, p. 32). This framework has its root in the philosophy and traditions of ancient Greece and Rome, wherein the heart of public life lies a process of active participation in discussion and collective decision making that is carried out within a framework of fundamental solidarity and equality. It is based on concepts of Western democracy and highlights the role of citizens and their self-determined opinions in the civic society.

> *"In this context, dominant thinkers contribute to the philosophical construction of civil society: Hobbes by emancipating opinion, identifying with conscience, and freeing it from religion; Locke by emphasizing reason and criticism as key elements of an informed and educated opinion; Rousseau by re-establishing consensus; and Kant by proposing the public sphere as the means through which the conflicting private will of rational people could be brought into harmony. Within this context, Hegel questions the ability of public opinion to function outside the confines of prejudice, ideology, and irrationality; Marx further problematizes it as a mask for bourgeois class interests." (Papacharissi 2010, p. 32)*

The structure of civic society has been influenced by liberalism, which emphasizes the role of the citizens and the rational expression of an individual's opinions, so that these actions accumulate as public opinions and collective actions. The typical character of a public domain, argued by Weintraub (1997, p. 14), is the "terrain of active citizenship", which indicates that "the public" equals to politics in the *Republican/Classical Framework*. However, it's hard to dissociate the private domain from all activities in the social life because what is outside of the state cannot be easily defined as "the private". Only until Habermas (1991a, p. 1–14) introduced the notion of the public sphere, which is located between the private domain (home, market) and public domain (state/government), did this framework finds its clear private/public distinctions. The expression of opinion plays an essential role in civic society, but only rational opinions can contribute to the public sphere and further influence policies.

In the *Feminist Framework*, the boundary between "the private" and "the public" is distinguished according to gender, using terms of social structure and ideology. The traditional life ascribes femininity to the home, such that the domestic space is commonly associated with the feminine and is a special place "in which women may exert and negotiate any amount of power or agency afforded them by the current socio-cultural setting"; on the other hand, the social individual in the public space is thought to be masculine and commonly ascribed to only men (Weintraub 1997, p. 27–29, Papacharissi 2010, p. 34). Because of this social structure and different gender roles, the public/private distinction is becoming an ideology – one that prescribes social rules for proper behavior and standards of gender identity. The public life, generally outside of home, is dominated and masculinized by the male, whereas the home, a typical domestic place for the womenfolk, is correspondingly feminized. The distinction between "the private" and "the public" is also a central question for feminist studies and social movement during the past two hundred years (Pateman 2006, p. 155). Even now, feminists are still pursuing to propose a theory or construct a theoretical model for gender equality.

Unlike the prior introduced frameworks, the *Semiotics Framework* is derived from linguistic studies. Gal (2002, p. 79–84) argues that "the private" and "the public" cannot be simply and directly interpreted as "particular places, domains, spheres of activity, or even types of interaction", but instead, are "co-constitutive cultural categories". Besides, the "the private" and "the public" are also important "indexical signs", that is to say, their "referential meaning" is closely related to the communication context in which interaction happens (p. 79). In any given society, the meanings of "the private" and "the public" are rooted in and emerged from its social environment and culture, which can change across different historical periods. However, when these concepts have been established, they can be utilized to categorize words in the languages. Some will be categorized as "private" while others will be categorized as "public". While every society has its own language, it also has its own concept and definition of what is private or public. The words that fall under either the private or the public categories in various societies sometimes exhibit stark distinctions. As expected, the distinction between "the private" and "the public" also varies across different societies, countries and cultures. Of course, as the notions are ever-changing, skewing and redefinition exist such that there is sometimes an overlap.

Finally, the *Sociability Framework* understands the boundary between "the private" and "the public" as *social behaviors,* which are "enabled and restricted by cultural and historical conventions of what is termed private and what is considered public" (Papacharissi 2010, p. 33). Sociability refers to the ability to interact with others, or to socialize (Preece 2001, p. 351–356, Preece 2006). "The private" and "the public" are related to the social roles and activities of individuals. In "The Fall of Public Man", Sennet (1976, p. 33) explains that a "role" is generally defined as a set of socially "appropriate" behavior. Similarly, Goffman (1959, p. 1–16) distinguishes between private and public roles according to behaviors in any given situations. In social drama terms, a person presents himself the way an actor assumes a role in a drama – by appropriating a different person according to front stage (public) and backstage (private) situations. Goffman also notes that the symbolic demarcation of interactional space is a key constitutive feature of social reality.

Altman (1975, p. 3) develops Goffman's theory by suggesting that social behaviors are related to the "physical environment". In social interaction, the "concepts of personal space" and "territorial behavior" is highly related. He views privacy as "a central regulatory process by which a person (or group) makes himself more or less accessible and open to others". People exchange personal information by communicating. In this process, they decide which piece of information is accessible to others other than themselves (input) and what to disclose to others (output). That is to say, "privacy is an interpersonal boundary-control process" (Altman 1976, p. 3–4). The parameter of "the private" is determined by a social and dynamic process that allows an "access to the self" by filtering pieces of information through a selective system that works out which member on the same platform is allowed or denied access to the private information of another. The interaction within the sociability framework includes what George Herbert Mead terms "symbolic interaction", that "the individual mind can exist only in relation to other minds with shared meanings" (1982, p. 5). Mead's study of human behaviors mainly focuses on social interaction and social roles.

In the framework of sociability, "the private" is a domain where a person can keep away from others, as well as his or her worries and pressures in daily life; separately, "the public" is "opened to the community and subjected to the authority of its magistrates" (Veyne 1987, pp. 8). "The public", as understood within the framework of sociability, can be conceptualized as the space that any social group or individual can enter into, and in which recognition through expression and interaction of information can be attained. "Public space" in this frame work is thus recognized as a civic character. The public space associated with sociability emerges from a complex interplay of spatial and social arrangements and allows more diverse individuals and groups "to dwell in peace together on civilized but essential dignified and reserved terms" (Weintraub 1997, p. 23).

Table 1: Theoretical Frameworks of Private and Public Distinction

Frame	Public	Private	Main Research Filed
Liberal-economic	government/state	independently owned/ managed companies and organizations	Economics
Republican/ Classical	political action	family and home	Politics
Feminist	masculinized	feminized	Gender Studies
Semiotics	co-constitutive cultural interactional context	categories dependent	Linguistic
Sociability	behavior in public place	behavior in private place	Sociology

Studying the private/public distinction is a complex process involving knowledge of various research fields. Among these five frameworks, the *Sociability Framework* is the only one that displays ideal characteristics that are appropriate for a discussion on the division between "the private" and "the public" on SNSs. The *Liberal-Economic Framework* concentrates on a negotiation between state/ authority and individual economic behavior from a macro perspective, yet it lacks micro observational capacities with respect to the behaviors of SNSs users. The *Republican/Classical* approach deals only with the civic society and political discussion. Although Papacharissi developed this framework in 2010 and described it as a convergence of media environment, democracy and civic engagement in temporary democracy, it merely discusses the public side of the boundary and neglects the private side, which deals with the domains of family and market. Furthermore, the *Republican/Classical Framework* considers privacy as a type of property and correlates it to personality rights. This research field legitimately belongs to the discipline of law studies. For decades, several policy makers and law scholars have been discussing whether law should grant individuals a right of property that enables them to bargain over which personal data to reveal to which firms and for what purposes (Samuelson 2000, p. 1127, Zittrain 2000, p. 1201). However, this framework cannot adequately account for the flow of information from a private to a public space on SNSs during the process of social interaction, neither does it explain how individuals manage their property. The *Feminist Framework* considers gender as a decisive factor for the classification of the private/public dichotomy, and contends for more female prerogatives. However, gender is merely one out of many factors that influence the private/public distinction. To investigate social interaction within private and public spaces, additional factors must be considered. The *Semiotics Framework* is helpful towards distinguishing "the private" and "the public" but only according to interactional contexts. It operates by first establishing several co-constitutive cultural categories of words, and then determining whether the situation is a private or public one based on that. However, the meanings of these words are fluid in nature and shift according to different cultures and contexts. Consider the word "sofa". If a set of sofa is placed in the bedroom, it naturally connotes a private context; but if the same set of sofa is placed in the office, then it becomes contextually "public". Hence, the problem of the *Semiotic Framework* lies in the lack of stable context in which the word can be categorized as either "private" or "public". An extended problem of the *Semiotic Framework* is the lack of fixed deciding factors that inform the context of the word. As factors such as nationality, race, gender, age, and many more, all play a part in determining the meaning of any word in particular, the informative environment is fluid. Therefore, only when the myriad of deciding factors can be narrowed down to a single one can the context of a particular word stabilize sufficiently for us to establish a concrete meaning that categorizes this word as belonging to "the private" or "the public".

Having explained the flaws of the above four frameworks, we are left with one last remaining structural type: *Sociability*. The *Sociability Framework* refers to social contexts differently from the *Semiotics Framework*: the former claims that the receiver of the information contextualizes it; while the later understands contextualization as a categorization of cultures. The *Sociability Framework* assigns social behaviors to corresponding environments. In short, the social roles of the participants in any given interaction correlate to the social environment where this interaction takes place. Consequently, we can translate the distinction between "the private" and "the public" into the difference between any two given communication roles. Family members and friends are classified as private relationships; whereas striking up a conversation in a crowd or with strangers, or even engaging in a discussion on political policies with other citizens, are categorized as public interactive roles; classmates or colleagues are generally mixed with private and public relationships, and we can interpret them as people in semi-public context.

Another advantage of the *Sociability Framework* is the freedom of control it affords an individual in terms of behavior and "accessibility to self". This is mediated through the management of the disclosure of personal information during interaction. Compared to other media platforms, the most important attribute of SNSs is that participants have uniquely identifiable profiles provided by themselves. In other words, participants play active roles in deciding how much personal information is exposed to family, friends, colleagues and strangers. Although, there is a loophole in this system as SNSs users are not hundred percent in control and private information may sometimes be collected by commercial organizations. This flaw is mitigated slightly by user-awareness of its existence. As such, user-control still plays an essential role in the management of private/public boundary. The division between "the private" and "the public" is a dynamic process that controls the flow of personal information to respective communication targets engaged in interaction. Because of this quality, the *Sociability Framework* is better suited for an analysis on the boundary between "private" and "public" spaces of SNSs.

2.3 Private/Public Distinction: Decision by Social Contexts

The *Sociability Framework* indicates that the private/public distinction is related to types of appropriate behaviors in certain situations. The situations here are equivalent to the social contexts in which an individual reveals personal information about himself or air his opinions about a particular issue. In this process, the person who is supposed to receive the revealed information plays a decisive role in setting the boundary between "the public" and "the private". The role and nature of an audience evolve under the effects of ICTs, which highlights the multirole of Internet users as contributors to the problem of a public/private boundary. The audience in the social media context is not only the information receiver, but also the generator. Therefore, before we discuss the boundary issue, we need to reconsider the relationship between media and people.

In the Mass Communication Model, the communicating process is "one way" so that people can only be touched by information passively. Journalists and mass media collect and select contents for the audience. Nevertheless, when every user can publish content on social media platforms, the function of mass media is radically transformed. A new model that explains this new communication process is subsequently needed. Beck (2006, p. 45–47, 2013, p. 136–140) argues that the model of "Mediated Social Communication" (soziale Zeitkommunikation) appropriated by Wagner (1998, p. 187–240) and Schönhagen (2004, p. 117–120) is much better than the model of Mass Communication in explaining communication within the CMC parameters. Instead of separating the transfer of information between the media organization/journalist and the public, the *Mediated Social Communication* model understands the communication process as an interactive procedure of social dialogue/talk of the time (Zeitgespräch der Gesellschaft) to mediate information, during which journalists function as mediators to transfer information (Beck 2013, p. 137–138). Journalists are not "gate keepers" that control the selection of information for audiences; rather, they become simple mediators who facilitate information.

The main difference between the *Mediated Social Communication* model and the traditional model of Mass Communication lies in the changing audience. The traditional model of Mass Communication indicates that communicators and media are separate roles that carry out different functions in the communication process, by which we interpret to mean that only journalists and media organizations can collect and send information. Meanwhile, the *Mediated Social Communication* model presents both journalists and mass media as mediating forces that constitute a part of the communications system. Beyond the mediation system stands the output partner (Ausganspartner, AP, source) or target Partner (Zielpartner, ZP, addressee), who generates and receives content. In the following Figure 1, the grey portion on the left represents one cycle of information circulation. The mediator system (Vermittelungssystem, VS) mediates information from output partner to target partner. However, in the communication process, not everyone receives the mediated information because they may be not interested in it and neglect it. The person who finally receives content from output partner in this model is therefore called the representative target partner (repräs. ZP). Correspondently, there is also the representative output partner (repräs. AP), which refers to people who release information on behalf of a party or a social group. Fürst et. al. (2015, p. 331–332) highlighted the crucial role of representation in the process of *Mediated Social Communication* as "[r]epresentation is understood as originating from statements of members of organizations or opinion-based groups (representatives), which are attributed to all others (represented) members of this group." The rest of the members of a party of a social group, of course, recognize the representative output partner as their advocator. The interactive communication process in accordance with the model of *Mediated Social Communication*, therefore, cannot be realized "by the expression of every single individual, but by the exchange of statements between the representatives of diverse groups in society" (Fürst et. al., 2015, p. 335).

On the mediating process, there is more than one circulation of information. Wagner added the same component to the black part on the right, as he did to the left, in this model, and the communication process is then extended from left to right. Sometimes a person gains access to information not from the media but from someone who has consumed information through certain avenue of media. That means, target partner (inactive role, deaktiviert) can also change his role to output partner (active role, aktiviert). Information is mediated and circulated between the grey and black parts. In each part, feedback still happens.

Figure 1: Model of Mediated Social Communication. Wagner (1998, p. 187–240) and Schönhagen (2004, p. 117–120)

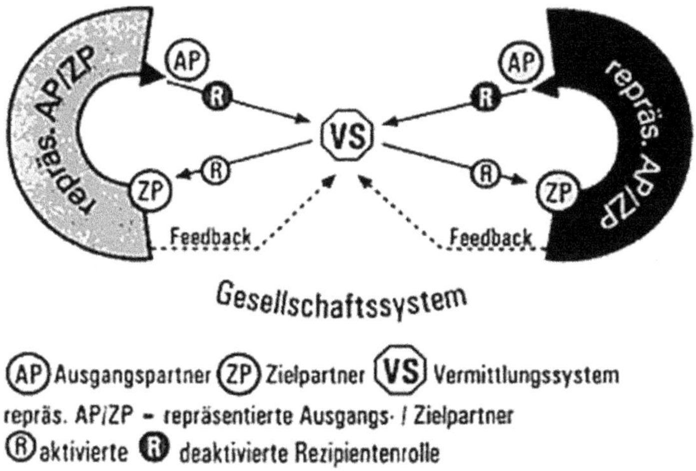

The model of *Mediated Social Communication* explains that information that is mediated by this system can reach the receiver and be transferred again to another level of receivers, who then perpetuate yet another transfer of this information, and so on. The act of communication in this model is thus a multi-leveled operation that functions based on the perpetuation of information. This can be used to explain not only mass communication activities, but also communication procedures in CMC. One of the most important advantages of the *Mediated Social Communication* Model lies in the separation of communication partner and mediator, which helps us to understand the relationship between media platforms and people. As such, SNSs is just a mediator through which information circulates within the output and target partners. However, SNSs itself is not related with to context; instead, the target partner decides on the boundary between "private" and "public", in accordance with the *Sociability Framework.*

The *Mediated Social Communication* model explains communication context as a correlation to the target partner. Goffman's (1959, p. 30–51) metaphor of the theatre indicates that people present themselves in many different manners, according to social contexts. This metaphor refers to the back stage as a private domain and the front stage as a public domain. However, the set behavior on the front- and backstage cannot be divided clearly due to the use of electronic media (Meyrowitz 1985, p. 93). Meyrowitz (1985, p. 71) argues that electronic media contribute to the loss of context, for example: when two people are watching an election debate (which is supposed to be a public event) in their own bedroom (which is supposed to be private), it becomes difficult to contextualize this act of watching as a private or public gesture. Similarly, when someone sits in the toilet, discussing public affairs with friends via Facebook or WhatsApp, the context seems to be lost. ICTs have changed the social network in which "information is disseminated, accessed and controlled" (Thompson 2011, p. 62). Media connects communication partners from different physical places so that the context of two physical places may overlap. This contributes to the loss of context and blurs the boundary between "the private" and "the public". Nevertheless, if we focus on the social role of the target partner (who determines the context), the boundary would be clear. Watching a TV election debate in the bedroom is a public act since the debate is mediated by the TV set and connects the president to members of the audience who are watching the program from the comfort of their bedrooms. Correspondingly, interpreting the private/public distinction according to Goffman's theatre metaphor is problematic. From a dramaturgical perspective, Hogan argues that Goffman interprete the social context bying integriting space-time and audiences. "That is to say, there is usually one specific front that needs to be presented in any given situation, because each region is not just a space-time locus, but a time-space-identity locus inhabited by a specific audience" (2010, p. 378). It doesn't matter whether the person who disseminates the information knows the audience, since the information is contextualized by the target partner. Therefore, instead of the blurred boundary between the private and public domains, the boundary is shifting dynamically according to different social contexts formed by social interaction (Gal 2002, p. 80–81).

When discussing the private and public context on SNSs, we need to shift our attention away from the media and the physical place where people behave to the target partner to whom information flows. Even on SNSs, people with different social roles, such as friends, colleagues and strangers, are engaged in communication. The private or public context depends on their roles when communicative behavior occurs; namely, the role of the target partner to whom the output partner decides to reveal information. Sometimes the target partner could be both a friend and a colleague of the output partner in reality. The role and nature of a target partner evolve under the effects of ICTs, which highlights the multirole of Internet users as contributors to the problems of a public/private boundary. However, the social role of SNSs users is clearly categorized. The user (output partner) first adds this target partner into his/her friend-list or colleague-list, or even both. When the user posts an entry on his personal page, he can choose only one category for which to make this post visible. Based on the list of the target partner to whom the SNSs users choose to make the posted information accessible, the boundary between "private" and "public" on SNSs is determined. In a way, this is similar to how a conversation in real-life is deemed as "private" or "public" on the basis of the conversational partner. In other words, regardless of physical or virtual spaces, the private or public context is decided by the target partner.

Communication technology that connects individuals has been changed, but interactional dynamics among people remains the same when the context is unchanged. Nissenbaum (2004, p. 103–107) raises an account of privacy in terms of *"contextual integrity"* and argues that privacy always has to be analyzed in relation to the different spheres or contexts in which individuals live out their lives. The social context of a physical space extends into the virtual space when an individual communicates with the same person on both physical and virtual spaces. This can also be changed by online interaction with someone from the virtual social circle that differs with the offline one. In a mediated environment, technology helps to shape context, although it is the target partner who decides whether to contextualize a particular piece of information as a private and public sort. In an interview with a group of American teenagers, Boyd (2008, p. 143) finds that the opinions of those whom the interviewees appropriate as their target audience influences the way they disclose themselves on SNSs. In other words, the audience of the information decides the context in which people adjust their behaviors appropriately. Teenagers present themselves online to "an imagined audience" (Boyd 2006). The answer to the question "who is watching" might turn out different from expectation. Under this circumstance, to create a personal profile on SNSs is also a process of managing the impression of the self upon others, during which individuals have to consider the potentiality of their audiences and the interpretive potential of the disclosed information (Boyd 2008, p. 130). Before revealing any information, users have decided already in their mind to whom they would like to reveal information. They also take into consideration the possibility of somebody (such as a random stranger or a commercial organization) other than the designated target partner may receive their information. Therefore, users may mitigate this risk by disseminating fake information or electronically limiting the visibility of this piece of information. Of course, some users may not care who is on the receiving end and hence, disregard this issue of privacy.

To conclude the discussion above, this dissertation argues that: (1) no matter how media transforms, the relationship between mediator/media and the communication partner remains the same, from the perspective of the *Mediated Social Communication* model; (2) as media transforms, a virtual space is established in our mind. Similar to a physical environment, the contextualization of information over social media platforms is determined by the target communication partner. Instead of studying the macro structure of private and public spheres online, I will concentrate on a micro-level examination of personal behavior, which comprise of thousands of disputants interacting at an interpersonal level. Altman's theory of privacy (1975, p. 1–8, 32–58, 103–123) proposes an original idea of an environmental mechanism of territoriality[2] that explains personal space and crowding. He combined concepts of social psychological with environmental psychology and came up with a theory that people use human spatial behavior techniques to regulate social interaction. The process of controlling the boundary between "the private" and "the public" is considered a regulatory behavior to control social interaction and incorporate both *input* – spatial control of who visits, and *output* – informational control of disclosure to another (Thompson 2011, p. 60–61). The boundary between "the private" and "the public" therefore conflates characters of both the *spatial* and the *informational*. The individual tries to control the accessibility to "the private" by managing the "environment of the self" and "information about self" (Thompson 2011, p. 61).

In this dissertation, the target partner is conceptualized as the social circles of an ego-centered network that is built upon interactional online relationships. By social circle, I refer to the group of people who are socially interconnected on SNSs. Due to the change in the privacy policy of SNSs, many platforms add a new function that enables users to control the visibility of shared information. Users are able to decide who can see the content of their personal pages. Take Facebook for example, users can control whether a new post is accessible to family, friends or the whole public. Google+ has a similar function. Altman (1975, p. 80) theorizes personal space in terms of distance. There are six different levels of social circles on SNSs, through which people can manage the extent of visibility in relation to shared information. These six levels are namely family, friend, colleague/classmate, acquaintance, and strangers. Although the understanding of "friendship" on SNSs may be fuzzier for some users, the social distance between a friend and the ego (self) within the model is much closer than that of a stranger. SNSs are relatively more private than other online forms such as online forums and public blogs. In order to differentiate between different types of friendship on SNSs, let's

---

2 Altman analyzes the human social behavior in relation to the physical environment from an ecological or social systems perspective. The personal space of an individual refers to the area immediately surrounding the body. People regulate their privacy by altering his or her distance and angel of orientation from others. Territoriality is conceptualized as personalizing, ownership, and defense of geographic areas. He proposes that privacy is a central regular process by which a person (or a group) makes himself or herself more or less accessible and open to others. The concepts of personal space and territorial behavior are mechanisms that are set in motion to achieve desire levels of privacy.

break the term friendship into "friends" and "acquaintances" so as to present a clearer distinction of their social distances within the social circle model.

Figure 2: Social Circles on SNSs according to Social Distance

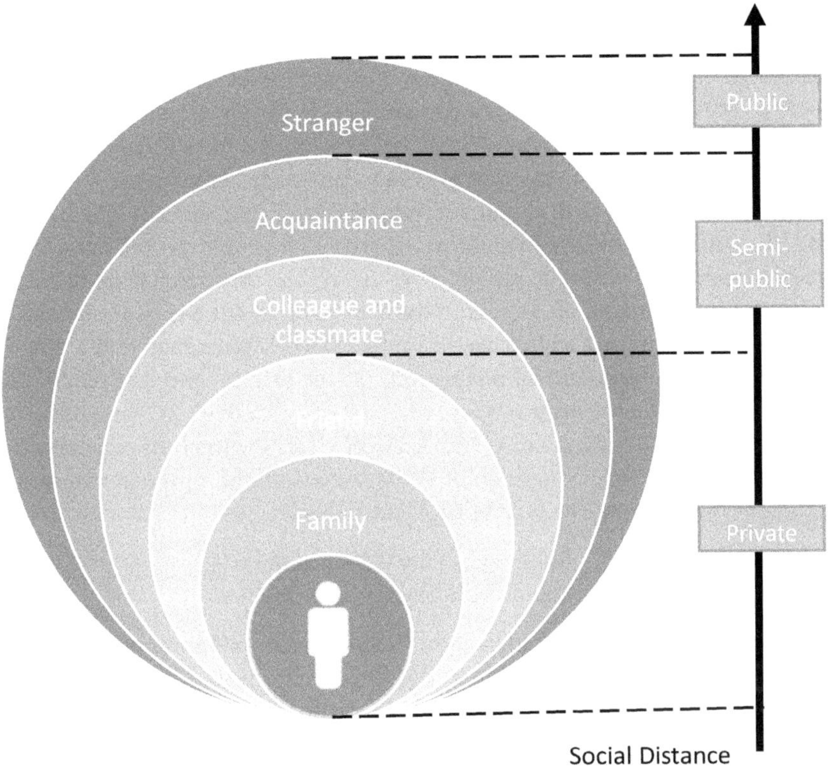

SNSs are generally considered the "backstage"[3] (Lewis, Kaufman et al. 2008, p. 83, Tufekci 2008, p. 21–22) or "private space" of an individual. This "backstage"

3 Lewis et al. (2008, p. 85–87) develop Goffman's theater metaphor and utilize the notion of backstage when analyzing information about personal interest and hobbies displayed on Facebook. An individual's favorite music, as an important component of personal interest, is loosely connected to the notion of backstage, namely, something inherently private. The process of displaying an individual's favorite music in Facebook is seen as an act to draw open the stage curtain to show the world his/her personal interest. This takes the act onto the front stage.

is a personal domain for what Wynn and Katz (1997, p. 306) call "an extension of the individual's mind and attributes". However, when users share their preferences for subjects such as music and films with other people on SNSs, they lift the curtain of this backstage and offer others a glimpse of their world. In that case, SNSs is no longer a backstage but a front. Some people carefully select which preference to reveal, and from the information that is visible to the public, the reasons for the private or public nature of their profiles become clear (Hogan 2010, p. 380). SNSs thus become a conflation of both private and public spaces. Under this assumption, it is my objective to locate the boundary that divides "the private" from "the public", in order to clearly demarcate both spaces.

In accordance with the spatial and informational characters of "the private" and "the public", I define "the public" as a space where people stay collectively and where personal information and opinions are visible; "the private", on the other hand, is the "territories of the self" (Goffman 1971, p. 40) where an individual keeps herself or himself withdrawn from the external. Weintraub (1997, p. 4–5) summarized two fundamental distinctions of "the private" and "the public": 1). "hidden or withdrawn" versus "open, revealed or accessible"; 2). "individual, or pertains only to an individual" versus "collective" or "the interests of a collectivity of individuals". In an extension of Weintraub's findings, I present two simple equations that explain "the private" and "the public":

Public=visibility + collectivity
Private=withdrawal + individual

Due to the evolution of communication technology, the private or public space is not stable anymore. Instead, it shifts according to various social contexts. From a traditional perspective, the family belongs to the domestic domain, which is classified as a private place. However, when this domestic region is connected to the mass public via the Internet, it ceases to be private. In some cases, watching a live show of a presidential debate at home, or expressing a political opinion on Twitter while sitting on the toilet-bowl with a smartphone, are instances of an extension of "the private" into "the public" through performing actions. The shifting meaning of what is "private" and what is "public" is decided by the ways that target partners contextualize information: to whom and to what extent should a SNSs user disclose personal information and political opinions? Under some special circumstances, the private and public spaces may overlap but they are still largely determined by social contexts. Returning to the aforementioned examples, watching a live show of a presidential debate in the bedroom alone or with family members privatizes the scene. However, if there is an additional presence of colleagues or acquaintances, this act of watching becomes public. This is because the relationship of a colleague or an acquaintance is beyond the inner realm of an individual (that constitutes "private"). In an extension of this view, although the cyber-world presented by SNSs are virtual realities, the social relationships and roles of the real world continue. The only difference is that more relationships are defined as "weak ties", such as colleagues/classmates, acquaintances and strangers, as virtual social networks operate with more flexibility and mobility (Beck 2006, p. 169–171).

In an effort to clearer present the constituents of "the private", it is necessary to draw distinctions among "the private", "the intimate", "the personal" and "the secret". *Privacy* is the noun of "private" and refers to "the state or condition of being alone, undisturbed, or free from public attention", as well as "a matter of choice, right, and freedom from interference or intrusion" (OED 2014). Its legal meaning as *rights* is more commonly used today. The word *intimate* indicates a "close connection by friendship or personal knowledge" and is "characterized by familiarity with a person or thing", when pertaining to relationships. Often, *intimate* has a meaning that pertains to, or is connected with, the inmost nature or fundamental character of a thing (OED 2014). Intimate objects, such as our bodies, can be kept private from public exposure. *Personal* is that which is of or pertaining to a "particular person's own affairs" (DeCew 1997, p. 56–58). Not everything that is private is also personal. For example, the password to my Email account is private because it is knowledge that is confined to myself. However, it is not personal for me since it is only meaningless numbers. Likewise, if my personal pictures and details are available to the public on my SNSs profile, they are not private things. The meaning of *private* also differs from that of *secret*. Privacy is the state of being unobserved and prevented from public view. Secrecy is the act of keeping things hidden, where it extends beyond the mere private into the hidden. Secrecy spills into privacy, but not all privacy is secrecy. The word *secret* connotes a deliberate withholding of information from others out of fear, and usually consists of information that has potentially negative impact. A secret may even cause harm to the secret-keeper and people around him or her.

According to the *Sociability Framework*, the examination of the boundary separating "the private" and "the public" on SNSs concentrates on the ways in which social interaction and relations influence social behavior. The establishment of a boundary between "the private" and "the public" is a negotiating and coordinating process that manages the tension between them in different social situations and relationships (Petronio 1991, p. 330). The control of the boundary between "the private" and "the public" is therefore largely based on the regulation performed by social interaction on the communication of personal information. In addition, this social interaction is influenced by culture. Altman (1975, p. 12) suggests that there are cultural-based privacy mechanisms, like the customs, norms, or styles of behavior by which members of different cultural groups regulate their contact with others. The suggestion of privacy as a cultural product treats privacy as a social construction by which the meaning of "the private" is *situational, contextual,* and influenced by *historical factors*. As Kisselburgh (2008, p. 28) suggests, culture influences the ways in which people interpret language and construct meaning, and this cultural context plays a pivotal role in the ways in which an individual understands the message. Over SNSs, the prevailing culture of the information source plays a crucial role in the regulation of the private/public boundary. SNSs users in countries of individualist culture (e.g. Germany, USA) reportedly disclose more personal information than that in countries of collectivistic cultures (e.g. China) (Wu and Lu 2013, p. 106).

2.4 Focus of Research

This dissertation explores the social behavior of an individual so as to distinguish "the private" from "the public" through the framework of sociability. Here, the boundary between "the private" and "the public" can be interpreted as two mechanisms: (a) a distinction based on communicative and social interaction; (b) a product or construction of social and cultural experiences. It is important to note that my discussions will not explicitly focus on issues of privacy and privacy concerns; instead, I engage with the participants of the study in a dialogue about information-sharing practices. Building on Altman's dialectical concept of privacy as a process of opening and closing a boundary to others, and sociability framework, my dissertation focuses on the following two questions:

Q1: What is the boundary between "the private" and "the public" on SNSs?
Q2: Is there a difference or similarity in the boundary between "the private" and "the public" on SNSs across countries?

III. Boundary Management Pertaining to SNSs

In the previous two chapters, I have formulated the theoretical basics for the construction of a boundary between "the private" and "the public", with regards to SNSs. This chapter will analyze the characteristics of "the private" and "the public" as defined in SNSs within the framework of sociability, particularly focusing on the public character of SNSs. The first part of this chapter will argue that SNSs only provide a public "space" but not always a public "sphere". According to Jürgen Harbermas, the construction of a public "sphere" can only occur under a deliberation process and involves the compliance of several conditions, such as rationality, user equality and inclusiveness. The second part of this chapter will investigate two main classes of information that channel the flow of data from a private to public space, namely: self-disclosure, and political expression. Both of these sets of behavior operate on the basis of self-imposed restriction; meaning users can set up a boundary protecting the viewership and dissemination of their personal information and political opinions on SNSs.

3.1 "Private" and "Public" on SNSs

It's difficult to clearly demarcate a public or private space on SNSs because these platforms possess characteristics that sometimes overlap with each other. In other words, a piece of information that appears to be private in nature can at times become public due to the medium of its presentation, and vice versa. However, according to the framework of sociability, we can differentiate "the private" from "the public" by assigning a particular set of social behavior to a corresponding social role. Although not entirely foolproof, this method proves to be largely effective in segregating the two polarities. Users view SNSs as platforms that facilitate the development of relationships with families and friends. To protect their personal information, users can control the extent of visibility of their profiles by customizing their privacy settings, thereby contextualizing these behaviors as "private". Conversely, when a piece of data is selectively set as "public", it becomes accessible to everyone, including random strangers. Consequently, this changes the SNSs from a private communication space into a public space. This is especially true when users participate actively in discussion threads on public forums during which they reveal their sentiments towards current and social affairs such as politics, economics and institutions. In other words, the users' engagement in any sort of discussions that facilitate an exchange of information between themselves and strangers creates an opportunity for SNSs to assume the role of a public space for public discussion.

3.1.1 Private Character of SNSs

The guidelines of Sociability differentiate between "the private" and "the public" according to *social behavior*. In a private space, an individual's behavior is guided and appraised by his private role, which emerges out of intimate and familial relationships (Jones 1984, p. 604). The goals of specific individuals and their personalized relationships with others are the primary concerns in private space. In 2006, a research project by Pew Research Center indicated that 91% of teenagers use social media platforms (i.e. My Space and Facebook) to maintain contact with friends whom they often meet; while 82% used the sites to connect friends whom they hardly meet personally; additionally, 49% used the SNSs to develop new friendships (Lenhart and Madden 2007). SNSs especially promote connections among friends or acquaintances who people seldom meet in life by allowing users to post updates about their daily lives and personal interests. Also, SNSs allow users to establish contact or develop relationships with people whom they have never met in the offline world. With the development of relationship online, the quality of friendship increases as well (Chan and Cheng 2004, p. 312).

SNSs are considered private spaces because users interact with families and friends through the disclosure of personal information such as thoughts, feelings and attitudes. Relationships are thus developed. Ben-Ze'ev (2004, p. 102) explains that the cyberspace provides a private world, where people maintain personal and social relationships. Meanwhile, users can control the accessibility of their profiles and customize the audience of each piece of shared information, so that their personal domains on SNSs are kept relatively private. Although data and personal information are visible and eligible for collection by governmental and commercial organizations, most users still see SNSs as a private space, as demonstrated by their online behaviors. To exemplify the perception of SNSs as a private space, Lenhart and Madden (2007) conducted a research that revealed more than half of the teenage participants had in some way restricted the accessibility of their profiles, yet at the same time, while they might disclose personal information with up to several hundred casual acquaintances, they draw the line at sharing personal information with strangers. As such, these SNSs exist in between "the private" and "the public". Similar findings have been presented by Livingstone (2006, p. 138–140) after her interviews with participating teenagers. She contends that the way people perceived privacy is to selectively disclose certain types of information based on the target audience. Young users view their profiles as a private space in which they wanted to be "public" to friends but "private" (in-accessible) to parents (Livingstone 2008, p. 397). One of the interviewees even revealed that "I don't give away information that I'm not willing to share", which reveals an intense awareness of private space in these interviewees (Livingstone, 2008, p. 404). Another survey conducted by West et.al (2009, p. 624) produced results similar to Livingstone's. The use of Facebook involves making partial aspects of a user's private life public, but only under the condition of the user's authorization. By this, I mean that there is an understanding that information can remain private when a user limits access to his profile and creates a filter that only allows Facebook "friends" to view his posts. Such behaviors that control visibility of profiles and personal information indicate that SNSs are private spaces where a certain degree of privacy is retained by the users. This self-imposed restricted disclosure on SNSs sets up a boundary between "the private" and "the public".

To clarify, any personal political opinion belongs in the private space until it is disclosed on SNSs. In other words, private information is only made public when it is shared with others, regardless deliberate or not. Personal political views stay at the inner layer of personality (Altman & Taylor, 1973, p. 17). The central layer is intimate and only individuals themselves can see it before they exchange political opinions with others during social interaction (more theoretical backgrounds see Chapter 3.3.2). As a relationship develops and interaction proceeds, personal political opinion is revealed and transferred to more people, thus increasing its visibility.

3.1.2 Public Character of SNSs

Public factors, such as an openness to all users and public discussions, attribute to the character of SNSs. Burkell et al. (2013, p. 1) argues that online social spaces are definitely not private but public spaces, because the profiles on SNSs are designed to be accessible to all individuals, even though users can still limit the audience. Also, users sometimes view and treat SNSs as a public space, resulting in the social norms that "are inconsistent with the claim that social media is a private space" (Burkell et al. 2013, p. 1). Also, sharing information over SNSs, although mainly comprising weak social ties, are nevertheless largely dependent on social relationships, which differentiates them from the FtFC in a relatively publicized context (Lewis and West 2009, p. 1209). SNSs users may choose to publish their posts publicly such that their information is made visible to all users, while some may not be aware that the shared information has entered into the public domain due to the default privacy settings. Tverdek (2008, p. 68) argues that users might lose control over the creation and maintenance of different sorts of social relationships with different people. When personal information is shared on SNSs, it infiltrates every possible channel of the online social network. This becomes problematic as the information reaches receivers who are not included in the original target audience. In other words, users lose control over the dissemination process due to the networked effect, causing information that is deemed "personal" to become publicized. SNSs are therefore considered a public space on account of this uncontrollability, as opposed to the private space wherein information is kept within a certain territory. Recently, several SNSs platforms, such as Facebook, introduced new functions that allow more precise customization of user privacy settings. One of the new functions enables users to restrict the audience of specific posts as well as restrict the audience of any possible reposts; however, the default privacy setting is still "public". Users who are unaware of this new function will naturally not utilize it and so, their personal information will remain visible to the public. Therefore, the question of "public" or "private" in SNSs is ultimately not influenced by the available privacy functions of the platforms; instead, it is determined by the behaviors of users.

In addition to revealing personal information to the public, activities that take place in public spaces include commercial economics, civic discussion, political participation institutional and public service, which are open and influential to anyone. Therefore, the notion of "the public" often refers to of a collection of people or collective behaviors. The framework of sociability derives the meaning of public space out of a *civic perspective*. "The public" is "a space of heterogeneous coexistence, not of inclusive solidarity or of conscious collective action; a space of symbolic display, of the complex blending of practical motives with interaction ritual and personal ties, of physical proximity coexisting with social distance" (Weintraub 1997, p. 25–26). Personal political opinion can be disclosed in the form of information-sharing through a platform consisting of people or media, transgressing the boundary between what is "private" and what is "public", while at the same time being diffused to a collective group of people, and then shifted into a public space.

Political expression is an essential component of the public space and is influenced by interaction and interpersonal ties. Internet facilities, such as online forums and blogs, expand the public space for political expression, particularly on SNSs, where the development of the interactive and portable device enables citizens of "a playful modality of civic engagement" (Gordon, Baldwin-Philippi et al. 2013, p. 5). SNSs also provide a more casual environment for users who do not normally engage in politics to come into contact with, and explore political activities, a curiosity sparked by "witnessing" their friends' engagement in politics

(Vitak, Zube et al. 2009, p. 22–27). With these facilities, individuals are therefore able to come together to learn, acquire and process political information, as well as participate in a deliberation process. SNSs are not only platforms on which users "gather" to exchange personal information and to develop relationships, but also an alternative way to participate in political affairs and deliberation. The latter is a process which may involve more citizens.

In a networked public space, political expression may involve numerous people whose only connection is through SNSs. Some of these people in the network share similar interests and concerns, thus giving rise to more opportunities for further discussions, which may or may not be classified as political expression. SNSs users of such common social groups can access selective reviews or posts written by friends/strangers who are members of the same platform. This enables a highly selective branch of information to reach across users' subsets of social network in that users are able to customize the receiving audience of their posts on SNSs. Without question, the content of political expression is public in nature, especially from an informational perspective. However, the deliberation of its disclosure collaborates with the target audience to contextualize its privacy or publicity. In other words, if an individual restricts his political expression to an audience of close family members, this political expression remains civic in character. This is because the limited visibility declassifies this situation as a public space. In addition, some politicians create public profiles on SNSs platforms, most notably on Facebook, to take advantage of the extensive outreach potential of such domains to communicate with citizens and to campaign themselves. Also, organizations like NGOs create public pages on SNSs to advocate their ideals and promote social movements. These public domains are categorized as public space. SNSs thus become avenues to engage cyber-savvy people in political and social activities.

3.1.3 SNSs: Still at the Forefront of Evolving Public Sphere

The emergence of the Internet increases the frequency and intensity of discussions as it expands the public space for discussion and contributes to the construction of a public sphere. A public "space" and a public "sphere" are two totally different concepts. A public sphere is actually an ideal form, in which people congregate to share and exchange opinions of social problems and public affairs freely and rationally, and where those opinions can further influence political action (Habermas 1991a, p. 1–4). A public space, on the other hand, refers to a social space that is opened and accessible to every person. Political expression may assume the form of deliberation through which public opinions can be formed and discussions can influence political action. This also helps to foster an online public sphere. ICTs, especially, provide more platforms for discussants to express political opinion, and consequently, may facilitate political participation and increase the number of political voices. Expression under a pseudo-anonymous name also prevents identity confusion among users and provides a more widely inclusive and freely communicative environment to promote deliberation (Papacharissi 2002, p. 16).

For the individual, the pseudo-anonymous environment reduces social sanction of personal behavior and contributes to opinion expression. In the cyber world, individuals have more opportunities for a "self-evaluation of the information" (Cismaru 2010). People are less pressurized in the expression of personal opinions, which means that the minority groups, whose voices are seldom or never heard, are now able to give voice to their thoughts. In other words, the exchange of a diversity of ideas is made possible. Political subjects that are taboo, sensitive and discomfiting, about which individuals may experience difficulties in expressing in an offline context, become possible for discussion under the protection of anonymity. The Internet creates a conversational context with the absence of social cues pertaining to status and gender, and generates information exchanges and deliberations. As such, Papacharissi (2002, p. 16) and Khan, Gilani et al. (2012, p. 48) believe that the Internet has raised possibilities about creating a more democratic communication and facilitating grassroots democracy so that, despite its weakness, allow the congregation of people across the national borders in an utopian vision. In addition, as compare to the traditional mass media, the Internet provides possibilities of interaction among users that promotes interpersonal communication. Such exchanges among individuals can in turn influence "the reception and processing of political news when it comes to translating mass-mediated messages into meaningful individual action" (Scheufele 2002, p. 57–58).

The media performs a vital role within the public sphere by informing and guiding public opinion. With the emergence of ICTs in daily life, more platforms have been provided for those outside of the governing class with respect to governance. In the forms of email, newsroom, blogs, social network sites and microblog, online networked communication has been constructed to cater to a wider network of users. Several studies demonstrate that the internet provides unprecedented advantages that are different from previous media platforms in terms of facilitating political expression and expanding public sphere (Blumler and Gurevitch 2001, p. 3, Dahlberg 2001b, p. 621, Brundidge 2010, p. 681, Papacharissi 2010, p. 119–123, Himelboim 2011, p. 636). Additionally, Gimmler argues that the model of deliberative democracy developed by Habermas (1991a), support the concept that the Internet is an "efficient political instrument" for online deliberation in an open public sphere where people can express themselves freely (Gimmler, 2001, p. 21). Additionally, with the extension of topics to public discussion, the increment of a multiplicity of topics and diversities of participants, the Internet and ICTs contribute to the development of public sphere

Despite the contributions of ICTs to the public sphere and the ensuing expansion of available communicative spaces for political expression, several phenomena indicate that SNSs cannot be considered as a public sphere. The public sphere is a domain of social life in which rational deliberation can result in a public consensus. It is based on the liberal democratic tradition and is "normatively grounded upon a reconstruction of the (rational) intuitions of everyday communication rather than being drawn from out of the ideals of an exclusionary" (Dahlberg 2014, p. 23). Deliberation leads to the formation of public opinion, which then enables democratic scrutiny that further influences the process of policy making. Not all public spaces can be seen as a public sphere, because a public sphere contains three norms (Polat 2005, p. 448):

> *"First, it has to be equally open to everyone. Everyone has to be able to be member of the public sphere and join in deliberations so that a diversity of viewpoints can be ensured; Second, within the public sphere a rational accord is reached as a result of rational critical debate that is free from value judgments; Finally, the public sphere has to be independent from the intrusion of government and commercial interests and power."*

In addition, inclusiveness is also an important condition of a public sphere. This is achieved by ensuring that the information discussed is readily accessible to everyone. It remains a topic of controversy, however, whether the political expression on SNS has constructed a public sphere, or simply provided a public space for public opinion. Nevertheless, it is inevitable that alongside these conditions, some corresponding problems caused by the expression of political opinions online arise within the public sphere. The public sphere stands independent of governmental and commercial interests and power, but it's undeniable that many public figures, such as political representatives, government officials, companies and commercial organizations, exist in this online environment. As such, I contend that SNSs are considered public *spaces* but not a public *sphere*.

Equality among SNSs Users

The public sphere strengthens deliberative democracy by ensuring that information and interactive opportunities are equally accessible to all members of the public. SNSs are considered a public domain where people disclose information about themselves and express personal opinions. Compared to FtFC, users of SNSs have relatively equal access to available resources in an open quest for information pertaining to specific issues. The open policy of such online social network makes this possible. While this idea is tech-utopian, different authority, existing knowledge gaps, and varying conditions of technic al facilities may still lead to inequality of political expression. Despite the prevalent use of SNSs, the digital divide still exists in forms of unequal access to technology, as well as unequal participation opportunities, due to a disparity in the extent of knowledge displayed by each individual.

The distribution of power differs remarkably on SNSs. The flows of information on the web are "always, and necessarily, situated within the hierarchies and inequalities of communication capitalism" (Dean 2003, p. 107). A recent network analysis of websites predicted that a power-law distribution of linking, clustering, and the presence of a strongly connected core, as well as the "patterns of participation and attention attraction", are also heavily influenced by the power law (Himelboim 2011, p. 634). In other words, the distribution of power is unequal and never quite the same. Dahlberg (2007, p. 829–830, 832–834) suggests a rethinking of the deliberative public sphere that operates on a deliberative democracy and containing the symmetries of power through which deliberation and consensus can be realized. To better understand the online public sphere, we must also consider the "inter-subjective basis of meaning", the "centrality of respect for difference in democracy" and the influence of deliberative groups with similar opinion or identity on democracy (Dahlberg 2007, p. 827).

For SNSs users, intrinsic individual differences such as education background, gender, social and economic status, can also result in unequal political expression. Although some weaker social groups and grass-root clubs receive several benefits through the expression of their opinions (which results in an influencing of policy-making) online, we cannot deny the existence of a certain degree of social prejudice generated by knowledge gaps, a social elitist mindset, the special attractions of politicians. The voices of the minority group finally fall within common confines. Gender differences are also problematic for the equality of the opinion expression. A feminist, Fraser (1990, p. 115–116), criticized that Habermas' notion of the public sphere functions merely as a realm for privileged men to practice their skills of governance, for it excludes women and non-propertied classes. Therefore, political expressions are not equally powerful, articulate, or privileged, and cannot give voice to collective identities and interests.

Rationality of Political Expression on SNSs

Habermas (2005, p. 385–388) indicates that communicative rationality is rooted in an open flow of information within the public sphere and motivated by the aim of shared opinions that are accepted by the public. Individuals meet face-to-face according to legal or rational deliberating procedures in order to come to an agreement on a matter of public interest. A deliberative public sphere exists based on the rational expression and the procedures of open discussion aimed at achieving rationally motivated consensus (Habermas 1991b, p. 402, Gimmler 2001, p. 23, Papacharissi 2002, p. 11, Papacharissi 2009, p. 4–5). The ultimate purpose of a public sphere is to facilitate decision-making processes and guide public opinions. In any given public sphere, an eventual consensus and a rational deliberating procedure are "desirable outcomes" of public discussion (Papacharissi 2009, p. 5). While people express in ways that are not as rationally and tolerantly desirable as the public sphere requests, it could be even worse when they encounter oppositional opinions (Dahlgren 2005, p. 156). The Internet and networked technology have constructed various platforms for political expression. As such, it is unavoidable that the interaction taking place through these platforms does not assume the rational norm of public sphere; instead, we often find words full of incitement, irony, defamation and discrimination floating in cyberspace. Additionally, debating under a pseudo-anonymous name reduces the risk of punishment and creates a false sense of security that induces the users into believing in their anonymity. Consequently, it is not uncommon to find violent and extreme personalities online as people succumb to the exhilaration of free expression.

In spite of this, I would like to stress that such extreme behavior and general irrationality on online public spaces do not mean that rationality does not exist in cyberspace. Barton (2005, p. 184–185) analyzed the roles of blogs, discussion boards, and information providers of political expression, and found that political participation and discussion are constantly being generated on these platforms, fostering a critical-rational public sphere. Comments and reviews by public intellectuals are still of a high quality, while such arguments and rationality expressions can be found on SNSs, blogs and websites of mainstream media, playing vital roles in the influence of policy making. The existing rationality of political expression cannot represent the public sphere, but it, at least, provides the necessary condition to foster it.

The Problem of Inclusiveness on SNSs

Political expression is seen as a vital part of democracy that fulfills the public's essential need for debate, discussion and persuasion. Habermas originally suggests that a public sphere involves the discussions of those whom "have been previously excluded", and whose opinions are "considered on the basis of their merits, not on the social standing of the speaker" (Poor 2005). Online networked platforms are expected to provide more possibilities for the expressions of various opinions. When access is available, SNSs user can navigate among different platforms and groups to receive political information, as well as to make their voices heard. An online environment makes it possible to hold discussions with groups of higher diversity and to share and exchange opinions, as compared to an offline environment (Dahlberg 2001a). That is to say, the domination of discourse and exclusiveness of some groups can be dismantled.

SNSs provide information and platforms that offer opportunities for a widening of the role of the public in social and political interaction. They introduce alternative ways to be involved in groups and to pursue interests outside the traditional realm of offline public debate. Everyone should be included in the political expression according to the inclusive norm of public sphere. In practice, however, inclusiveness is a key point that has been criticized a lot. Heterogeneity and fragmentation are two problematic products of this inclusiveness of the public sphere.

The *heterogeneity of opinion* has been questioned as the authenticity of its claim has been disputed. While SNSs seem to provide open platforms that invite the participation of any and all citizens in public and social affairs, the diversity of opinions that is believed to influence policy makings is often challenged. In spite of the theoretical assumptions of heterogeneous opinion due to the benefits of online networked communication, there is much evidence to support the idea that the structure of Internet promotes a selective exposure to similarity, both politically and personally in online discussions (Brundidge and Rice 2009, p. 149–150, Iyengar and Hahn 2009, p. 19). A comparison between online discussions and news reports on the print media indicates that the former reflects little or no difference from the latter, and so, the Internet is actually not a better public sphere (Gerhards and Schäfer 2010, p. 143). Reports released on August 2014 by Pew Research Center and Rutgers University (Hampton, Lee et al. 2014, p. 3–4) revealed that SNSs users follow the "spiral of silence" and are more likely to express opinions that have already been agreed on by others; in other words, they are less likely to express their views if they believed their opinion to differ from those of their friends, family and colleagues. SNSs, therefore, are incongruent with the expectations of a public sphere, which connects heterogeneous people and gives the dissenters voices.

Studies also explore the problem of heterogeneity in an online public sphere. A survey by Brundidge and Rice (2009, p. 144) suggests that online political expression helps slightly in the formation of heterogeneous political expressions. In an online context, especially, political expressions and the facilitation of news have proven to be contributive towards the heterogeneity beyond the influence of "face-to-face" expression and traditional news media use (Brundidge 2010, p. 681). The use of SNSs is also associated with the "heterogeneity of discussion networks and activities in civic life" (Kim, Hsu et al. 2013, p. 498). Similarly, Benkler (2006, p. 256) argues that despite the "enormous diversities", some "mechanisms and practices" still exist within the online public sphere, so that people can find things in common when deliberating. Heterogeneity in online discussion demonstrates some harmful effects for the public sphere as the diversity of opinions is reduced. As such, the internet or ICTs are not ideal platforms for sufficient deliberation.

One other problem of inclusiveness is the fragmentation that existing heterogeneity can cause. This results in topics and orders that are possibly random and irrelevant, that distract instead of create a common starting point for political expression. In other words, when everything and anything is included on SNSs, there is a new problem of too many different voices but no consensus. Although there is a semblance of debate in the online space, commentators recognize that arguments are largely between 'like-minded' people who "share [a common] identity", causing the deliberating groups to become more or less insulated from the members of the opposition (Sustein 2001, p. 51–53, Sunstein 2009, p. 67–68). The ensuing problem, as Sunstein (2001, p. 67, 75) argues, is that the increasing social fragmentation can become a "breeding ground for group polarization" and "extremism." The discussion even transforms "towards a more extreme point" after the deliberation has been fully processed (Sunstein 2009, p. 60). This polarization, in turn, arises out of an understanding of the limitation of those who are differently situated, and therefore inflicts harm onto the public sphere.

From the arguments about heterogeneity and fragmentation of opinions above, it's clear that both "mainstream" opinions and diverse ideas exist on SNSs. The presence of these two facets helps to foster online public conditions. The public sphere, on one hand, needs a diversity of opinions to represent people of different social and political positions, so that democracy can proceed healthily; on the other hand, only by a consensus founded upon common interests and rationality can public opinion be formed and further influence public policies. That is the theoretical process proposed by Habermas about the workings of a public sphere.

However, it is imperative to mention that SNSs cannot be considered a wholly public sphere. Although the use of SNSs may contribute to the increasing possibilities of political expressions, and even help to foster the public sphere occasionally, ICTs only offer additional platforms for public discussion and cannot single-handedly transform a political and economic structure that has been established for centuries. New media is not a revolution; rather, it functions as an alternative for political expression in FtFC and on the traditional media. To sum up the arguments above, it's clear that SNSs are not complete public spheres because they cannot guarantee an equal, rational, independent and inclusive expression of opinion. Even if the rational expressions and diverse opinions have been deliberated by SNSs users, the question of sustainability remains debatable; especially since online networks are occupied by "consumerism, entertainment, nonpolitical networking and chat", which can totally eclipse democratic deliberation (Dahlgren 2005, p. 151). Where non-democratic political systems are concerned, although online platforms are relatively opened, different opinions can be delated through censorship. By analyzing the structural, the representational and the interactional dimensions of public sphere in Internet, Dahlgren (2005, p. 160) concludes that:

> *"The Internet is at the forefront of the evolving public sphere, and if the dispersion of public spheres generally is contributing to the already destabilized political communication system, specific counter public spheres on the Internet are also allowing engaged citizens to play a role in the development of new democratic politics. Discussion here may take the form of deliberation, with various degrees of success, but what is more important in this context is that talk among citizens is the catalyst for the civic cultures that are fueling this engagement."*

Therefore, what SNSs provide is not a public *sphere*, but rather, a public *space* where political discussions can increase. Unlike a public sphere, a public space allows a higher diversity of individuals and groups to engage in discussion with one another. This provides a more civilized atmosphere. It is therefore more meaningful to use the term "public space" when addressing a platform on which different social groups or individuals who participate and gain recognition through expressive forms of sociability congregate in cyber. As opposed to the Habermasian "public sphere" that is at once elitist, rational, and unitary, the sociability concept of "the public" attempts to engage people of different social strata (including the non-educated and grassroots) in public discussions. The framework of sociability conceptualizes "public space" from a civic perspective; "the public" is not a space for discussion which set goals for rational expression (Weintraub 1997, p. 25–27). This means that the framework of sociability is more suitable for the analysis of political expression on SNSs.

3.2 Information Flow on SNSs: from Private to Public Space

A contested boundary, believed to be affected by social environment and the interactions within, exists between the private and public domains on SNSs. A boundary has formed when users control the amount of information to be disclosed from the private to the public space. This information may contain details of an individual's personal data, daily lifestyle, feelings, thoughts and attitudes, as well as personal opinions regarding political affairs, public service and policies.

SNSs users disclose all possible kinds of personal information, attitudes and opinions in their profiles. In this section, I categorize the information that has been concealed or transferred from private to public space into two main parts:

a. Self-disclosure. This refers to the disclosure of all information about oneself, including personal data, things that happened in one's personal life, feelings and attitudes;
b. Political expression. This is the expression of personal political opinions, discussions with others about political affairs and policies. In general, anything that is related to public interest, the state and the government.

Any information relating to self-disclosure and political expression is always primarily located within the "territories of the self", in which personal information and opinions are concealed and isolated from people outside of the self. However, once SNSs users share this piece of information through the selection of the extent of visibility, they transfer this personal information to a region "outside of me". The extent of visibility varies according to social relationships. For example, if users allow access to only people who are closely related to the self, such as family members and friends, their personal information remains within a private space; however, if this accessibility is extended to people of a more distant relationships, such as acquaintances, colleagues/classmates or even everyone on the Internet, this piece of information is then considered to be transferred to the public space. In a brief diversion, it must be acknowledged that users can also discuss office affairs with colleagues or perform business-related dealings over professional SNSs, such as LinkedIn, XING or ResearchGate, that are meant for academic or professional purposes. However, these platforms are not my research targets due to their obvious public characters and specific functions as career or business improvement channels. Thus, my work will exclude these openly public SNSs and focus on social media SNSs like Facebook and Google+, which consist of both private and public characters.

3.2.1 Self-disclosure

Self-disclosure refers to the behavior in which one presents private information about the self. It highlights the quantity and the kind of personal information provided, and is necessary to develop relationship, build trust and construct self-identity (Berg and Derlaga 1987, p. 4, Ellison, Heino et al. 2006, p. 417–419, Krämer and Haferkamp 2011, p. 129). In the process of interpersonal communication, self-disclosure is an interactional behavior between two individuals in the form of exchanging information and facts about oneself, including personal expressions of feelings, opinions and judgments (Derlega, Metts et al. 1993, p. 1–4, Greene, Derlega et al. 2006, p. 411). During the first meeting, people introduce themselves by revealing basic personal information, such as name, age, working place and hometown, etc. Correspondingly, they expect the same level of reciprocity from their communication partners. This process is the beginning of the self-disclosure process, which helps individuals to make themselves known to and get closer to others. In other words, selective self-disclosure is a method of fostering relationships among people.

SNSs are platforms that help people to develop and maintain personal relationships. Communication on SNSs is an attribute of CMC that is also influenced by social network, both in the real world and in cyberspace. As a person's posting behavior on SNSs is strongly related to his personal relationships with others, self-disclosure has become part of the norms on SNSs. Some attributes of CMC, such as the "reduced nonverbal cues", control over time," the pace of the interaction", more equal to participate, hyper-personal interaction and anonymity, have effects on the online disclosure behavior (Walther 1996, p. 4–11, McKenna and Bargh 2000, p. 60–62, Schouten 2007, p. 11). Many studies reveal that individuals who get involved with online networks demonstrate an increase of sharing private information than those who do not (Joinson 2001, p. 179, Tidwell and Walther 2002, Van House 2004, p. 1). However, the process of self-disclosure on SNSs not only helps to develop personal relationships, but also results in a reduction in privacy. Especially in recent years, privacy and cyber-security have become the top concerns of SNSs users. They do not make the information posted accessible to everyone any longer; on the contrary, they manage their online personal information using the available privacy setting. This means that SNSs users have the option of posting their information or not, and even after this piece of information is posted, some private information, such as address, age and relationship, remain accessible to only certain people (family or close friends). It is common to see personal profiles on SNSs that are not opened to strangers. As such, self-disclosure is a way to explore how people transfer personal information and opinions from a private to a public space. By controlling the posting and visibility of information, SNSs users actually impose a boundary between "the private" and "the public".

3.2.2 Political Expression

Political expression, which comes from the freedom of speech in human rights, is defined as a commentary on matters of general public interest. Its forms include political discussion and expression of personal political opinion. On SNSs, it is common to see users revealing their personal opinions about social and economic policies. For instance, they may comment positively in a forum or in response to a public post to express support for their preferred president or chancellor electoral candidates; or conversely, they may express negativity or displeasure towards another candidate whom they view unfavorably.

SNSs are considered to be a better place for deliberation than other traditional public discussion platforms. The emergence of social media grants the resource-poor individuals in civil society – those denied access by the "old" media – access to the public sphere (Gerhards and Schäfer 2007, p. 211). A multitude of civic forums, on which views are exchanged and deliberated freely among citizens, provide platforms for an individual to express his opinions. They therefore expand the public domain and make an obvious contribution to the public sphere (Dahlgren 2005, p. 147). Empirical studies also demonstrate that people who use the internet politically are "much more likely to be invested in other forms of civic and political activism" (Smith, Schlozman et al. 2009, p. 7). Baym (2010, 28–38) agrees with this and points out that Internet users are more likely to participate in political activities, mass media consumption and voting action than non-users. Based on the research above, SNSs promotes political discussion. Taking into consideration the efficacy of traditional ways of civic or political participation, the influence of SNSs may not be strong enough. Admittedly, though, we cannot deny the extra facilitation brought by ICTs.

Political expression is the essential component of information circulation within a public space and is influenced by interaction and personal ties. The Internet expands the public space and provides enjoyment and convenience for political expression. In regards to SNSs, the advanced development of electronic devices make online civic participation "portable, interactive, context sensitive, connected and individual" (Gordon, Baldwin-Philippi et al. 2013). A more comfortable and joyful environment can be presented on SNSs in forms of social networks. People who previously avoided engagement in politics may become interested in getting involved in political activity due to peer pressure on SNSs (Vitak, Zube et al. 2009). Discussing politics with friends and sharing ideas are also important ways to socialize and to derive enjoyments, which helps relationships to grow as well. Individuals are therefore able to come together to learn, acquire and process political information, as well as deliberate over issues of public interest. Studies have indicated that users of SNSs are positively associated with an increase of political expression (Shen, Wang et al. 2009, p. 456, Gil de Zúñiga, Jung et al. 2012, p. 325–326, Bode, Vraga et al. 2013, p. 11–12). In a networked public space, political expression may involve more people who are connected through SNSs. They can be considered a social group, wherein they share similar attributes and opinions towards a specific topic. Hence, the political expression on SNSs has the potential to lead to further discussions on certain topics of interest. SNSs users can read selected information that has been disseminated from the participants of a common social network. This is permitted by a highly selective direction of information flow that is able to reach across the subset of social network of SNSs users.

In addition to expressing personal political opinions and engaging in political discussion, it is not unusual to for SNSs users to repost news reports or passages pertaining to public affairs. A study on SNSs usage during the 2008 US president election indicated that users shared links to news media such as CNN, the New York Times and the Huffington Post, and also cross-posted comments on their own Facebook profiles and on the main candidates' Facebook profiles (Robertson, Vatrapu et al. 2010, p. 14–15, 27–28). Posting opinions is, of course, a way of political expression, as is the sharing of news about public affairs. The Use and Gratifications Theory[4] explains that SNSs are utilized to seek information, socialize, and establish status and reputation, so that the social interaction and group discussion can be facilitated (Park, Kee et al. 2009, p. 729, Lee and Ma 2012, p. 331). Through SNSs, news content can be collectively shared by users with similar interests (Lee and Ma 2012, p. 332). As this shared information already preexists in a public space, I contend that the acts of sharing or reposting political news and passages without making personal comments is also considered a form of political expression. This is because through sharing political news and passages, SNSs users reveal unique personal political interests and opinions which reflect the inner layer of their personalities (Altman and Taylor 1973, p. 17). This is a way of disseminating information about themselves from a private to a public space.

3.3 Mechanism of Boundary Management

SNSs contain both private and public spaces. The boundary between "the private" and "the public" is implemented by the extensive management of personal information and political opinions flowing from a private to a public space that in turn determines the visibility of this information. Studies argue that self-disclosure

4 The use and gratifications theory analyzes why and how people actively seek out specific sources of media to satisfy specific needs from a social psychological perspective. It focuses mainly on processes of mass media and communication. This theory assumes that audiences are not passive consumers of media; instead, they have power over the consumption of media. Audiences play an active role in interpreting and integrating media into their own lives, so they can choose the appropriate source of media to meet their desires and achieve gratification.

and political expression on SNSs are different from those of FtFC and of traditional mass media. In this section, I'll introduce some theories to explain why SNSs users disclose personal information and express political opinions on SNSs, so that we can explore the mechanism of boundary management.

There are several kinds of interactions among individuals on SNSs. SNSs users disclose, share and exchange information and opinions in virtual communities and networks (Ahlqvist, Bäck et al. 2010, p. 3, Kaplan and Haenlein 2010, p. 60, Kietzmann, Hermkens et al. 2011, p. 242). Here, users share personal information, such as name, age, gender, location and profiles, to present an image of the self in an identity construction process in order to develop relationships with others. New communication technology, in the forms of hyperlinks, downloading files, videos, pictures and chats, has enhanced the ability of media to interact. Since traditional mass media (e.g. press, radio, TV) provides only a one-way information flow and allows a low capacity for feedback, the multimedia facilities of new communication technology lead to it being ranked higher on the interactive continuum (Kiousis 2002, p. 370, Rafaeli and Ariel 2007, p. 76). An exceptionally well-received feature of SNSs is the allowance for a higher degree of users' responses that seeks to improve the process of exchanging information and the level of communicative involvement of the users. With a simple click of the mouse, the user can upload personal pictures or initiate a video chat, thus creating a bi-directional flow of information. Psychologically speaking, the computer in no longer seen as a mere medium of communication, but as "an independent source of interaction" (Sundar and Nass 2000, p. 683).

The framework of sociability identifies the boundary between "the private" and "the public" as an interactional process that controls the "access to self" by limiting the extent of disclosure of personal information and political expression. SNSs comprise of both private and public spaces, of which the two realms are distinguished by the appropriation of social behaviors that relate to the role of the target partner. By disclosing or withholding personal information and political opinions, users are able to set a boundary that separates "the private" from "the public". From this knowledge, I deduce that the two controlling factors of the flow of information from a private to a public space – self-disclosure and political expression – are consequences of social interaction and behaviors as influenced by respective communication partners.

Several theories related to interpersonal communication explain why an individual reveals the self in the process of social interaction. Among them, the Social Exchange Theory (SET), the Social Penetration Theory (SPT) and the Communication Privacy Management Theory (CPMT) mainly explain how social interaction influences the acts of self-disclosure and political expression. SET provides a relationship foundation for information exchange while SPT transfers the key concepts of SET into an interpersonal communication context and constructs influential factors for self-disclosure and political expression specifically. CPMT proposes a boundary between "the private" and "the public", and emphasizes the right to control the boundary. It also considers the influence of the individual (micro) and social (macro) on one's personal behavior. The boundary is a dynamic process involving selective control over a personal boundary in a social environment. Like SET and SPT, CPMT also hypothesizes that the management of behavior itself is based on the judgment of costs/risks and benefits, as influenced by the communication partner and culture. As this chapter focuses on the relationship between the behavior of an individual and personal boundary, our discussion will concentrate on interpersonal interaction factors on the micro level. Cultural and macro-social environment will be discussed in the next chapter. It is imperative to make it clear that SET, SPT and CPMT are generally used for self-disclosure and privacy research, which is why they are also suitable to explain influential factors of political expression. I will venture deeper into these theories in an examination of the mechanism of boundary management.

3.3.1 Social Exchange Theory

SET understands *exchange* as a form of social behavior that can result in both economic and social outcomes (Lambe, Wittmann et al. 2001, p. 1–2). Providing an economic metaphor and an quasi-economic form to analyze social relationships, SET abides by a fundamental principle that humans in social situations choose behaviors that maximize their self-interests in any given situation (Worthy, Gary et al. 1969, p. 60–62). Homans (1961, p. 13) defines social exchange as "an exchange of activity, tangible or intangible, and more or less rewarding or costly, between at least two persons."[5] The process of social exchange is based on three assumptions that are human in nature: (1) human beings "seek rewards and avoid punishments"; (2) they are "rational beings"; (3) the standards used to "evaluate costs and rewards vary over time and from person to person" (West and Turner 2006, p. 188). Homans (1961, p. 19–22) emphasizes the individual behavior of action in interaction with one another, and explains that social behavior and the

5 The earliest discussion on social exchange from the perspective of social behavior see Homans, G.C. (1958). "Human Behavior as Exchange". American Journal of Sociology **63**(6): p. 597–606.

forms of social organization are produced by social interaction that reveals how one's behavior reinforces another's, and vice versa.

Blau (1964, p. 92–97), another important scholar of SET, focuses primarily on the reciprocal exchange of extrinsic benefits and the forms of association. Reciprocity is an "interdependent exchange" which "requires a bidirectional transactions" (Cropanzano and Mitchell 2005, p. 876). This means that when an individual performs a series of actions, he expects the receiver of these actions to mimic them back to him. SET assumes that human beings are rational creatures in their evaluation of risks and costs of a behavior. It is a principle of social behavior that the benefits/rewards must be greater than the costs (Homans 1961, p. 39–49). Interdependent reciprocity highlights the "interpersonal transactions", which functions based on the assumption that the initial behavior of an individual will result in a corresponding reaction of another (Cropanzano and Mitchell 2005, p. 876). Before engaging in acts of revealing, people already have concepts of equity and reciprocity that help to estimate the costs and benefits of communication on SNSs. SET suggests that the perceived reciprocity helps to keep people satisfied with and to maintain their social relationships (Chibucos, Leite et al. 2005, p. 139). In other words, people who observe a balance in the give-and-take front of a relationship are more likely to initiate and put effort into maintaining one. Individuals are motivated to gain rewards in social exchanges, making reciprocity a key factor for the self-disclosure in social interaction. If the benefits are higher than the costs, the relationship can continue developing.

Reciprocity in social exchange is measured by the quality of social interaction. It is not only individual-oriented, but can also become a social norm. Studies showed that reciprocity was considered a cultural mandate: anyone who does not comply will be punished (Mauss and Halls 1990, p. 47–48, Malinowski 2013, p. 8–9). The norm stipulates the behavior of an individual in society, which can vary according to different social propriety. People from different cultures can have different expectations of reciprocal behavior as well as perceive benefits by different degrees, although reciprocity can be considered a universal expectation. Therefore, reciprocity also varies within cultures and individuals.

For decades, SET has been used to explain the motivations for self-disclosure and the levels of intimate reciprocity (Worthy, Gary et al. 1969, p. 59, Derlega, Harris et al. 1973, p. 273, Collins and Miller 1994, p. 457). Since the end of 1990's, SET has become a key theory in the exploration of the costs and benefits of information disclosure, and to further discuss the issue of privacy protection on the Internet (Dwyer, Hiltz et al. 2007, p. 2, Cheung, Lee et al. 2015, p. 279). The studies mentioned above focus on the discussion of how reciprocity and costs influence disclosure behavior. On SNSs, especially, SET is extended in a discussion of privacy concern and online self-disclosure. Trust, risk beliefs and anonymity are adopted in the calculation of perceived costs, and reciprocity is considered as benefits. When exchange is perceived to be beneficial, the individual will likely share more about themselves and participate in an exchange relationship (Metzger 2004, Dwyer, Hiltz et al. 2007, Posey, Lowry et al. 2010, p. 185).

The framework of sociability views the boundary between "the private" and "the public" as a result of social interaction. In line with this framework, SET emphasizes the process of social interaction and explains the motivation that facilitates the exchange of information. The calculation of cost and reciprocity of information exchange decides the extent of disclosure behavior. SET, SPT and CPMT then develop this behavior to explain concepts of self-disclosure, political expression, and boundary control.

3.3.2 Social Penetration Theory

SET provides general motivations of information exchange in social interaction. However, there is a need for a theoretical basis that focuses on interpersonal interaction and concrete social behavior. For SNSs users, the boundary between "the private" and "the public" is formulated by the exchange of information between an individual and his communication partner during the process of interpersonal communication. The Social penetration theory (SPT) is an extension of SET that theorizes influential factors of self-disclosure and political expression in an interpersonal interaction. According to SPT, the act of revealing the self is a key component in the development of personal relationships and one that fosters closeness (Altman and Taylor 1973, p. 25–104). The term "social penetration" refers to a process of interpersonal exchange with the disclosure of intimate information (Altman and Taylor 1973, p. 27). Personal relationship begins with this exchange of information. As an individual discloses more regarding themselves to others, the relationship develops. SPT employs the metaphor of an "onion" to explain the development of a relationship. Just like an onion, a personality is conceived as a series of layers which differ along a central – peripheral or depth dimension (Altman & Taylor, 1973, p. 17). The outer or the peripheral layers are items having to do with more visible information, such as biological characteristics (e.g. age, sex and personal history), about the individual; and the inner central layers contain core properties, such as fears, self-concepts, and basic values.

Similar to SET, SPT also emphasizes the costs and rewards, satisfaction and dissatisfaction, gained from interaction and inhibition, all of which heavily influence a relationship (Altman and Taylor 1973, p. 6, 32–38, Taylor and Altman

1975, p. 18, Altman, Vinsel et al. 1981, p. 120). Benefits or rewards happen in the process of disclosure behavior between individuals, and fondness or affection increases with the development of their relationship; however, disclosure itself can also generate vulnerability and risks (Altman and Taylor 1973, p. 32–38). Here, the basic disclosure benefit is reciprocity, and on the contrary, the basic disclosure costs refer to risks. An important aspect of social penetration concerns the reciprocity of exchange between persons. "The greater the ratio of rewards to costs, the more satisfying the relationship" (Altman and Taylor 1973, p. 32).

There is an interactional social norm for information exchange in the theory of social penetration. In the process of relationship development, especially at the beginning and end of the relationship, individuals disclose the same level of intimacy which is regarded as an interactional norm since self-disclosure is often reciprocated and frequently serves to strengthen the ties that bind people in relationships (VanLear 1987, p. 299). Especially in the early exploration stages of a possible relationship with a stranger, social norms prescribe some equality of participation and disclosure, and individuals are supposed to exhibit reciprocity of exchange, so that the relationship can proceed further. "Those in close or longer-term relationships will not exhibit as much reciprocity, nor will they perceive an obligation to reciprocate" (Altman 1973, p. 256). When individuals disclose more information about themselves, they also expect others in the relationship to disclose information of an equal amount and of the same quality; if not, the relationship might come to the end. Consequently, the disclosure behavior of individuals affects the disclosure decisions of their communication partners. On SNSs, disclosure is frequently considered a norm of interpersonal interaction (Houghton, Joinson et al. 2013).

Altman and Taylor (1973, p. 27–30) understand the process of social penetration as the development of interpersonal relationships where self-disclosure is the key variable that measures the extent of revealed private and intimate information. SPT is first used to analyze the development of personal relationships, such as romantic relationship, friendship, doctor-patient relationship. In recent years, SPT has also been used to study privacy concerns and online relationship on the Internet. The increasing popularity of SNSs is causing users to share more and more personal information online (Gibbs, Ellison et al. 2006, p. 159, Posey, Lowry et al. 2010, p. 184).

Personal political views are usually located within the deepest recess of a person's personality (Altman & Taylor, 1973, p. 17). The central region is a highly intimate one that contains information which the individual would be less willing to reveal; whereas the peripheral or outer regions are opened, common and involved in the "public" life of the individual. As the relationship develops, more central layers are revealed (Altman & Taylor, 1973, p. 39). Former studies focused solely on the disclosure of personal information during social interaction, but neglected to deal with the revealing of political views during interpersonal interaction. In the process of social penetration, the divulgence of personal information and political views are taken to be separate but equally important behaviors. Especially since SNSs connect a large number of people who exchange not only personal information online, but also share personal political views and propagate interesting political news.

People are connected to, and interact with, one another on social networks. Similar to self-disclosure, political expression is also a behavior based on the balance of benefits and costs. Expressing political opinions can be interpreted as a reciprocal behavior as follows: SNSs users reveal their favorite political figures or mention some political news, so that a conversation can get started and they can develop relationships with their communication partners. Through this act of expression, SNSs users can exchange information and extend political knowledge. Furthermore, because SNSs is a platform for public discussion, this may cause an effect on policy-making. Online political expression can also be risky, especially as politics is often a sensitive topic and opposing ideas may give rise to argues and quarrel, which may in turn cause harm to personal relationships. In addition, illegal words on SNSs will not avoid punishment by law, or to express an opinion that is different as the majority's may be condemn by other SNSs users. This way, personal political views and interests, both of which are located within a private space, are transferred to a public space through the act of disclosure on SNSs. Former studies on political expression focus merely on people's willingness to express political opinions and participate in political discussions (Scheufele 2007, p. 233–238, Woong Yun and Park 2011, p. 212–213, Halpern and Gibbs 2013, p. 1161, Gil de Zúñiga, Molyneux et al. 2014, p. 614–616), but an important perspective is neglected: political expression happens both in the development of personal relationship and political participation. As such it is quite necessary to add this perspective into this dissertation, where the boundary between "the Private" and "the Public" is interpreted as the result of social interaction.

SPT treats social benefits and costs, as well as social norms, as motivations for the disclosure of personal information and political views during interpersonal interaction. Although most of the past studies merely concentrated on self-disclosure pertaining to the development of a relationship and within the spectrum of privacy concerns, SPT has already provided a special perspective of interpersonal interaction to observe the flow of information from a private to a public space. This theory conflates the divulgence processes of self-disclosure and political expression in order to explain how they are revealed from the "self-territorial" region to an "outside of me" region through cyber participatory behavior. After analyzing disclosure behavior from an interpersonal interactive lens, I find that SPT best suits the framework of sociability. Hence, this theory will be integrated into my models.

3.3.3 Communication Privacy Management Theory

Built on SPT, the Communication Privacy Management Theory (CPMT) uses the metaphor of boundaries to illustrate the division between being "private" and being "public". SPT mainly focuses on self-disclosure as the primary way to develop close relationships. Whereas self-disclosure treats openness as only one issue for consideration, another existing consideration is the desire for privacy. Within the demarcated space, people keep selected pieces of information private and believe that they own and assert a right over this data. During interpersonal interaction, people manage their personal information by using personal privacy rules, which are "guides for interpretation rather than ironclad laws" (Griffin 2012, p. 170).

Individuals may withhold personal information out of "fear of the repercussions that accompany a divulgence of such" (Derlega, Metts et al. 1993, p. 67). On the other hand, the extent of disclosure is dependent on the level of trust between themselves and their communication partners. In other words, the act of disclosure relies heavily on whether the divulged information can be kept "safe" upon disclosure. Let's assume that there is a communication channel linking the private and the public spaces of an individual. It provides a means for the transfer of information between both spaces. "By altering the degree of openness of the self to others, a hypothetical personal boundary is more or less receptive to social interaction with others" (Buchmann 2013, p. 17). Here, privacy can be interpreted as "a dynamic process involving selective control over a personal boundary either by an individual or by a group" (Derlega, Metts et al. 1993, p. 6, Buchmann 2013, p. 17). CPMT adopts five primary principles that inform how people regulate private information (Griffin 2012, p. 168–169):

> *"1) People believe they own and have a right to control their private information; 2) people control their private information through the use of personal privacy rules; 3) when others are told or given access to a person's private information, they become co-owners of that information; 4) co-owners of private information need to negotiate mutually agreeable privacy rules about telling others; 5) when co-owners of private information don't effectively negotiate and follow mutually held privacy rules, boundary turbulence is the likely result."*

CPMT highlights the "right" and the behavior to "control" based on social interaction. In this theory, individuals, who are the subjects of privacy, have autonomy over their personal information.[6] When there is a flouting or abuse of privacy rules, the individuals will try to construct new privacy rules to re-coordinate. Privacy in CPMT is also an interpersonal boundary-control entity born out of a "restriction of interaction and a seeking of interaction"(Altman 1975, p. 11). A boundary between "the private" and "the public", on the other hand, is a consequence of negotiation and interpersonal interaction to control the "access to self". In the dynamic process of managing the boundary, Griffin (2012, p. 170–172) summarizes the five factors presented by CPMT that collaborate to formulate a customary set of privacy rules:

Culture. Altman (1975, p. 77) points out that the differences and similarities of different cultures influence the social behaviours of individuals and the way in wich they perceive personal space. Similarly, Petronio (2002, p. 40–42) believes that culture influences the evaluation of openness and disclosure. Thus, people of different cultures manage the boundary between "the private" and "the public" differently. Culture also influences the processes of self-disclosure and political discussion in any given country.

Gender. Some studies suggests that women are more likely to disclose personal information than men (Gitter and Black 1976, p. 327, Hacker 1981, p. 385). However, a survey by Dindia and Allen (1992, p. 115) argues that one's behavior of self-disclosure can vary according to respective relationship partners. When a woman is developing a familial, friendly, or spousal relationship, she is prone to disclosing information about herself; but when the target is a stranger, a woman's willingness to disclose personal data is really no difference from that of a man. By virtue of gender differences, boundaries are sculpted differently according to men and women.

Motivation. People own the information and through the process of self-disclosure, form bonds relating to the data they reveal. By extension, when people disclose their personal interests, they are in some way revealing private information about themselves. People, therefore, will always have some form of motivation (such as reciprocity) that accounts for their acts of disclosure.

Context. The context is shaped by physical and social environments in which the information is shared. Additionally, social contexts influence behavior.

6 Although it is still controversial if an individual really has autonomy over their information, because the companies who own SNSs may collect users' data or even abuse it. However, user can still choose to post or not and this is also a way to regulate their privacy.

Risk/benefit ratios. Similar to how people judge the costs and profits of disclosure actions in SET, the risk/benefit ratios are the results of calculating the disclosure or withholding of private information. Generally, benefits of acts of revelation reduce stress after revealing, receiving enjoyment, encouragement and social support, or gaining social capital; on the contrary, risks are, for example, embarrassment, loss and failure, possible repercussions of secrets and some vulnerable data.

CPMT suggests that the boundary between "the private" and "the public" is negotiated and coordinated among various communication individuals, and is dependent on the perceived benefits and costs of boundary management. When others are given access to a person's private information, they become co-owners of that information and there "arises a need to negotiate mutually agreeable privacy rules" pertaining to the status and nature of this secret (Griffin 2012, p. 173). This process emphasizes the importance of interaction in the formulation of privacy rules with communication partners. By gauging the benefits of revealing personal information and political expression, SNSs users rationally control the boundary between "the private" and "the public".

In recent years, the study of CPMT has changed its focus from offline interpersonal interaction to the Internet, in order to explore issues relating to privacy management and motivations of disclosure on social media platforms. Interaction on the Internet is distinct from interaction on older media platforms in that bloggers develop different privacy rules and self-centric bloggers exhibit less motivation to delete blog entries (Child, Haridakis et al. 2012, p. 1869). On Facebook, the aforementioned five factors that inform the establishment of privacy rules are also evident. Facebook has a "*culture* of its own", which is made obvious by the users' compliance with its unique disclosure/privacy regulations; the *gender* of the user motivates his/her cyber personality and behavior differently as reflected by the different contents of disclosure; the desire to show off contributes to the *motivations* of self-disclosure; the *context* of Facebook decide the boundary and its privacy rules; and finally, the *risk-benefit ratio* start to function during online communication (Waters and Ackerman 2011, p. 112–113). CPMT serves numerous studies about Facebook and other SNSs, particularly studies pertaining to motivation factors, such as reciprocation and costs. Online privacy rules and privacy management are also explored. However, regarding social media platforms, there are still no clear solutions to the quest of locating a boundary between "the private" and "the public" and marking its changes dynamically. In line with CPMT and privacy rules with respect to SNSs, I will disregard the motivations of privacy management and focus on an exploration of the risks and benefits that is unique to the male and the female SNSs users of different cultural backgrounds.

3.3.4 Boundary Management on SNSs

Within the framework of sociability, the management of the boundary between "the private" and "the public" is a dynamic process and is a result of interpersonal interaction. Based on such interaction, SET interprets information exchanges as rational choices that are direct results of the calculation of respective benefits and costs. It provides a theoretical foundation for information transfer from a private to a public space. SPT extends the application of SET to interpersonal communication. Consequently, acts of specific self-disclosure and political expression become two key components of information exchange in social interaction. As a further development of SET and SPT, CPMT formulates a boundary between "the private" and "the public". People have ownership rights over private information, and deciding whether to reveal or conceal private information is part of the process of boundary management. In this dynamic process, people negotiate with and abide by privacy rules that are established based on results of the risk/benefit calculation, and which are influenced by gender and culture. In an application of these three key theories, I derive three factors which influence the boundary between "the private" and "the public": norms and influences, benefits, costs/risks. Let's contextualize privacy rules within SNSs and explore the mechanism of boundary management.

Figure 3: Theoritical Framework of The Boundary between The Private and The Public on SNSs

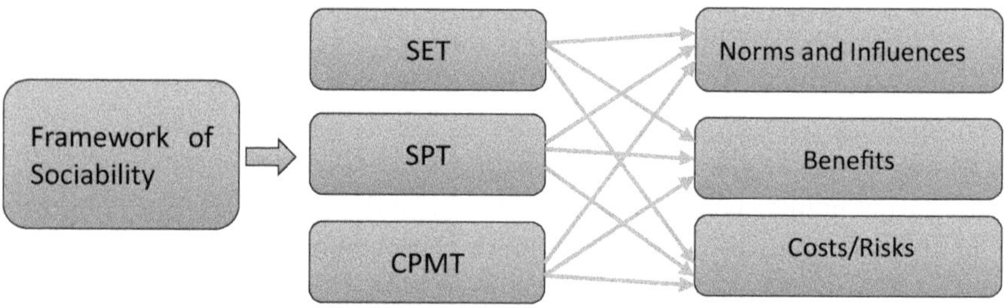

SPT postulates an "onion-skin" structure, in which personality is conceived as a series of layers which differs along a central-peripheral dimension (Altman and Taylor 1973, p. 17). As the relationship develops through social interaction, people venture closer to the more central layers and begin to develop a deeper understanding of their target communication partners. The central layers are the facets that people only want to share with those who are in a close relationship with them. People also only disclose personal information of similar intimacy level as that of their partners (VanLear 1987, p. 299). Consequently, the extent of self-disclosure increases with the development of a deeper relationship, causing the disclosure behavior of an individual to become predictable within the parameters of his/her social circle. Strangers, colleagues and acquaintances are located in the outer layers furthest from the self. As such, SNSs users may reveal less about themselves to members within these outer regions. However, an individual may disclose information in their inner space of intimacy to friends and family members who are situated near to the self within the structure. Studies we mentioned in Chapter 3.2 indicate that users disclose more on SNSs than on CMC, but it's still unclear how the different types of disclosure behavior displayed to these seven social circles differ from one another. To explore how SNSs users disclose information to people in different social circles, I propose the following question:

RQ 1: How does self-disclosure differ within different social circles on SNSs?

SNSs, as a social space, exhibit both private and public characters. People can choose the audience of their personal profiles and posts. Political expression, although public in content, forms an informational perspective that is contextualized by its audience. In other words, the target audience decides whether a particular political expression remains in private or is revealed to the public. It is not a convincing argument as this conclusion is derived by virtue of the default public setting on SNSs. Thus, I combine factors of frequency and visibility in an examination of users' political expression on SNSs, so that a clear boundary can be implemented between "the private" and "the public".

RQ 2: Within which level/s of closeness within the social circle should an individual reveal his/her political expression?

IV. "The Private" and "The Public": Differences and Similarities in a Globalized Germany and China

Economic development, globalization and the diffusion of ICTs reconfigure cultural and social differences so that countries all over the world become more similar in the ways they approach the issue of privacy concerns and freedom of speech in the cyber world. By extension, many countries also subscribe to the belief that SNSs expand the parameters of public discussions, political or not. With the rising popularity of the Internet across the globe, people of different nationalities begin to adopt similar attitudes towards privacy protection and freedom of opinion expression. Consequently, the location and interpretation of the boundary between "private" and "public" in different countries may also reflect some similarities. This chapter analyzes the private and public concepts of "private" and "public" in a cross-cultural context, using the framework of sociability as a reference point. I contextualize the concepts of "private" and "public" historically and socially within Germany and China to analyze the respective differences and similarities of how these two nations view the respective boundary between "the private" and "the public", and examine the ways in which processes of globalization and digitalization influence both German and Chinese cultures and social behaviors on SNSs.

4.1 "The Private" and "The Public" in German Society

I have selected Germany and China as the basis of my comparative study as these are countries that exhibit starkly contrasting cultures and social traditions. As such, we may assume that these two countries display some obvious differences in the ways each of them appropriates the boundary between "the private" and "the public". Furthermore, the process of globalization and the influence of ICTs introduce more privacy concerns along with their functions as platforms for public discussions and deliberations. This may indirectly result in more similarities than differences between the Western and the Eastern societies. The rapid development of the Internet and the change in social structure in China (a collectivistic and Eastern country) make the Chinese society an ideal sample piece for the analysis of the influences of digitalization and globalization. On the other hand, Germany, with its traditional notion of *public* and *public* sphere, is a qualified representative of the individualistic Western country. In recent years, the ICTs have brought about a transformation in the boundary between "the private" and "the public". This has raised many concerned discussions within the German society. To understand the changes in the differences and similarities between the notions of "private" and "public" in Germany and China, I will examine the historical transformation with respect to the influences of digitalization and globalization.

4.1.1 Historical Transformation of Concepts of "Private" and "Public" in Germany

The concepts of "private" and "public" in Germany are relatively young. Schiewe (2003, p. 60–61) describes the developing and transforming process of the word "public (Öffentlichkeit)" in German history as such: From the medieval times to the 17th century, the word "offenlich" (later "öffentlich") referred to an article that can be clearly seen by everyone. The antonyms of "offenlich" are "secret (geheim)", "sneaky (heimlich)" or "hidden (verborgen)". The word "publicus" first appeared in the Roman law and was associated with the rights and duty of a ruler, as well as being the equivalent of a government. With the implementation of Roman laws in Germany, the words "öffentlich" and "publicus" grew to be associated with the "state (staatlich)". In the 18th century, the notion of an "audience (publikum)" was created alongside the development and diffusion of the press. At first, the "audience" referred to the recipients of state regulations. This notion was derived from the Latin expression "publicum, publica". However, the Age of Enlightenment saw a great influx of French literature that heavily influenced and distorted its initial meaning. "Publikum" thereafter referred to all those who allowed themselves to be enlightened through new forms of sociability (Geselligkeitsform), such as Arts and Literature, as well as public opinion, that educated the "audience" and empowered them. Since the middle of the 18th century, "audiences" had access to education, literature and arts. Consequently, a "literature public sphere (literarische Öffentlichkeit)" was formed. Following that, the French Revolution introduced the concept of "public opinion (öffentliche Meinung)", which includes political discussions among citizens, to Germany. From then on, *public (Öffentlichkeit)* begin to take on a more political meaning. 1812 is a very special year for the Western society. It was the year that the Spanish Constitution established the principles of universal male suffrage, national sovereignty, constitutional monarchy and freedom of the press, and supported land reform and free enterprise. After that, liberalism became the trend in Europe. The meaning of "public" transformed into a place where public opinions are formed and where public demands work as counter-reactivity to the rules of the state. The 19th century generally understood the meaning of "public" in terms of Marxist theory and worker movements, so that the "public opinion" became associated with the critics. Between the 19th to 20th centuries, mass media further changed the meaning of "public opinion", which was at that time interpreted as "suggestibility (Beeinflussbarkeit)". Public opinion in the 20th century referred to thoughts and ideas formed with the help of the electronic media, and which exert a degree of influence on public institutions. This process is thought to be the fundamental construction of a "public sphere (öffentliche Sphäre)", as suggested by Jürgen Habermas (1991, 181–210).

A modern concept of "privacy" developed with the emergence of law in the USA in 1890. Privacy became a human right. Since there is no word in the German dictionary to represent "privacy", the words with the closest meaning are "Privatsphäre" or "Privatheit".[7] The Sphere theory (Sphärentheorie) indicates that personality rights can be divided into three different spheres:

- The *social sphere*: Sozialsphäre, also known as the public or individual sphere (Öffentlichkeits- oder Individualsphäre), is the space in which an individual interacts as a community-related and community-bound person in the context of public life with other members of society[8].
- The *private sphere* (Privatsphäre, privacy) contrasts directly with the social sphere and refers to a range of private autonomous way of life in which the individual can develop and preserve his individuality[9].
- The *intimate sphere* (Intimsphäre) is an absolutely protected, inviolable, core area of private life, resulting from the guarantee of human dignity and guarantee of essential content of each relevant freedom fundamental[10].

Here, privacy is conceived as an "informational autonomy" (informationelle Selbstbestimmung) instead of the "right to be left alone" in Germany. Capurro (2005, p. 40–41) explains that the German idea of privacy is based on the Western concept of autonomy, at least as a "regulative idea"[11] that is "related at the same time to the society in which such autonomous individualities live". He further argues that people are able to formulate their own ideas if they are permitted to exchange

7 The original meaning of "Privatheit" is defined by Hannah Arendt as the sphere of property (Eigentum, different from estate, Besitz) that includes one's own household (in the sense of working life, the family, including all slaves, property, etc.) and the area of the necessities of life.

8 Entscheidungen des Bundesverfassungsgerichts (BverfG) 65, 1 (44).

9 BVerfG 35, 202 (220).

10 Ständige Rechtsprechung des BVerfG, and BVerfGE 109, 279 (313 f.).

11 Coinciding with the ideal that Kant himself stresses in his opusculum, "An Answer to the Question: What is Enlightenment?"

ideas and opinions freely. This can be realized only when the information transfer in media (including digital media) is not censored. Here, the material being censored is thought to contain an "implicit" or "explicit" violation to privacy. In networked communications today, "the ethics of informational autonomy is being conceived as an ethics of knowledge sharing" (Capurro 2005, p. 40–41). The beginning of legal data protection in Germany dates back to 1978. Later on, in 1983, the German Federal Constitutional Court (Bundesverfassungsgericht) made a decision for a Volkszählungsurteil (National census judgement) to fight against "what was seen as excessive state interference in the field of personal data" (Capurro 2005, p. 41). However, there are no laws like the *US Freedom of Information Act* (went into effect in 1967) in Germany, which allows for the full or partial "disclosure of previously unreleased information and documents controlled by the United States government".[12]

4.1.2 Increasing Privacy Concerns and Expanding Public Space on SNSs

The process of digitalization in Germany began in 1990's, when communication technology, such as DVD, CD and MP3 increased its stakes in the German market (Schildt and Siegfried 2009, p. 488). Since the mid 1990's, the number of Internet users has increased as well. Between the year of 1998 and 2000, the Germans, particularly, experienced the highest increase in terms of Internet users. In 2003, German TV underwent a remarkably important transformation. When Digital Video Broadcasting Terrestrial (DVB-T) replaced Analogue Terrestrial Television, televised programs became transmittable over the Internet. By the beginning of 2005, 69% of the entire German population were Internet users. This figure grew steadily until 2013, when Internet users in Germany increased to 54.2 million, with 77.2% of the German population having access to the Internet (ARD and ZDF 2014). 74% of the German Internet users are also registered on a SNSs platform, while 66% of them are active users (Huth, Arns et al. 2011, p. 6). SNSs expand the range of interaction possibilities among individuals on the Internet. Corresponding to this change in the media environment, the emergence of the Internet and SNSs within the German society evoked an increase in concerns pertaining to privacy.

---

12 Freedom of Information Act. retrieved May 10th, 2015, from http://www.detroitpubliclibrary.org/sites/default/files/attachments/Freedom%20of%20Information%20Act_0.pdf.

The use of new communicational technologies also involves new risks to the privacy protection of individual users. The reasons could be as follow (Fraunhofer 2008, p. 10): (1) SNSs usually require a lot of private information and sensitive data from users but this data is unprotected and available to others; (2) central data storage with an Internet service provider ensures easy access and high service availability, but personal data are easily accessible and may be selected as well; (3) there are few or no conditions for the creation of new user accounts; thus increasing the number of users and exposure; (4) strong linkages of data are formed with the relationships among online users. These links allow the extraction of new information from and about the information content of individual data objects; (5) it is easy to identify users and their corresponding data using these platforms, making it easy for others to steal personal information. These benefits of software enable personal data and information to be easily collected and abused. Therefore, users who have registered accounts with several SNSs choose platforms that meet their needs. The security of personal data (96%) and privacy setting (92%) are two of the most important deciding factors (Huth, Arns et al. 2011, p. 22). In a survey with German Internet users conducted in 2011 by BITKOM, almost all of the respondents (94%) believed that the networks should provide better data protection, and 86% of the respondents suggested the implementation of a privacy seal for social networks; a further 78% are in favor of the adoption of state regulations or laws on data protection on SNSs (Huth, Arns et al. 2011, p. 29).

SNSs provide alternative platforms for the expression of political opinion. Although fewer SNSs users from democratic countries read up on political news or engage in opinion expression as opposed to their non-democratic counterparts, political engagement is proven to be related to Internet access (Kroh and Neiss 2013, p. 174). The Internet enhances people's interest in politics, especially where the younger generation is concerned, and provides an accessible platform for people who are poorly integrated into traditional political process, such as the poor, the young and the political minorities. This empowers every individual in terms of political participation (Norris 2003, p. 38–40, Kroh and Neiss 2013, p. 175).

Although SNSs are supposed to be an extended space for public discussion, there are only a few Germans who actually express their political opinions or participate in political affairs online. A survey on German SNSs in 2013 indicates that the most important motivation to use SNSs is to stay contact with friend. In the 23 items of motivation list of SNSs use, to seek or search political information or to discuss political issues is excluded (BITKOM 2013a). In 2014, a report released by ARD and ZDF reveals that only 6% of German Internet users seek political or economic news on SNSs daily, and only 21% do so weekly (ARD and

ZDF 2014). As compared to private purpose, German SNSs users do not spend much time on political expression.

Figure 4: Reasons for using social Networks (Multiple choices possible, n=684) (BITKOM 2013a)

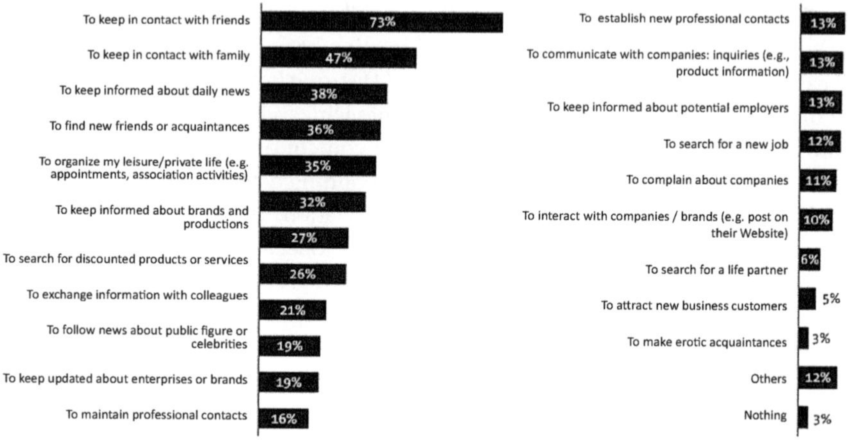

The utilization of SNSs is supposed to facilitate interaction between candidates and voters, as well as to garner more attention for political figures during the election period. This has become a top research topic of German political communication. SNSs for political purpose has produced obvious effects, especially on political motivation and on informing users about political information. However, the reality is that German political parties and voters are not so active on SNSs. In 2010, CDU, FDP, SPD and Grüne opened official Facebook accounts but only Grüne used the account to interact with users. Die Linke did not even register for an official Facebook site (Elter 2010, p. 64–66). In 2012, the situation improved with the widespread use of Facebook. 368 (59,4%) of 620 deputies in German Parliament (Bundestag) have an official profile on Facebook (Siri, Melchner et al. 2012). A recent survey published by GESIS reveals that Facebook is widely used for Bundestag election from 2009 (last election) to 2013 (the latest election), while the Facebook profiles and official sites increased to 1,669; correspondingly, the number of posts also increased to 468, 914 while the number of comments hit 596, 569 (Kaczmirek, Mayr et al. 2013).

As the studies on the ways in which Germans express political opinions on SNSs is still limited, it is difficult to calculate to the extent that which SNSs is used for political expression in Germany. However, we can still assume that the use of SNSs for political purpose is quite limited in the German context, when taking all the above data into consideration. We will survey how German discuss political affairs and find out more details pertaining to the boundary between "the Private" and "the public" in this dissertation.

To sum up the meaning of "private" and "public" in the German society, there is traditionally an association of "the private" with "informational autonomy" and "the public" with "public opinion" or "public sphere". The prevalence of SNSs and the Internet change the notions of "the private" and "the public", as well as provide a chance for people to rethink the boundary between them. "Informational autonomy" provides a broader understanding of shared information and emphasizes the ability of a person to think independently. In addition, the expanded online public space is beneficial to the diversity of opinions as it creates room for discussions and deliberation.

4.2 "The Private" and "The Public" in Chinese Society

If Germany is considered a representative of the Western traditions of "private" and "public", China, with its fully oriental understanding of the two polarities, must be its corresponding Eastern counterpart. The Chinese society is more collectivistic in its obvious non-observance of privacy. This contrasts sharply with the individualist Western society that has its own definition of *private*. However, as the "ethics of knowledge sharing" brought about by ICTs began to make its appearance in the Chinese society, people began to share their private information. Meanwhile, they have to consider the security of this personal information that is now floating in cyberspace. In order to understand the transforming concepts of "private" and "public" within the contemporary Chinese society, we need to return to ancient Chinese history.

4.2.1 Cultural Backgrounds and Historical Review of "The Private" and "The Public" in China

Countries that observe the collectivistic cultural trend do not view personal interests as importantly as group interests. As such, not enough attention is paid to the notion of privacy. China, as a collectivistic country, had no equivalent concepts of "private" and "public" to that in Western society. This was before the 20th century. In the 1st century AD, an early book "Shuo Wen Jie Zi" (说文解字) explained the genealogical meaning of Chinese words and related the idea of "private" (Si, 私) to treachery. "Public" (Gong, 公), on the other hand, was interpreted as the opposite of "selfish" and suggested "equality" in terms of property. After the Qin Dynastic

(221–207BC) union of the state, the "public" became a concept associated with the empire and the king (沟口雄三 2011, p. 5–6).

During the 10th century Song Dynasty of China, the idea of "public" was changed by Neo-Confucianism philosophy. Neo-Confucianism tried to guide its development in a "rationalistic and humanistic" manner by eradicating the "religious and superstitious elements" that prior dominated Han-Confucianism (202BC–220AD) (Blocker and Starling 2001, p. 64). It employed metaphysics as a guide for developing a rationalist ethical philosophy and focused on the personal psychological world, outer society, morals and ethics (沟口雄三 2011, p. 11). "Public", from a Neo-Confucian perspective, refers to a neutral situation that was generated naturally and without bias. "Public" as a regulator of nature therefore combined everything in nature together in an orderly manner. In the human society, "public" was characterized by humanity, reliability, mannerism and wisdom. Whereas in the Chinese feudal social relationships, "public" was the moral guardian that kept social statues in order (沟口雄三 2011, p. 13). The Neo-Confucian idea of "private", as the opposite concept of "public", referred to human behaviors or biases towards people of lowly social status who disturb this neutral situation. Here, "Private" emphasizes on the difference between the desires of an individual during the process of socialization. Any human desire and initiative were considered to be against the "public" and so, against the natural order of things. People should not possess any human desire and must behave according to social propriety. The concept of "the private" was therefore denied by the philosophy of Neo-Confucianism.

Human desires could be categorized into "natural desire" (desire for sex and food) and "social desire" (desire for survive and property, and the material desire). The concept of social desire did not exist until the late Ming Dynasty and early Qing Dynasty (17th century AD). As the Ming Dynasty prospered economically, the types of commercial products and materials grew in proportion with the people's desire for property and other material goods. The natural desires were no longer as important as before as "private" at that time referred to social desires (沟口雄三 2011, p. 13–20). Accordingly, the notion of "public" also changed to mean equality. By that, it meant that when conflicts between the lords and the proprietors or between the tenants and the landlords occurred, privileges should be forbidden.

Although the concepts of "private" and "public" varied across different Chinese eras, one recurring distinctive feature between them is the respective association with the family and the country. The "private" referred to the private lives of not just an individual, but of a whole family. People lived collectively as a family in ancient China. The family was the basic unit of society so that the goal of the family was more important than the goal of an individual. Conversely, the "public" stood for the power of heaven[13] and the country. The most powerful person in ancient China during was the Emperor, who was also known as "the son of heaven (天子, Tianzi)" and was recognized as an embodiment of the power of heaven. He or she[14] ruled the country comprising "all under heaven". In those days, the public life of ancient Chinese men revolved around the daily morning meetings held in the palace that were chaired by the Emperor, during which the officials would discuss national affairs with the Emperor. The "public" was an extension of the family, and the whole country was conceptualized as a big family helmed by the Emperor (the father-figure who is the most powerful person of a family); all the Chinese folks were members of this big family.

The boundary between private and public spaces in ancient China was clearly embodied by the typical Chinese architectural structure of the Kong Family Mansion. This is the historical residence of the direct descendants of Confucius. The Kong Family Mansion is divided into two parts: the southern part functions as a front office where discussions or actions pertaining to political and public affairs could take place, while the northern part acts as a living room for familial interaction. The Kong men were conferred the highest status in a family and concurrently held official posts within the region. They dealt with political affairs in the front office during the day and returned to the private quarters to interact with family members after work. The spatial boundary between private and public spaces, or rather, between the front office and the living room, was extremely clear. To emphasize the immutable quality of this boundary, only the Kong men were allowed to physically transgress the division separating the front and the back of the mansion. Other substitute officers who were not members of the Kong family were allowed to enter only the office and not the living rooms; hence, these visitors would never get to meet or interact with any of the Kong womenfolk and children. All of the residences in Chinese history, including the Forbidden Palace (where the Emperor lived), shared a similar structure. Therefore, we can conclude that the private family lives of Chinese political figures were well-protected by this architectural structure and political system. One thing that we should keep in mind, however, is that unlike Western society, the public region in China was not accessible to everyone; it was reserved only for

13 The "Power of heaven" refers to ancient China that was operated under the Mandate of Heaven.

14 China did come under the rule of a female Emperor (Wu Ze Tian) during the Tang dynasty (618–907AD).

officials and the aristocrats. This is one marked distinction between "the private" and "the public" outside of the family nucleus.

Within a family in ancient China, on the other hand, there was no clear distinction between "the private" and "the public". The concept of "family" is deeply rooted within the traditional Chinese culture. The basic understanding is that family members share common properties and personal information within the familial nucleus. Only intimate issues (e.g. sex) are kept within the territorial of a person. Macgowan (1908, p. 180–181) explains:

> *"Fortunately, the Chinese do not believe in the privacy of a home as we do. They do not mind having the whole details of their daily experience seen by everyone that cares to look. How they live, what they eat, and even the family jars that we try to hush up from the public are things that seem to be common properties and not to belong exclusively to this particular family who is most concerned."*

As such, there is no Chinese word encompassing all the meanings of the English word "privacy". "Privacy", in the English context, as discussed in Chapter 2.1, is highly related to the individual, family and inner layer of personality. Due to the influence of collectivistic culture, the concepts of "inner", "personal" and "family" (that resembles Goffman's "territorial of self") of "the private" are ambiguous to the Chinese population.

At the beginning of the 20th century, the current Chinese society modernized the original concept of "public". The term "public" now refers to a collection of people who share common interests and features in a country. This is really quite similar to the modern definition of citizens. "Private", on the contrary, refers to individually and privately owned properties and interests. By the late 20th century, the transfer of economics in China from central planning to market-oriented changed the "power relations" of individual, social groups and state institution. Consequently, the increased social mobility gave rise to the change of social structure and resulted in a growing individualization amidst the Chinese society (Yan 2009, p. 25–56, 273–281). The traditional and collectivistic society of the olden days changed rapidly when people started to leave their families in search of work in the big city. They are removed from the familiarity of their familial and social groups for the first time, and thrown into a new and unfamiliar territory where they have to watch out for themselves. This shifts the traditional culture of collectivity into a modern culture of individuality. The Chinese society thereafter began to place more emphasis on personal well-being, personal interest and personal value. The concept of "private" thus becomes clearer for Chinese people as they now possess a heightened sense of entitlement to privacy rights and protection of personal interests.

The notion of privacy as a right has been sanctioned by Chinese laws as of the 1980's. Article 75 of the General Principles of The Civil Law (GPCL) of the People's Republic of China became effective on 1st January 1987. This act protects the citizen's lawful property, including "lawfully earned income, housing, savings, articles for daily use, objects art, books, reference materials, trees, livestock, as well as means of production" that the law permits a citizen to possess and other lawful property. Privacy, thus, operates as an extension of personality rights. As the Internet grew more prevalent, the Chinese government recognized that some form of measure had to be undertaken in order to protect the privacy of internet users. This resulted in the introduction of the Personal Information Protection Act. Furthermore, the Internet and SNSs raised privacy breaches such as stolen bank information, online credit card fraud, and big data techniques of sneaking into SNSs accounts to rip off personal information, to the attention of Chinese people. Under such pressing circumstances, privacy protection became an important imperative of the Chinese legislative body. This urgency is reflected in two "milestones" of Chinese internet laws: firstly, the Chinese government established the China National Information Security Testing Evaluation & Certification Center (CNISTEC)[15] in 1999; then, in 2005, the News Office of the State Council and Ministry of Information Industry co-implemented the Regulations for Administering the Internet News and Information Services[16] (Wu, Lau et al. 2011, p. 609). All these measures were taken in hope of reducing, if not eradicating, internet crimes and making the cyberspace a safer place for Chinese users.

15 CNISTEC is an independent, government-sponsored organization that is the designated national certifying authority for 11 security-related items, including: Access Control Products, such as firewalls, routers, proxy servers/gateways; Authentication Products; Security Auditing Products; Security Management Products; Data Integrity Products; Digital Signature Products; Non-repudiation Products; Commercial Encryption Products; Tempest Products; Information System Security; and Information Security Services.

16 Regulations for Administering the Internet News and Information Services aim to standardize internet news information services, satisfy the needs of the public for internet news information, safeguard national security and public interests, protect the lawful rights and interests of internet news information service units, and promote the healthy and orderly development of internet news information services. This applies to the provision of internet news in services in the People's Republic of China.

4.2.2 "The Private" and "The Public" as Merging Concepts on SNSs

The Internet and its ensuing privacy concerns help to develop the Chinese's understanding of "private". A survey conducted by Beijing Youth Daily in 2002 revealed that over 55% interviewees believed that it became harder to maintain privacy over the Internet; and 29.3% of interviewees believed that their personal information has been revealed without permission[17]. During the early developmental stages of the Chinese Internet, most privacy issues were related to scandals of Chinese entertainment stars. As SNSs got more popular, people found it easier to share more personal information but harder to control their privacy. As an increasing number of college students and young working adults register accounts with the Chinese versions of Facebook- Renren (www.renren.com, named Xiaonei before)[18], the influence of SNSs increases in Chinese society. As a result of rapid registrations, Renren received 160 million users in 2011 (Hille 2011).

Many discussions and suggested solutions about privacy protection were suggested by Chinese people. A recent survey reveals that a large percentage of the Chinese population is willing to prosecute any violator of their privacy (He 2011). In a semantic network analysis on issues of privacy in Weibo, Yuan, Feng et al. (2013, p. 1027) concludes that:

> *"Contemporary China is in a period of rapid social transformation. An expanding market economy, the growing importance of new forms of sociality, and an emerging sense of individuality, along with the fast development of ICTs, are all part of the contemporary environment that is cultivating and reframing people's understandings of privacy. The discourse on privacy on Chinese social media not only reflects but also constitutes changes in people's lifeworlds."*

In addition to the concept of "the private", the diffusion of new communication technology in China also changes the way that people express political opinions and generate discussions. After more than 20 years of fast development of ICTs in the forms of websites, news portals, online instant message tools (i.e. QQ, MSN), blogs and online forum-BBS (Bulletin Board System) in China, SNSs broke into the Chinese society in 2006. Channels to express opinion have also been

17 Beijing Youth Daily: Survey reveals that Privacy protection is getting more and more difficult over the Internet. Retrieved from http://news.xinhuanet.com/newscenter/2002-12/02/content_646092.htm.

18 Besides Renren, Kaixin (www.kaixin001.com) is also a Chinese SNSs that issimilar to Facebook. Unfortunately, it lost its market soon after establishment. Kaixin slowed down its expansion from the 13th most popular website in 2010 to the 45th in 2013 (ALEXA, 2013). Thus, I only mentioned Renren here.

reinvented with changes in communication technology. BBS and the review sections of news portals, such as Qiangguoluntan (http://bbs1.people.com.cn/) and Tianya (http://www.tianya.cn/), provide opportunities for Chinese people to discuss social and political affairs. However, these online forums are being monitored by board managers (Banzhu), who are authorized to set online rules and control the contents of the forums. Studies suggest that the public sphere in China is in its emerging stage (Yang and Calhoun 2007, p. 211, Zhou, Chan et al. 2008, p. 759). Although the online public sphere cannot be fully developed over the Internet due to an insufficient diversity of opinions and fragmentation, it does provide an alternate access to Chinese political information, as well as function as an alternate platform for deliberation. The same can be said for blogging platforms in China. Some politically sensitive contents may be deleted by board managers or blocked by automatic online systems, but users have come up with several ingenious ideas to navigate these systems by avoiding sensitive words through substitution with other words of the same pronunciation or by using the abbreviations of these offensive words. The meaning of these messages is thus preserved while eluding the obliteration of censorship systems. If all else fails, there is always the option to change platforms since there are so many different hosts in China. MacKinnon (2008, p. 31) argues that "blogs may be a catalyst for long-term political change" by extending public space for political discussion and activism in China.

Faced with strong competition from other online platforms, blogging finally lost its edge. By the end of 2013, Blog users comprised of only 14.2% of all Internet users and blogging exhibited a strong declining trend (CNNIC 2014, p. 42). The new emerging Chinese micro blog "Weibo" eventually replaced the original Blog in 2008. Facilitating numerous discussions on social problems and public policies, Weibo evolved into one of the dominant online channels of expression for Chinese netizens. Public intellectuals and celebrities post their opinions on Weibo, which are then reviewed and reposted by other users. Weibo users demonstrate more willingness to express political opinions online than offline (Wu 2013).

By now, China is already processing a transformation of social structure and personal relationships. In this non-democratic country, political and civic participation emerge on SNSs platforms. When traditional mass media is not allowed to report on crises that occur within the Chinese society, Weibo works as an alternative platform for the news to be disseminated and as a platform for public discussion; this may further influence the agenda of traditional mass media.[19] Weibo is

19 A typical for this situation is the Wenzhou train collision in 2011, more details about this accident please see p. 175–176.

also a place to publish articles on controversial topics and to generate discussions. In the first half of 2014, 43.6% of the Internet citizens in China have used Weibo; 80.3% of users read news articles on Sina Weibo, which places the first one motivation of Sina Weibo utilize (CNNIC 2014). Weibo has become the most important source of breaking news and is now a public platform for public discussion. Although Wechat is increasing its social influence by converging the function of SNSs and Instant Message Software, Weibo is still irreplaceable, especially as a platform for public discussion.

Through a historical overview of the notion of "the Private" and "the Public", it is obvious that German and Chinese societies have totally different understandings about the boundary. The process of the transforming notion of "the Private" and "the Public" in Chinese society demonstrates a rising public sphere that is constructed by the media (first by press and electronic media, and later extensively by digital media). This process is similar to "the structural transformation of the public sphere" in German society. The Internet plays an especially important role in the construction of a space for public discussion, which further contributes to the diversity of opinions in China. Although a mountain of differences exists between the traditional German and Chinese interpretations of "the Private" and "the Public", globalization, modernization and the diffusion of Internet worldwide, all contribute to a transformation in both societies and bring about similarities in them. In order to look deeper into these differences and similarities, we need to analyze the changes in German and Chinese societies from the social, economic and cultural perspectives.

4.3 Globalization: Digital Differences and Similarities of the Boundary between "The Private" and "The Public"

As previously mentioned, Germany and China observe different cultures and social traditions. Nevertheless, people in these two countries have demonstrated a surprising number of similarities in the ways they conceptualize "the private" and "the public". This could be due to the influence of the Internet. Due to the formation of a common set of values and attitudes related to the online freedom of expression, privacy, trust and security across the globe, "a global internet culture" is forming (Dutta, Dutton et al. 2011, p. 3). The use of the Internet increases with "world-system status, privatization and competition in the telecommunications sector, democracy and cosmopolitanism" (Guillén and Suárez 2005, p. 45). The global outcry for online privacy also suggests that levels of apprehension with regards to privacy concerns are mostly homogenous in many countries, "so that governments and corporations must be cognizant of the prevailing cultural and individual differences that influence internet users' behavior vis-à-vis online privacy" (Cho, Rivera-Sánchez et al. 2009, p. 411). Additionally, Internet users across countries feel that people should be able to freely "criticize their government" and "express their opinions anonymously on the Internet" (Dutta, Dutton et al. 2011, p. 12). Also, studies demonstrate that the diffusion of the Internet, which is considered an effective forum for fostering deliberation, gathering information and exchanges among citizens, has motivated political opinion expression and deliberation (Jennings and Zeitner 2003, p. 312, Hardy and Scheufele 2006, p. 73). The BBC World Service poll conducted in 26 countries in 2010 revealed that 78% of adults feel that the Internet has given them more freedom (BBC 2010, p. 1). Echoes of such similar beliefs across different countries can be seen as the effect of globalization.

The unified internet culture is a phenomenon brought about by globalization. In the book "Cosmopolitan Communication: Cultural Diversity in a Globalized World", Norris and Inglehart (2009, p. 6) reveal that the wide influence of globalization has intruded into the field of mass communication. Globalization here is defined as "the process of expanding networks of interdependence spanning national boundaries, which follows the increasingly swift movement of ideas, money, goods, services, ecology, and people across territorial borders." This effect is also termed "cosmopolitan communication" to represent the diversity and extent of information that flows across the national borders, including the breadth and scope of interaction within a globalized social group and its localization (p. 136). Both German and Chinese societies are experiencing the influence of globalization, commonly brought about by the consumption of Hollywood films and American blockbusters that are infiltrating the regional cinemas and television screens. Working hand in hand with popular media is the food industry: local residences and busy city streets are populated with numerous American franchises such as McDonalds and KFC. American popular international music channel, MTV, also brings Pop culture into these two countries. As the local German and Chinese traditions assimilate this foreign culture, more similarities are produced.

In particular, the rapid expansion of new information and ICTs from the mid-1990s onwards and the "multi-media convergence" across platforms increase the interaction across national boundaries through usage of electronic and new technical products that connect the global with the local (Norris and Inglehart 2009, p. 11–12). SNSs backed by international big enterprises are widely available to local users worldwide. For example, Facebook, Twitter and Google+ broke into and soon replaced the roles of the original local SNSs within the German society. In China, although the "digital Great wall" prohibits some international

SNSs such as Facebook and Twitter from entering the Chinese market, a few SNS platforms like LinkedIn, Instagram, Xing are still able to break through. Moreover, Chinese local SNSs have been deeply influenced by the concepts, designs and managements of the international enterprises. They are quite similar to the international SNSs, to the extent that Renren is also known as "Chinese Facebook" and Sina Weibo as "Chinese Twitter". The prevalence of SNSs in the German and Chinese societies give rise to privacy concerns and an awareness of data protection in these two countries; both governments are making efforts to establish laws that protect digital security. Further, the question of whether SNSs usage extends political expression and benefits democracy attracts very much attention and broaches extensive discussion in both societies.

Base on the strong evidence above, it seems that countries all over the world share more similarities than differences due to globalization. After comparing 90 societies, Norris and Inglehart (2009, p. 35) finally conclude that an astonishingly "substantial digital divide", in forms of a huge gap of media consume and communication devices between the poorest and the richest countries, still exists nowadays. In contrast to the cultural diversity mentioned by Norris and Inglehart, Yuan, Feng et al. (2013, p. 1027–1029) argue that China, as a developed Oriental country without a prior tradition of privacy, is in a period of social transformation which sees an increasing preoccupation with the idea of privacy concerns, as brought about by the new concept of individuality and process of globalization. Under the effect of an expanding economy, the growing importance of new forms of sociality and an emerging sense of individuality in all parts of the social environment help to enhance people's understandings of privacy in China. Based on the transforming social relationship between the "self" and "others", the "individual" and the "collective", the "private" and the "public", the Chinese society seems to display more characteristics of individualism in the process of globalization and by extension, develop similar concepts of "private" and "public" as members of the German society.

Norris and Inglehart (2009, p. 141–167) constructed three levels of cross-national comparison to examine the cultural differences and similarities produced by globalization. These levels are: *media freedom, economic development* and *globalization*. "The level of media freedom influences the availability of news and information within any country. And levels of economic development shape investment in modern communication infrastructures and thus access to the media"; finally, the level of globalization measures the ride integration and "determines whether countries are in cooperated into global markets" (Norris and Inglehart 2009, p. 30). These three levels provide a broad perspective for the understanding of globalization and its influences across countries. To analyze the differences and similarities between German and Chinese societies, we must delve deeper into these three aspects of each country.

4.3.1 Media Freedom and Media System

The level of media freedom is an important aspect in the determination of availability of news and information within a country and is influenced largely by the political and commercial stance of the owner, as well as the regulatory and control bureau of the country (Norris and Inglehart 2009, p. 30–37). The recent Press Freedom Index from the Reporters without Borders in 2015 showed that Germany ranked No.12 with an overall score of 11.47, while China ranked No.176 with an overall score of 73.55.[20] Based on the rankings and scores, there are many obvious differences shown in the *pluralism* (the degree to which opinions are presented in the media), *median independence* (the degree to which the media are able to function independently of sources of political, governmental, business and religious power and influence), *environment and self-censorship* (the environment in which journalists and other news and information providers operate), *legislative framework* (impact of the legislative governing news and information activities), *transparency* (transparency of the institutions and procedures that affected the production of news and information), *infrastructure* (quality of the infrastructure that supports the production of news and information) and *abuse* (the level of violence and harassment during the period assessed). The lower the overall score, the freer the media environment. The Press Freedom Index reflects a huge gap between the media freedom in Germany and that in China. The Press is one of the most important platforms on which members of the public express political opinions and deliberate. A low level of Press Freedom in China means that the platform for political expression is limited.

In addition, the media systems in Germany and China are totally different. Hallin and Mancini (2004, p. 143–145) categorized the German media system as a Democratic Corporatist Model, within which there exist "a high degree of political parallelism" and "a strongly developed mass circulation press". Meanwhile, strong commercial media markets developed in Democratic Corporatist countries where a high level of autonomy characterizes other social powers. In Germany, people have the right to freely express and distribute their opinions in the forms of speech, writing and pictures, and to access information for themselves without

20 Reporters without Borders: 2015 World Press Freedom Index. Retrieved March 10th, 2016, from https://index.rsf.org/#!/index-details.

hindrance from generally accessible sources. Freedom of the press and freedom of reporting by means of broadcasts and films are guaranteed. Article 5 of the German Basic Law Sector even proclaims that "[t]here is no censorship". Additionally, there is a "dual media system" that combines public service broadcastings with commercialized TV and Radio in Germany. The public broadcastings are publicly funded through license fees. They "act as a medium and factor in the process of the formation of free individual and public opinion through the production and transmission of their offers, thereby serving the democratic, social and cultural needs of society" (2009, p. 10). The other type, the private and commercial broadcastings, are mostly financed by advertisements.

In contrast to the German Media system, the Chinese media observes its own system. The leaders of the Chinese Communist Party (CCP) make use of the media to propagate positive views of the party and the government, henceforth appropriating the media as the organ of CCP. However, due to the growth spurt in Chinese economy, there is an availability of foreign news and shows. Other contributive factors include the influence of globalization and the diffusion of ICTs, as well as the mobile crowds who pass through China's borders. In addition, a lot of international companies invest in Chinese Media and the Internet so that they contribute to the infiltration of Western cultures and values into Chinese society. These factors loosen the iron-fist control that the Chinese Communist Party exerts over information (Nhan 2008, p. 38). The Chinese state-owned media also faces the imminent danger of commercialization. The first step of commercialization started with the Chinese regional party press in the 1980s and this process accelerated during the 1990s. Commercialized sub-party newspaper, in the forms of morning and evening city newspapers, were created and heavily financed by advertisements. In 1979, the first Chinese advertisement was broadcasted on television in Shanghai; commercialization followed suit (Redl and Simons 2002, p. 22). In 2001, shortly before China joined the World Trade Organization (WTO), the Chinese government created an objective out of "promoting media amalgamation by establishing trans-regional multi-media news groups", and also "instituted detailed regulations on media industry fund-raising, foreign-funded media cooperation and trans-media development" (Kops. 2006, p. 26–27). Tai (2013, p. 140–142) explains the process of international interaction between the Chinese media market and WTO as:

> *"On November 15, 1999, after 15 years of arduous, on-and-off negotiations, China and the United States signed a bilateral agreement on China's accession to the WTO; on May 19, 2000, China completed its WTO talks with the European Union. China's bilateral negotiations with all WTO members were concluded on September 13, 2001, after reaching agreement with the last country, Mexico. The WTO Ministerial Conference approved*

China's terms of membership on November 11, 2001, in Doha, Qatar, and China officially became a member on December 11, 2001."

By the end of 2001, the Chinese media industry was cooperating with several overseas media groups. By 2003, 30 overseas television networks, such as Phoenix Television, Bloomberg Television, STAR TV, Eurosport, BBC World, CNBC had entered China's media market under certain limitations. They are regarded as a branch of private Chinese TV, which is different from the Chinese state-owned CCTV and provincial TV. The rise of commercial media in China means more media products for the audience.

Although various sources of press and broadcasting have provided a diversity of information for the Chinese audience, the general media is still under the control of the state. This limits the platforms that facilitate the expression and exchanges of opinions whereas "the introduction of new technologies has transformed the Chinese public sphere in ways that make a more open and reasonable debate more likely" (McCormick and Liu 2003, p. 142). ICTs have changed the media environment in China as well. According to Norris's (2001, p. 223–227) cultural hypothesis, the internet will influence the predominant values and attitudes in the society, and when possible, affect values of both new groups and new individuals. This potentially increases the importance of opinion expression in Chinese society. A survey conducted by the China Academy of Social Sciences in 2005 revealed that there are 8 aspects of daily needs demonstrated by Internet users within the Chinese community, two of which are the expression of personal opinions (views) or the publication of one's works, and the exchange of opinions or information with others (CASS 2005). The Chinese media is experiencing the influence of globalization and the changes brought about by technological developments. At the same time, there is a trend of the Chinese society becoming acclimatized to the Western cultures and behaviors as more international media products (such as Hollywood films, music, live football game) break into the Chinese market.

In summary, although the German and Chinese media systems are different fundamentally, globalization and new forms of technology have created more possibilities for people in these two countries to share common media cultures and products. This is especially obvious for the Chinese audience as the extended distribution of ideas and platforms of opinion expression create a new environment for the establishment of a boundary between "private" and "public".

4.3.2 Economic Development

The economy of a country accounts largely for the various channels of information dissemination used by its citizens. Norris and Inglehart (2009, p. 137–138) profess that "economic underdevelopment is a barrier to information". This is because the introduction and implementation of communication structures require monetary support. A poor country generally lacks the necessary resources for the development of communication technology, mainly because any source of funds would go towards agriculture or food resource purposes rather telecommunication, which is considered a luxury. Mostly, the general public would also lack the proper education that is required to handle or utilize such modes of mass media. As such, a poor economy would almost always mean a corresponding underdevelopment in terms of new media technologies. China came in second in the GDP ranking of 2015, just after the United States, while Germany was came in fourth (The World Bank 2015). Based on this, we can safely assume that the economic development of Germany and China are on comparable grounds. In terms of economy, it seems that there is a certain similarity shared by Germany and China that may be beneficial towards this comparative study.

Since the end of 1970's, China has opened up itself to international markets and products. The 1990's witnessed an increasing cash flow from overseas investors in China, an important factor that accounted for China's integration into global economy. However, the Chinese government was well aware that the free economic market might be a risk towards political stability and so, it restricted the freedom of the press. Within the Chinese media environment, however, the opened windows of opportunities and economic developments shaped investments in modern communication infrastructures by means of access to the mass media.

> *"As an integral part of its economic liberalization plan, the Chinese government has made a sustained effort to promote the development and use of information technologies in all industries and professions across the nation, and it has also been keen to boost China's global profile politically and economically in a national Internet strategy." (Tai 2013, p. 138)*

Meanwhile, the "economic liberalization" in China has "created social conditions favorable to the Chinese civil society" (Tai 2013, p. 143). The Internet transfers new information that functions as an optional news channel alongside the Chinese traditional and state-controlled media. Additionally, an expanded public place was provided through the expression of opinions and discussions on online platforms. Although a cyber "Great Wall" stands between China and the rest of the world – and prevents foreign information from flowing into the Chinese society – the Chinese commercial companies nevertheless managed to create their own versions of virtually every kind of international social media platforms. Some examples include Renren (Chinese Facebook), Weibo (Chinese Twitter), Youku/Tudou (Chinese Youtube) and Qzone (Chinese My Space). Therefore, Chinese people can still engage in cyber activities on international media platforms, albeit those of their own creation. On the other hand, with the emergence of the Internet and its new form – the social media –, on which people share all kinds of details about their lives, Chinese users are also faced with the concern of privacy protection.

As previously mentioned, Germany and China are on comparable economic grounds that may create a false impression of similarity in the ways they constitute the boundary between "the private" and "the public". However, as I delve deeper into the respective cultures of these countries, I realize that there are still some very valid differences between them in terms of cultural values.

4.3.3 Globalization and Culture

An obvious phenomenon of globalization is the worldwide flow of global trade in terms of cultural goods and services. International cultural products or rather, the United States predominant cultural products, have been introduced to and widely received by the markets of Eastern countries. This has brought Western social values to the front of mass world culture, and even influenced and changed the regional and local cultures of other countries. The globalization of mass communication is driven by the spread of satellite and cable TV, mobile telephones, the Internet and multimedia convergence. To compare different levels of globalization, Norris and Inglehart (2009, p. 146) looked at the KOF Index of Globalization provided by the Swiss Economic Institute, according to which, Germany ranked No.27 (KOF Index 78.86) and China was No.75 (KOF Index 61.51). The KOF Index contains three dimensions: *social globalization* (which refers to the spread of personal contact, information flows, and cultural proximity); *economic globalization* (which measures the actual long-distance flows of goods, investment capital and commercial services, as well as restrictions through import barriers, taxes, and tariffs); and *political globalization* (which is measured by integration with international intergovernmental organizations, the number of embassies based in a country, and national engagement in UN peace mission).

Table 2: 2015 KOF Index of German and China

Country	**Globalization Index(ranking/ index)**	**Economic Globalization (ranking/index)**	**Social Globalization (ranking/index)**	**Political Globalization (ranking/index)**
Germany	27/78.86	63/64.10	15/83.75	17/92.17
China	75/61.65	120/49.80	90/52.61	43/85.32

Table 2 reveals a consequential number of differences in the economic, social and political globalization of German and Chinese societies. Although the globalization index of China is not as high as that of Germany, China is experiencing rapid social changes and cultural value transformations due to processes of globalization and modernization. Globalization brings Western cultural values, such as individualism, into the Chinese society. Moreover, China's state sponsored quest for modernity raises the value of the individual and accounts for the consequential individualization of Chinese society. Yan (2009, p. 490–491) reviews the profound social changes during the three decades of the post-Mao reforms from 1979 to 2009. Her analysis points out a number of similarities between the individualization process in Western Europe and that of China, but at same time, demonstrates some important differences.

> *"China and Western Europe were both forced into the current round of individualization through the impact of globalization, especially due to the global triumph of neoliberalism and the capitalist mode of production. In both cases, the states were forced to reduce the previous dependence of individuals on state-sponsored institutions, and the individual either strived to or was compelled to create a life of her own. The four basic features of individualization[21] manifest themselves in China and Western Europe alike." (Yan 2009, p. 507)*

In the first part of this chapter, I have reviewed the social changes and the shifting meanings of "the private" and "the public" in German and Chinese societies. The influences of globalization and ICTs have obviously impacted the traditional boundary between "the private" and "the public" in both countries. Should they have more similarities then? Can they adopt cultural values of a more similar nature and establish, by extension, a similar boundary between "the private" and "the public"? Or, is there any better framework that can be used to explain the differences and similarities pertaining to the boundary issue?

Cultural Value: The Problem with Cross-cultural Comparison

The *Sociability Framework* interprets the distinction between "the private" and "the public" as social behaviors that are restricted by cultural conventions (see Chapter 2.2). These cultural differences have influenced the personal space of an individual (Altman 1975, p. 76–79), while members of various cultural groups

---

21 The four basic features of individualization process are: 1) Detraditionalization or 'losing the traditional'; 2) Institutionalized dis-embedding and re-embedding; 3) Compulsory pursuit of a 'life of one's own' and the lack of genuine individuality; 4)The internalization or psychologicalization of risks due to the precarious freedoms and uncertainties that the individual is facing Yan, Y. (2009). The Individualization of Chinese Society. Oxford and New York, Berg.

are distinguished by spatial habits (Hall 1966, p. 62). Cultural values are widely accepted or established beliefs that influence "attitudes" and "behaviors" that are then eroded by "changes in economics, politics, technology", and other "external pressures" (Hofstede 1980, p. 18–21, Long and Quek 2002, p. 327–329). According to different levels of perception and identity in a social group, and giving priority to in-group goals, national cultures are classified as either individualism or collectivism. In an individualistic society, people are autonomous and independent of their social groups. They are able to prioritize their personal goals over the goals of the group, and behave primarily on the basis of their attitudes rather than norms that are shared within the group. The ties among individuals in this kind of society are weak. On the contrary, people who observe a collectivistic culture are interdependent within their social groups (e.g. family, nation or tribe). In a collectivistic group, the goals and interests of the group remain always a priority. Individuals sometimes have to give up their personal interests and conform to the norms of group so that the markers of the group identity remain unchanged. Also, people who observe a collectivist cultures are likely to "focus on the context, more than the content" of communication and "pay less attention to the internal than to the external processes as determinants of social behavior" (Triandis 2001, p. 907). Over a period of 30 years, Hofstede (Hofstede 1980, p. 65–72, 1997, p. 129–130, 2001, p. 209–214) has compared more than 70 countries and concluded that the German society is generally labelled as an individualistic one, while the Chinese society is known as a collectivistic one.

Figure 5: Comparing the Cultural Value of Germany and China[22]

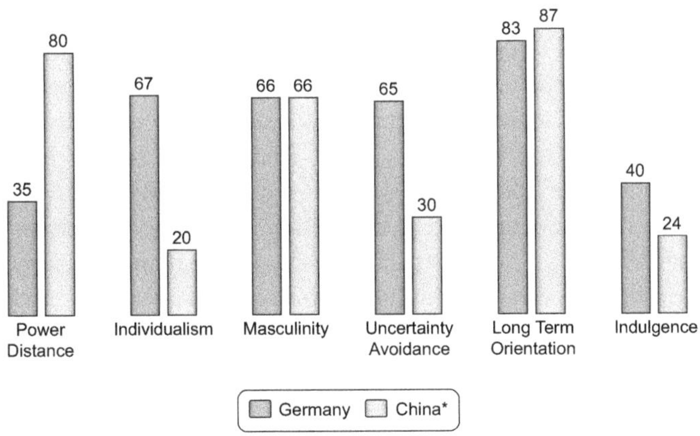

22 Retrieved May 10th, 2016 from https://geert-hofstede.com/countries.html.

Cultural values influence the personal behaviors of individuals and the boundary between what is "private" and what is "public". Studies have indicated that a person in an individualistic society shows a keener perception of and a higher desire for privacy (Kaya and Weber 2003, p. 301, Capurro 2005, p. 37) and feel less pressurized to express personal political opinions (Hofstede, Hofstede et al. 1997, p. 81–83). These differences can directly result in different behaviors of expressing personal information and political opinions. Several studies have also demonstrated that self-disclosure is related to cultural factors. Therefore, culture should directly affect the degree to which people feel comfortable with and inclined towards self-disclosure. Disclosure behavior is demonstrated to be positively influenced by an individual's perception of reciprocity, which is in turn determined by the individual's cultural background (Posey, Lowry et al. 2010, p. 184). An individual living in a highly individualistic country exhibits a higher level of concern over information privacy (Milberg, Burke et al. 1995, p. 130, Milberg, Smith et al. 2000, p. 47, Bellman, Johnson et al. 2004, p. 8, Cho, Rivera-Sánchez et al. 2009, p. 404). Privacy concerns vary in terms of individualism versus collectivism, power distance, and uncertainty avoidance (Cao and Everard 2008, p. 30, 44–45).

Compared to people who observe a collectivistic culture, individuals who observe an individualistic culture are more active-oriented, and therefore, more inclined to interact and share information with their communication partners. The individualistic culture emphasizes more on self-disclosure on contrary to the collectivistic culture. As such, members of a collectivistic culture display lower levels of self-disclosure as compared to those living in an individualistic society (Gudykunst, Matsumoto et al. 1996, p. 518, Marshall 2008, p. 143). Studies by Chen (1995, p. 88) demonstrate that American students disclose more than Chinese students, and this difference may be the "consequence of cultural values". A cross-cultural comparison reveals that "Koreans are less likely than Americans to reciprocate self-disclosures by discussing the same topic as that initiated by the other person" (Won-Doornink 1985, p. 97). Pertaining to self-disclosure within a circle of friends, the Japanese demonstrate a lower willingness to self-disclose than the Americans (Schug, Yuki et al. 2010, p. 1471). This significant evidence suggests that North Americans generally disclose more than the Asians do.

The above-mentioned studies discuss self-disclosure in an FtFC environment, while the differences in self-disclosure among different countries in CMC are still unclear. Studies of self-disclosure on SNSs are limited as compared to those conducted about the offline world. Yet self-disclosure behavior, particularly in the context of social software communication platforms (e.g., online communities, blogs, social network sites, etc.) is not well understood. Additionally, compared with studies on cross-cultural social behaviors, the exploration of cross-cultural self-disclosure is still limited (Markus and Kitayama 1991, p. 247–248, Zhao, Hinds et al. 2012, p. 69).

Hofstede points out that cultural value also affects political discussion and civic behavior. In a collectivistic society, people are inclined to agree with the opinion of the majority, while collective interests instead of individual interests are prioritized. In other words, the interest and opinion of an individual are compromised in favor of the group. On the other hand, an individual from individualistic society is more willing to express a private opinion. "Individual interests prevail over collective interests, and everyone has a right to privacy" (Hofstede, Hofstede et al. 1997, p. 81–83). In contrast to the theoretical assumption, Shen and Liang (2014) argue that cultural value exert no effect on the expression of opinion on the online bulletin boards across the world; this is the findings of their comparative research of online political discussion across 75 societies. Empirical studies on the relationship between culture and online political expression is quite limited. As social media platforms continue expanding into spaces of political discussion and collective action, it is perhaps advisable that future studies should focus on individual behaviors on social media platforms. Therefore, a cross-national study on opinion expression on SNSs is vital in the exploration of the cultural differences evident in political expressions of different countries.

After discussing the empirical studies above, we need to evaluate if Hofstede's cultural value is suitable for a cross-national comparison on the boundary between "the Private" and "the Public". Setting aside the differences and similarities between Germany and China that were discussed in the first two parts of this chapter, I would like to address the limitations of the framework in my cross-cultural comparison. The most serious problem remains the validity of cultural value. Although cultural value is widely used in many cross-national/cultural studies, it fails to describe the transforming society across a long period. Hofstede merely provides the score of cultural value for each country without observing how this changes over a long period. For example, the Chinese society is getting more individualistic with the process of modernization, but this transformation is not shown through the scores of cultural value shown in Figure 5. If the process of modernity brings individualism to the traditional and collectivistic countries, could there be more similarities among countries? Also, the influence of culture on the acts of self-disclosure and political expression on FtFC and CMC is quite different. Cultural value seems to lose its effect in an online environment. How can the cultural difference be interpreted in a digitalized and globalized world? To deal with these problem, this dissertation introduces another framework for a long-term interpretation of cultural effect.

Kultur and Civilization: Differences and Similarities in a Globalized World

A number of former studies suggest that there is a global trend of people in different countries exhibiting similar values and attitudes towards privacy and online freedom of expression (Bellman, Johnson et al. 2004, p. 3, Dutta, Dutton et al. 2011, p. 6). People from all over the world support the measures taken to protect cyber privacy and agree that the Internet has awarded them with more freedom. The use of Internet increases with world-system status, privatization and competition in the telecommunications sector, as well as democracy and cosmopolitanism. These factors result in an illusion of cultural similarities in a globalized world. Nevertheless, differences still exist among different countries, especially when considering the different accessibilities to mass communication and information technologies across the world. This disparity in telecommunications accessibility is reflective of the disparity between "the richest and poorest societies", especially in recent years (Norris and Inglehart 2009, p. 133). In other words, despite numerous similarities in terms of cyber culture and attitudes, there is a great disparity in the form of the private/public boundary on SNSs between Germany and China. Based on these differences and similarities, the global cyber world seems to be confused about its own nature. Is the globalized world becoming more homogenous or heterogeneous?

In studies of cross-cultural communication, there are generally three hypotheses that explain the differences and the similarities in the globalized world. The *convergence thesis* posits that globalization "threatens cultural diversity" and increases public support for "universal principals accepted by the international community" (Norris and Inglehart 2009, p. 289). An asymmetrical flow of cultural produces and services, in which entertainment, news, and advertising are exported disproportionately from the global North to the South, may consequently reduce the national diversity and wipe out cultures of the minority. With the effect of global communication, the historical traditional and indigenous belief systems of developing countries are seen to be homogenizing the world's culture toward American or Western values. On the contrary, the *polarization thesis* argues that "the loss of national autonomy associated with globalization is generating local resistance and counter movements, and catalyzing new culture wars between and within societies" (Norris and Inglehart 2009, p. 289). Instead of homogenization, the emergence of globalization generates a global culture, which reduces local diversities and bring changes to regional customs and traditions; consequently, large gaps exist among countries.

In a conflation of the above hypotheses, the *fusion or hybridization thesis* argues that "both convergence and polarization may be occurring simultaneously among different countries" (Norris and Inglehart 2009, p. 290–291). The process of globalization increases the cultural exchange among different countries, and promotes *cosmopolitanism*, particularly when various regions share similar values, life styles and enjoy similar culture. However, these values or cultures are "neither traditional nor modern, but a new synthesis of both" (Norris and Inglehart 2009, p. 291). The *fusion or hybridization thesis* highlights both cultural diversity and similarity, drawing upon the possible influence of a mainstream culture on several regions or countries. For example, the American popular culture is becoming dominant in the process of industrialization and modernization while the regional residences resist this culture and keep their lifestyles and traditions free of globalized convergence. Nevertheless, by coming into contact with popular culture and resisting conformity, a new synthetic culture is formed. This new culture is a synthesis of both its contact with and resistance towards the mainstream. In other words, while on one hand it maintains a certain traditional and regional aspect, on the other, it experiences some inevitable changes that are within expectations.

Among those three theses above, the *fusion or the hybridization thesis* seems to explain why there are not only differences, but also similarities, among countries in the world. Globalization and Western culture heighten the awareness of national culture and identity, and shift the local into an international context. However, it remains unclear what exactly the distinctions in different countries are, and what similarities do globalized countries share. Beyond the convergence, polarization and hybridization of national culture in a globalized world, Norbert Elias (2010, p. 1–8) introduces the concepts of *civilization* and *Kultur* to explain national commons and differences. He compares the development of the German concept of *Kultur* (which can be interpreted as "culture") with the French and English concepts of *civilization*, and concludes that "the French and English concepts of *civilization* can refer to political or economic, religious or technical, moral or social, facts"; however, the German concept of *Kultur* refers to "intellectual, artistic and religious facts", while avoiding political, economic and social facts (Elias 2010, p. 11). *Kultur* is a process of figuration based on the interdependence of individuals, which in turn shapes the social habitus of individuals by effecting a rational and reasonable control over themselves, others or groups. Additionally, *Kultur* transcends the boundary of nations and brings about long-term social influence.

"To a certain extent, the concept of civilization plays down the national differences between peoples; it emphasizes what is common to all human beings or—in the view of its bearers—should be. It expresses the self-assurance of peoples whose national boundaries and national identity have for centuries been so fully established that they have ceased to be the subject of any particular discussion, peoples which have long expanded outside their borders and colonized beyond them. In contrast, the German concept of Kultur places special stress on national differences and the particular identity of groups." (Elias 2010, p. 7)

The concept of *civilization* highlights the common of all countries and contends a wide variety of facts, such as the level of technology, the type of manners, the development of scientific knowledge, religious ideas and customs. The *self-consciousness of the West* is really the general function of the concept of *civilization*, and the common quality that leads to all these various human attitudes and activities can be described as "civilized" (Elias 2010, p. 5). *Kultur* tends to demarcate, emphasize on, and detail, the differences between groups, which then corresponds to this historical process. The question of "what really is our identity?" is a specific concern of *Kultur*, and people are able to determine the self-consciousness of a nation (namely its differences with other nations) by asking themselves this question (Elias 2010, p. 6). In the last two or three centuries, Elias postulates, the Western society has been seeking an appropriate word that can describe the uniqueness of its social characters. The word is *civilization*. Then, it finds the level of its technology, the nature of its manners, the development of its scientific knowledge or view of the world. These characters of *civilization* are also considered as Western standards, which has expanded with "colonizing groups" and eventually arrived at a stage of "political unification and consolidation" (Elias 2010, p. 7).

However, Elias mainly focuses on the nineteenth century and although his work is universally relevant, it is relatively distinctive to every state. Robertson (1992, p. 120–122) points out that Elias's concept of the civilizing process is fairly limited as it mainly refers to the discernible trends in the direction of the self while largely ignoring the ways in which the process of *civilization* came to take on a global 'life of its own'. To apply the concept of *civilization* in a globalized world, particularly to specify how this concept transforms at the turn of the twentieth century, Gong (1984, p. 24–81) analyzes the prehistory of globalization and the ways in which the Western concept of *civilization* comes into contact with and impacts Eastern countries. According to Gong, the standard of *civilization* was established during the nineteenth century, when Asia and Africa were brought within the compass of the expanding Eurocentric international system. International cooperation and numerous conferences after the two World Wars gave rise to the emergence of the relatively autonomous legal principles of humanity – human rights as international law[23]. The freedom of speech and the protection of privacy, both of which are related to the private/public boundary, were rooted in the general legal principles and the ensuing international law. The preamble of the Universal Declaration of Human rights adopted by the UN General Assembly on 10 December 1948 declares the freedom of speech as an essential part of human rights:

> *"Whereas disregard and contempt for human rights have resulted in barbarous acts which have outraged the conscience of mankind, and the advent of a world in which human beings shall enjoy freedom of speech and belief and freedom from fear and want has been proclaimed as the highest aspiration of the common people." (UN 1948)*

Article 12 of the Universal Declaration of Human rights also declares an act to protect the privacy of individuals:

> *"No one shall be subjected to arbitrary interference with his privacy, family, home or correspondence, nor to attacks upon his honor and reputation. Everyone has the right to the protection of the law against such interference or attacks."*

Last but not least, Article 17 of the International Covenant on Civil and Political Rights (UN 1966), which is adopted and opened for signature, ratification and accession by General Assembly of United Nation (UN) resolution in 1966, protects the privacy, home or correspondence, honor and reputation. Germany and China, as two civilized countries, joined the UN and adopted similar legal systems that were influenced by international laws. In 1973, West and East Germany, and then the reunited Germany, was admitted as a member of the UN. China had joined the UN earlier in 1971. In the 1970s, both Germany and China signed the Universal Declaration of Human rights and International Covenant on Civil and Political Rights. The freedom of speech and privacy protection law has been adopted in both countries in the form of first international law, and then, civic law. China, as an Eastern country with a distinctive social environment and unique

---

23 In 1899, nineteen European, five Asian and two American 'civilized countries' made the general principles of law as the standard of civilization, which became an essentially regulative principle concerning inter-state relations during the 1920s. The emergence of the relatively autonomous legal principles of humanity (human rights as international law) traced back to the period when the standard of civilization was in its most explicit phase during the Paris Peace Conference, following World War I. In 1919, 32 countries and nationalities made decisions to create the League of Nations, signed five peace treaties and established some universal principals such as equal rights of nations. After World War II, the UN was established to foster international co-operation and prevent future conflicts.

social/cultural traditions, is especially influenced by the universal principles. The process of civilization, in the forms of a development in global market, diffusion of technology and international cooperation, effected more similarities in different countries. Meanwhile, each country has its own culture, traditions, and costumes, all of which contribute to the diversity of a globalized world. The differentiation of *Kultur* and *civilization* provides a long-term perspective to observe the differences and similarities in the cross-cultural comparison. The transforming notion of "the Private" and "the Public" in German and Chinese societies also resonate with *Kultur* – each has its own definition about "Private" and "Public" and "Civilization" – global economic development, international cooperation and the transformation of media technology increase the shared value of countries.

This chapter has reviewed the historical and modern concepts of "private" and "public" in Germany and China, and analyzed their similarities as consequences of globalization. By comparing the cultures and conventions in instances of media freedom, media systems, culture values and economic development in these two societies, there are many clear differences between them. However, through an evaluation of their economic developments, we find their similarities. These differences and similarities can both contribute to the boundary between "the private" and "the public" on the German and Chinese SNSs. After introducing the theoretical framework of sociability in Chapter II and analyzing the information transfer from a private to a public space on a micro level in Chapter III, this chapter wraps up our discussion by analyzing the cross-national boundary on SNSs from a macro perspective. This chapter is also the last part of a theoretical analysis of the distinctions between "the private" and "the public" on SNSs. In the next chapter, I will construct models in an examination of factors influencing the management of the boundary between "the private" and "the public" on SNSs.

V. Proposing Models of the Boundary Between "the Private" and "the Public" on SNSs

In chapter III, I applied SET, SPT and CPMT to explain the motivations behind the disclosure of personal information and the expression of political opinions. In accordance with our previous discussion, *social norms and influences*, *social benefits* and *costs/risks* are three theoretical basics that account for the mechanisms of boundary management on SNSs. In this chapter, I will construct two models that help to explain the influential factors of boundary management. One of these models pertains to self-disclosure, while the other to political expression. I will then contextualize these two models in a digital world to explore the digital differences and similarities between Germany and China.

5.1 Proposing a Model for Self-disclosure

To construct a model for self-disclosure on SNSs, several key factors of SET, SPT and CMPT must be taken into consideration so as to determine the best way to represent the cost-benefit approach of self-disclosure. These key factors are:

- *social norms and influences*: social influence that tempts an individual to use SNSs and to disclose information
- *social benefits*: perceived reciprocity and trust
- *social costs/risks*: perceived risk believes and anonymity.

As my discussion on the boundary between "the private" and "the public" pertains specifically to SNSs, the usage and size of SNSs play an important role in guiding online self-disclosure and political expression. Hence, these factors will be included in the models.

Figure 6: Variables and Hypothesis for The Model of Self-disclosure

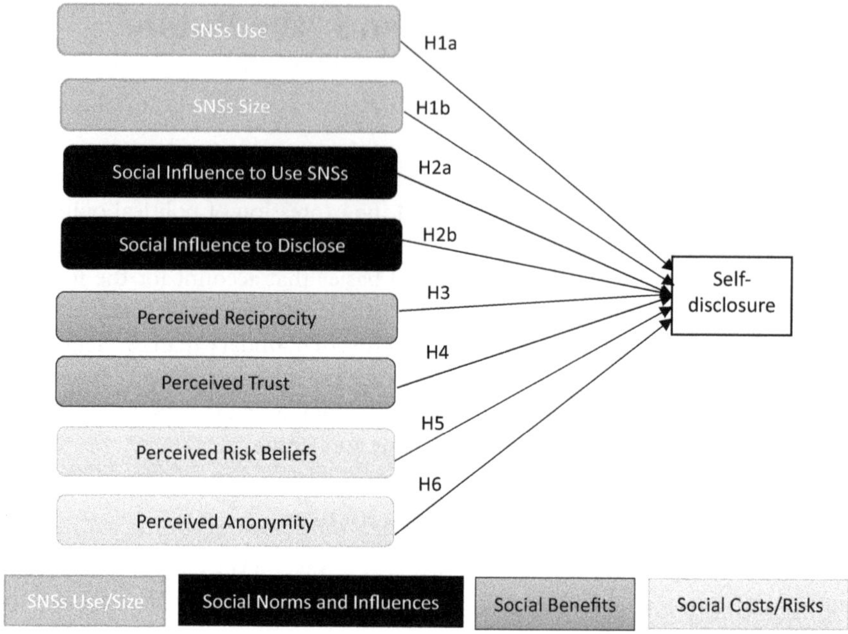

SNSs Use and SNSs Size

In Chapter 3.2, I have pointed out that self-disclosure in CMC is more active than in FtFC. Sufficient evidence and studies reveal that SNSs usage influences disclosure behavior. A survey conducted by Katz and Rice (2002, p. 317) contributes strong evidence to support the claim that "the Internet has already been used to powerfully enhance self-expression and interaction." People who are avid users of certain social web applications tend to reveal a wealth of personal details (Taddicken and Jers 2011, p. 145). Many recent studies have also demonstrated that the use of SNSs is positively related to self-disclosure (Barak and Gluck-Ofri 2007, p. 407, Reinecke and Trepte 2008, p. 16–18, Trepte and Reinecke 2012, p. 1102). As expected, Facebook users who often check their accounts also demonstrate a higher regularity in sharing personal information (Young and Quan-Haase 2009, p. 266). Based on these studies, I propose the first hypothesis:

H1a: SNSs usage is positively related to the extent of self-disclosure.

The *size* of an individual's SNSs friend-list, as well as his usage of SNSs, can influence his acts of self-disclosure on SNSs. By "size", I refer to the number of people on the SNS user's friend list who is able to see the user's updates and posts. Studies of Facebook have revealed that users with wider social networks tend to reveal more information on their profiles (Lampe, Ellison et al. 2007, p. 441). This is a double-edged sword because on one hand, SNSs users post personal information on their profile to identify themselves so that their friends can "find" them; on the other hand, a large social network size invites a lot of interactions, updates and posts among friends, which may entice the user into exposing far more than he may be comfortable with. According to SET and SPT, the size of a person's social circle on SNSs is an important factor for self-disclosure. Users with an extensive social network usually receives more social support from these cyber-friends and gain more social capital through intensive social interactions and the expectations of future social resources engendered by such (Ellison, Steinfield et al. 2007, p. 1143, Burke, Kraut et al. 2011, p. 571). If users connect with a lot of strangers over SNSs, there is a potential privacy concern when they want to post any personal information. Jones and Soltren (2005, p. 18–21) study of US University students reveal that a user with more than 300 friends is more likely to disclose more information about their personal interests, favorite music and clubs, than those with comparatively fewer friends. Therefore, as the number of people on a user's friend-list on Facebook increases, more risks are presented. In a bid to further my contention that the size and use of SNSs influence an individual's self-disclosure behavior, the following hypothesis is proposed:

H1b: The size of a user's SNSs is related to self-disclosure.

Social Influence to Use SNSs

SET and SPT hightlight the influence that other people have on an individual's social behavior. This is termed as *social influence*. Social influence refers to the amount of control that a social environment exerts over an individual's attitude, judgement and behavior (Deutsch and Gerard 1955, p. 635, Tesser and Shaffer 1990, p. 409). It comes from the impact of observing social norms, which are formed in the process of interaction among group members. If an individual wants to be involved in a social group, he needs to readily conform his own behavior to fit into the expectation of this particular group of people. Since this inidividual will not be familiar with the expectations of the group prior to his participation, his perception of the acceptable group norms drives the intention to engage in a specific behavior (Ajzen 1991, p. 179). Group members often face some form of peer pressure that motivates their conformity. When the new member is uncertain of what is expected of him, he chooses to mimic the behaviour of the majority (Cialdini 2001, p. 111–117). In addition, studies reveal that people are inclined to communicate with someone who is physically attractive and with whom they share similarities (Cialdini 2001, p. 148–151). This phenomenon motivates the conformity of individuals' behaviors to social norms.

Recent studies suggest that social influence still exists in CMC. "The use of the Internet has now shifted from an exhaustive information store, to another means with which to create and maintain group and individual social relationships" (Okdie and Guadagno 2008, p. 478). On contrary to the popular notion that CMC "liberates individuals from social influence" and group pressure, it actually has the potential to "accentuate social influence" (Postmes, Spears et al. 2002, p. 14–15, Lee 2004, p. 234, 256)."Privacy behavior is an upshot of social influences" (Lewis, Kaufman et al. 2008, p. 79). Consequently, the social influence to be part of an online community is positively related to self-disclosure within such an environment (Posey, Lowry et al. 2010, p. 181). People who are easily influenced are more likely to conform to norms and fulfill stereotypes of self-disclosure behavior on SNSs. Therefore, SNSs users can be influenced by both the use of SNSs and the disclosure behavior of other users. In order to maintain social relationships, individuals may adjust the frequency and the extent of self-disclosure to an equivalent level with that of their social groups so that they disclose a similar level of personal information in a bid to appear more socially attractive. In addition, due to the lack of social cues on SNSs, users are often oblivious to the more intimate details of their communication partners. Disclosure helps to reduce uncertainty and promote interactions, which in turn faciliate further acts of revelation. Based on the effect of social influence, I propose two hypotheses:

H2a: The social influence to use SNSs is positively related to self-disclosure.
H2b: The social influence to disclose is positively related to self-disclosure.

Perceived Reciprocity on SNSs

CET, SPT and CPMT regard reciprocity as an important element for benefits/reward in social communication as well as a factor that motivates disclosure and maintains a relationship. Disclosure behavior is based on the perception of reciprocity. Several studies demonstrate that the reciprocal perception of "relationship worth" is a positive factor that builds intimate relationships and increases the user's benefits from social exchange and the construction of social networks (Dindia 2002, Ellison, Steinfield et al. 2007, p. 1143, Ko and Kuo 2009, p. 78). Reciprocity is a social norm during interaction. When people share personal information and reveal opinions, they also expect this disclosure behavior to be returned in a similar extent so that their relationship can grow stronger. Disclosure is an interactional behavior which requires actions from both communication partners. People often respond and reveal information about themselves to those who disclosed personal information to them (Savicki 1972, p. 271, Collins and Miller 1994, p. 458–459). Those who share their information usually encourage one another to disclose more. This exchange of personal information, thoughts and feelings, helps people to gain social support, joy and satisfaction, reduce psychological pressures and receive useful information. These benefits are considered the reciprocal results of disclosure. On the contrary, the end of a relationship can be attributed to a lack of reciprocal feelings.

Even in an online context, perceived reciprocity is also an important motivation for self-disclosure. Early studies examined reciprocity of self-disclosure in Internet chat rooms and reported that reciprocity is a positive indicator of length and type of personal statement (Rollman, Krug et al. 2000, p. 161, Rollman and Parente 2001, p. 617, Barak and Gluck-Ofri 2007, p. 407). Reciprocity is also an established norm for SNSs users in that the perpetuated reciprocal feelings increases the likelihood of personal information disclosure and the sharing of ideas (Posey, Lowry et al. 2010, p. 181, Trepte and Reinecke 2012, p. 1112). Several evidences for both perceived reciprocity (positive correlations between self-reported disclosure and perceived partner disclosure) and actual reciprocity (correlations between each partner's self-reported disclosures) have been found (Dindia 1988, p. 737–743, Dindia 2002, p. 169). As the interaction on SNSs is related to the number of people and various processes of relational development, it is difficult to focus on each partner's self-reported disclosure. As such, I will examine only the perceived reciprocity.

H3: Perceived reciprocity on SNSs promotes self-disclosure.

Privacy Risk Beliefs on SNSs

Risk, as one of the elements opposed to social benefits, influences the control of how individuals disclose information about themselves during social interaction. The disclosure of personal information, thoughts and opinions goes hand in hand with the risk of the individual losing control over his privacy. The process of social exchange involves uncertainty and risk (Molm, Takahashi et al. 2000, p. 1422–1424). Individuals may wonder whether their partners are withholding information or question whether the information disclosed is real (Boon and Pasveer 1999, p. 323–329, Derlega, Winstead et al. 2008, p. 160–161). Consequently, participants in social exchange processes must accept the risk of providing "benefits" while receiving little, or even no, returns.

SNSs increase opportunities for online disclosure. People reveal and exchange information about themselves over such social media platforms. In online environments, it's easier to elicit self-disclosure that is related to many positive aspects, such as the opportunity to maintain relationships with friends who are physically absent, to establish new friendships, and to find support and information (Ellison, Steinfield et al. 2007, p. 1164). Meanwhile, a certain risk exists in online social exchange in various forms, such as the abuse of personal data by some commercial organization. The potential risk of encountering a stalker or an online criminal means that any disclosure of personal information or sharing of a personal profile threatens personal safety (Gross and Acquisti 2005, p. 73, Gibbs, Ellison et al. 2011, p. 77). Due to the use of a large data based (also known as "big data"), personal information in profiles can be collected by any third party. This results in the loss of privacy. Individuals can also be "tagged" by others on SNSs, which cause information about themselves to be revealed without their knowledge. This enables other people to obtain information about the unsuspecting user. In this way, self-disclosure may be dangerous because others may use this information as a basis to fabricate their own disclosures (Gibbs, Ellison et al. 2011, p. 77).

According to Dowling and Staelin (1994, p. 131), risk beliefs are defined as the expectation that a high potential for loss is associated with the release of personal information to others on SNSs. The more a person believes that disclosing personal information online is risky, the less information he or she will likely disclose (Malhotra, Kim et al. 2004, p. 346, Posey, Lowry et al. 2010, p. 190). Therefore, individuals who believe that they can manage the boundary between "private" and "public" and lower the risk of such online behaviors are potentially more likely to engage in conversation and acts of information disclosure.

H4: *An individual's risk beliefs on SNSs exert a positive effect on behaviors of self-disclosure.*

Perceived Trust on SNSs

In interpersonal communication, the relationship between trust and self-disclosure is a classical research topic. Trust is a prerequisite for honest communication and a positive implication for self-disclosure in the context of SET (Wheeless and Grotz 1977, p. 250, Joinson, Reips et al. 2010, p. 1). In a social exchange, trust is used to calculate the perceived cost. High trust may result in a perception of low cost, and vice versa, because trust can reduce perceived risks when people disclose private information about themselves (Metzger 2004). In fact, as Pistole (1993, p. 94) puts it, the "extent of and comfort with self-disclosure" that two people display in a personal relationship is highly dependent on how much they trust each other.

With regards to FtFC, Wheeless and Grotz (1977, p. 250) also suggest that there is a positive correlation between trust and the amount, depth, and honesty of self-disclosure. With the diffusion of the Internet and SNSs, studies begin to focus on the relationship among trust, privacy concern and self-disclosure. The Internet has some structural characteristics such as anonymity and a lack of social cues, such that interaction on the Internet has the potential to threaten one's privacy and perhaps even threaten one's physical safety; i.e. if a dangerous individual learns where a person lives or if an in-person meeting is arranged. As such, interaction in online social network may give rise to privacy concerns.

The link between privacy concern and self-disclosure is mediated by trust (Malhotra, Kim et al. 2004, p. 347–348, Metzger 2004). On an online social network, a primary form of trust may involve sharing information. In Green (2007, p. 44) words, "Individuals may trust others to provide honest and accurate information, or to keep private information confidential" (2007, p. 44). Although a certain risk still exists during the process of disclosure, users are generally willing to reveal personal information. This is because they desire the benefits that such interaction offers them, such as the development of a relationship or the gaining of emotional support, both of which require users to respond with kindness. Moreover, online communication based on trust is also a significant way to reduce uncertainty and to promote self-disclosure. As Sheldon (2009) reports, Facebook users are rarely unsure of the behavior of their chosen self-disclosure partners. In other words, trust between online communication partners promote a higher level of disclosure behavior (Posey, Lowry et al. 2010, p. 186). In FtFC, uncertainties can be reduced through both verbal and nonverbal cues in the communicational process. However, uncertainty-reductive behaviors on CMC are "text-based only" and display higher levels of both question and disclosure (Joinson and Paine 2007, p. 240). Since the limitation of CMC requires individuals to adjust themselves to the "uncertainty-reductive behaviors", they have to "skip the usual asking of peripheral questions and minor disclosure and instead require for more direct, intimate questioning and self-disclosure" (Joinson 2007, p. 78). As such, direct acts of disclosure help to reduce the uncertainty and risk of divulging personal information during the interaction process, as well as help to develop interpersonal trust. In other words, the level of trust is directly proportional to the extent of self-disclosure and vice versa.

Although a significant amount of studies has demonstrated the effect of trust on self-disclosure, Dwyer, Hiltz et al. argue that trust is not as effective in CMC as in FtFC, and that "online relationships can develop in sites where perceived trust and privacy safeguards are weak" (2007, p. 1). Based on these controversial results, this dissertation focuses on the interpersonal communication that aligns with the definition provided by Mayer, Davis et al. (1995, p. 712): trust is "the willingness of a party to be vulnerable to the actions of another party based on the expectation that the other will perform a particular action important to the trust or, irrespective of the ability to monitor or control that other party". With this definition in mind, I propose a hypothesis to examine the relationship between trust and self-disclosure on an online social network from the perspective of interpersonal interaction.

H5: The perceived trust of SNSs users is related to behaviors of self-disclosure.

Perceived Anonymity

Anonymity has been conceptualized as a state where a person is not identifiable (Marx 2001). It reduces the risk of being recognized in the social interaction, according to SET and SPT. Before the diffusion of new media, anyone could make a telephone call or write letters to a newspaper anonymously. Later, the progress of Internet technology, the prevalence of internet usage and the use of SNSs saw the genesis of a telecommunication-savvy era by "providing many channels for communication between people separated in time and space" (Qian and Scott 2007, p. 1429). With a "de-individuating"[24] effect, anonymity may lead to unruly behavior (Jessup, Connolly et al. 1990, p. 314). Users are able to register with a fake name, generally termed as "guest" on SNSs. Consequently, their personal information in offline social network and real life cannot corroborate.

There are two different types of anonymity that are constructed based on different attributes. One is known as *visual anonymity*, which refers to the condition where the "physical presence of a message source cannot be detected"; the other is termed *discursive anonymity*, referring to the condition where verbal communication "cannot be attributed to a particular source" (Qian and Scott 2007, p. 1430). Visual anonymity on SNSs typically takes the form of an absence of any visual representation of a person, such as profile photos or real names. This lack allows users to control their social interaction, and choose with whom and when to communicate. Furthermore, users have the luxury of taking their own sweet time to formulate and edit responses to earlier communication (Morahan-Martin and

24 De-individuation refers to the collective behavior of people in a group that erases the individuality of each member. Group members usually do not think that the others can single them out for their behavior. De-individuation may result in a reduction of normal inhibitions, enabling group members to engage in ways that they would not normally behave.

Schumacher 2003, p. 662). This luxury of time allows users to create an illusion of perfection or what Joinson calls "an idealized impression of one's communication partner" (2001, p. 179). Meanwhile, discursive anonymity on online social network is more complicated. Through acts of revealing information on online social network, users may disclose, to a certain degree, some sort of impression about themselves or the message source. However, when they deliberately leave out personal information about themselves, the message takes on an anonymous tone (Qian and Scott 2007, p. 1430). Through a study on blog users, Knoll and Bronstein (2014, p. 175) argue that visual and discursive anonymity is not related to, and thus exert no effect, on behaviors of self-disclosure. Similarly, Qian and Scott's (2007, p. 1428) study also suggest that "increased visual anonymity is not associated with greater self-disclosure". When compared to visual anonymity, however, discursive anonymity might exert some influence over how bloggers self-disclose, although the result is not significant.

SNSs provide various options for users to register pseudonymously or with their real names. For instance, newly registered Facebook account holders are required to provide their names, gender and Emails to identify their personal profiles, but other demographic information (location, school/company, etc.) and pictures are optional. The profiles on SNSs are therefore a little different from those on other online forums which require no registered accounts (usually showed as "guest"). Users can also provide real names, personal pictures, addresses, ages and genders, when registering for accounts. The various functions of the privacy settings incorporated by different SNSs platforms enable users to select different levels of publicity when revealing personal information in the cyber world. Pseudo-anonymity of online interactions provides more possibilities for users to disclose and to present themselves. It reduces the risk of self-disclosure, and disclosers should be much less fearful of potential condemnation or rejection. Under the protection of anonymity, users can express how they truly feel and think (McKenna and Bargh 2000, p. 63). In addition, anonymity encourages users to explore different aspects of their identity in a way that is not possible or sanctioned according to traditional social rules and norms (Turkle 1997, p. 255–270). The perceive anonymity that the internet provides encourages users to engage in further acts of disclosure by reducing possible concerns of privacy and identities.

In this dissertation, I am not going to use visual and discursive anonymity to explore the relationship between relationship and self-disclosure. This is because users remain recognizable to people with whom they are familiar even if they adopt a pseudo-anonymous name. Thus, it is difficult to completely consider the different types of full-, pseudo- or non- anonymous, that will affect this study. Instead, I will focus on the *perceived anonymity* that a user of SNSs thinks he is presenting to others in the online world, and use this perception to test the relationship between perceived anonymity and self-disclosure. Here is my proposed hypothesis:

H6: Perceived anonymity on SNSs is related to behaviors of self-disclosure.

5.2 Proposing a Model for Political Expression

Many democratic theories interpret political expression as the civic participation that benefits society on a macro level. However, new media forms quickly change the ways in which people participate in civic action and acquire political information. In these processes, an individual's personal behavior, instead of the whole society, plays an important role. Therefore, it is meaningful to analyze the motivations of political expression based on social behaviors and interactions from a micro perspective.

Making use of SET, SPT and the framework of sociability, I construct a model for political expression to examine the motivation of individuals who share personal political opinions and political information on SNSs. SET and SPT provide a "slightly more nuanced description" of motivation (Gordon, Baldwin-Philippi et al. 2013, p. 6) by emphasizing the costs and rewards, satisfaction and dissatisfaction, gained from interaction and inhibition, which have heavily influenced political expression. When individuals find that they are rewarded for their actions, they tend to repeat the action; the more rewards they receive, the more encouraged they feel and the more they respond (Homans 1958, p. 603–605). Consequently, social benefits contribute to political expression. On the other hand, several potential social risks that may lead to negative results also explain the reason behind why people sometimes withhold political opinions. Additionally, the framework of sociability highlights the influence of social interaction on behavior, and suggests that political expression is affected by social norms of the society. Political expression, as an important element of political participation, is therefore influenced by civic culture, social and individual factors. I construct the following model to analyze how expressions of opinion is influenced by the social media.

Figure 7: Variables and Hypothesis for the Model of Political Expression

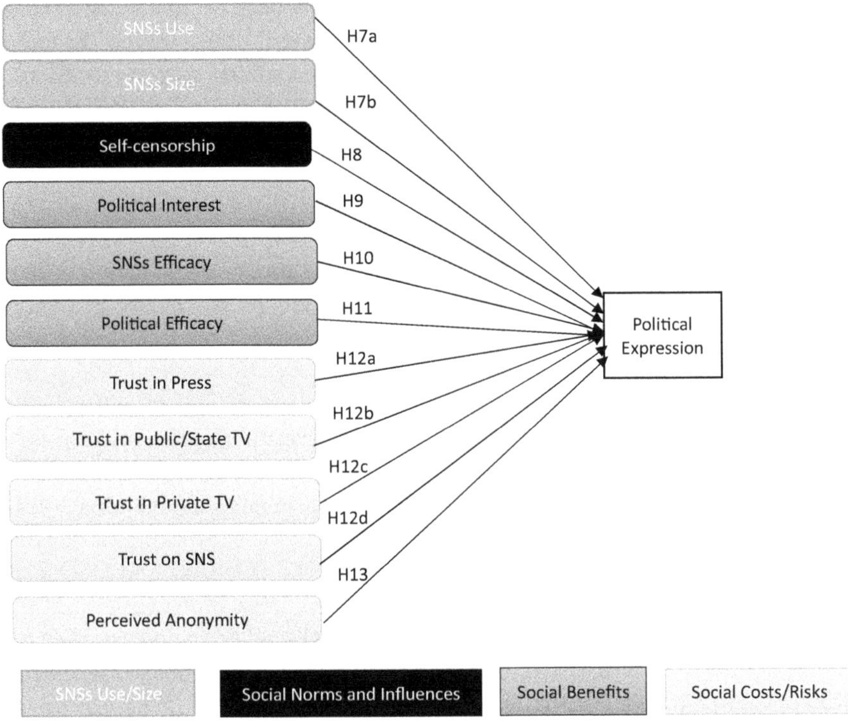

SNSs Use and Its Size

The use of social media influences "democratic participation" and can generate "citizen participation" in the form of political discussion (Zhang, Johnson et al. 2010, p. 75, Vitak, Zube et al. 2011, p. 107). For users, social media is not only a way to gain political information, but also an important platform on which to express and exchange their political opinions. Take Facebook for example, users can express themselves politically in various ways, such as sharing political interests and expressing political attitudes and opinions. Twitter and blogs are used by candidates and voters to comment on social and political issues, to share information, and to encourage civic participation. The use of the Internet is a strong predictor for new forms of political participation (Mou, Atkin et al. 2011, p. 341, Gil de Zúñiga, Jung et al. 2012, p. 319). The Internet provides a source of political information and a sphere for political expression (Dahlgren 2000, p. 328–331). This is especially true in non-democratic countries, where social media and online platforms increase the number of opportunities for the expression of personal political opinion. The use of the Internet in China has been demonstrated to have a positive effect on political expression (Shen, Wang et al. 2009, p. 451). The more frequently the Chinese people use Weibo, the more willing they are to discuss issues about the government and politics (Chan, Wu et al. 2012, p. 345). In this dissertation, we are going to explore how SNSs influence political expression with the following hypothesis:

H7a: SNSs usage is positively related to political expression.

In addition to SNSs usage, the number of people on a user's friend list (or rather, the SNSs *size*) is another influencing factor of political expression. The SNSs size is the number of people with whom users express political opinion. It can be conceptualized as a sort of social capital, which is characterized by Putnam (1995, p. 66) as "features of social organization such as networks, norms, and social trust that facilitate coordination and cooperation for mutual benefit" Putnam (1995, p. 66). Political expression on SNSs produces benefits in terms of starting conversations, developing relationships, facilitating political engagements and obtaining political information, according to SET and SPT. On FtFC, the network size is directly related to political participation and deliberation (La Due Lake and Huckfeldt 1998, p. 580, Eveland and Hively 2009, p. 217, Gil de Zúñiga, Molyneux et al. 2014, p. 620). On CMC, however, the online network size also reflects a positive effect on online political participation behavior and discussions on civic affairs (Valenzuela, Kim et al. 2012, p. 163, Halpern and Gibbs 2013, p. 1159, Gil de Zúñiga, Molyneux et al. 2014, p. 620). In fact, Halpern and Gibbs (2013) go as far as to claim that "Facebook expands the flow of information to other networks, and consequently enables more symmetrical conversations among users" (Halpern and Gibbs 2013, p. 1159). Political expression is a part of political participation and is believed to be influenced by online network size. Therefore, I propose H7b to examine the relationship between the social network size and political expression on SNSs:

H7b: SNSs size is related to political expression.

Self-censorship

An individual's expression of personal political opinion and involvement in political discussions can be affected by others' attitudes, behaviors and social norms. This is otherwise known as the role of peer and social influence on communicative acts in opinion expression (Neuwirth and Frederick 2004, p. 669). Over the last three decades, the Spiral of Silence Theory attempted to explain how an individual's own expression of political opinion is influenced by the opinion of the majority group (Noelle-Neumann 1993, p. 1–7, 167–169). In a "quasi-statistical sense", people perceive which opinion is held by the majority and which by the minority. If one's opinion is perceived as the latter, he or she becomes uncomfortable to voice it. As a result, individuals sometimes choose to keep their opinions to themselves, causing the voice of the minority to become obscure. In this process of keeping silent, the fear of isolation is considered a key factor in the withholding of personal opinions. Although this theory is still largely corroborative with the previous explanation that addresses one's motivation behind the expression of opinions, here, the fear of isolation enters the equation and changes the operation (Salmon and Neuwirth 1990, p. 576, Shoemaker, Breen et al. 2000, p. 66–67, Hayes, Matthes et al. 2011, p. 4–7). A recent study by Hayes, Glynn et al. (2005, p. 311) argues that:

> *"Spiral of silence theory attempts to explain public opinion as a social process by postulating that minority viewpoints gain or lose support as a function of how willing people in the minority are to express their opinions as a function of how willing people in the minority are to express their opinions publicly. According to spiral of silence theory, fear of isolation is the guiding mechanism leading people to self-censor in a hostile opinion climate, but it is constructed in this context as a social constant that everyone experiences. However, Noelle-Neuman did acknowledge that not everyone is actually silenced by the feeling that his or her opinions are not widely shared."*

The "willingness to speak out" is associated with the fear of isolation in that it meshes well with the realities of social discourse and explains little about behaviors in micro-contexts within which the study has been tested and Spiral of Silence-like processes can operate. Hayes (2007, p. 786–787) points out that "most researchers have tested the theory in a social context by ascertaining a person's willingness to voice an opinion or enter a conversation as a function of information about the climate of opinion on that topic" Hayes (2007, p. 786–787). However, social discourse often takes place in conversational contexts in which interaction partners are required to exchange and express their ideas instead of keeping their opinions to themselves. The fear of isolation does not include situations of social discourses. Hayes argues that there are other reasons for the *Spiral of Silence* in a hostile climate of opinion to be discovered, especially those that explain behaviors in micro-contexts.

Traditional studies on *Spiral of Silence* lack discussions on how people avoid expressing their opinions in a social context. An "individual difference" exerts an influence over an individual's decision to express opinions, or not (Hayes, Glynn et al. 2005, p. 302). Maslach, Stapp et al. (1985, p. 729) indicate that the different levels of willingness that people demonstrate in expression predict how they behave in situations where the social pressure to conform is present. To examine how individuals can affect the expression of opinion, the concept of *self-censorship* is introduced. *Self-censorship* refers to the "withholding of one's true opinion from an audience perceived to disagree with that opinion" (Hayes, Glynn et al. 2005, p. 298–300) and serves as a useful tool for the expression of public opinion and political participation. Although people in democratic societies are free to speak without fear of political repercussions, this does not always mean that people in free societies will always speak what they think. Unlike the fear of isolation, self-censorship focuses on perceptions of the *audience* and the "congruence between the beliefs of that audience and the person's own beliefs". In other words, the notion of self-censorship is based on a "conscious choice" to deliberately withhold one's opinion, not out of an absence of opportunity to speak out but out of want (Hayes, Glynn et al. 2005, p. 300).

In accordance with the *sociability framework* of this dissertation, self-censorship contextualizes political expression in an interaction and shifts our attention from the macro to the individual level. The *sociability framework* focuses on the target and communication partner (otherwise known as "the audience") and resonates with Hayes's emphasis on self-censorship. It is not a fear of isolation but rather self-censorship that is the reason for the *Spiral of Silence*. Especially on the Internet, a fear of isolation has been demonstrated to be unassociated with the willingness to speak out (Liu and Fahmy 2011, p. 52, Woong Yun and Park 2011, p. 214, Wu 2013, p. 13). Therefore, I propose self-censorship as an influential factor in my model and further examine its effect on an individual's behavior of political expression.

H8: Self-censorship affects political expression on SNSs.

Political Interest

Lupia and Philpot (2005, p. 1122) define political interest as "a citizen's willingness to pay attention to political phenomena at the possible expense of other topics". Being interested in politics is one of the most important features of a democratic society and is considered as a form of reciprocity for both society and its people. A healthy democracy depends on an electorate that exhibits interest in the political process. As van Deth and Elff profess, "without a minimum level of curiosity about politics, citizens would not even be aware of the political process or of opportunities to defend their well being and contribute to collective decisions" (2004, p. 478). Studies has revealed that increased interest in politics has been linked to higher levels of civic and political participation (Verba, Burns et al. 1997, p. 1060, Eggert and Giugni 2010, p. 181, Bode, Vraga et al. 2013, p. 12) and opinion expression (Lasorsa 1991, Baldassare and Katz 1996, p. 181).

From a personal perspective, a political view belongs to the inner layer of personality and contributes to developing relationships (Altman and Taylor 1973, p. 17). Personal political interest helps people to find common topics that in turn help to expand the dimensions of disclosure among individuals. Political interests of the social network (i.e., family and friends) in turn generate an individual's interest in politics (Dostie-Goulet 2009, p. 405). Through this, it would not be incorrect to claim that political interest can be taken as a form of reward in the process of relation development and political participation, which may be beneficial to further political action. Communication technology facilitates opinion expression and exchange, and links the use of SNSs positively to political participation (Shen, Wang et al. 2009, p. 456, Gil de Zúñiga, Jung et al. 2012, p. 325–326, Bode, Vraga et al. 2013, p. 11–12). In my model, I will examine the political interest that is a dependent variable in a relationship with political expression.

H9: Political Interest is a positive predictor of political opinion expression on SNSs.

Trust of Press, Public/State, Private TV and SNSs

Trust, according to Suh, Yee et al., accords an individual who is "willing to rely on the actions of another person or agent" (Suh, Yee et al. 2013, p. 3). In social interaction, trust can reduce complexity and further reduce the costs or risks of communication and increase feelings of security, especially when an individual expresses his personal opinions and further develops a relationship with another person. These effects promote people's sense of well-being and enable individuals to increase interaction (Warren 1999, p. 1–12). Different media platforms provide ways for citizens to express their political opinions and to discuss political affairs, so that people can deliberate and form a public opinion. Trust on media is based on interaction and can ultimately affect political and civic participation. We categorize trust on media into three types: 1) *trust relating to the press,* which refers to traditional print media like newspaper and magazine; 2) *trust associated with public or state TV*, which are financed by the state or the public and is responsible for qualified TV programmers; and 3) *trust in private TV*, which targets commercial profits and are financed mainly by advertisements. People's trust in different media platforms may lead to different behaviors of political expression. As radio is not often used for political expression, it will be excluded from my examination of trust in press and TV.

H12a: Trust in press is related to online political expression.

H12b: Trust in public TV is related to online political expression.

H12c: Trust in private TV is related to online political expression.

In addition to the press, private and public TV, the development of media technologies provides more platforms for citizens to receive information and participate in political expression. The contents provided by traditional media has been demonstrated to influence citizens' civic and political participation (McLeod 2000, p. 136–140, Dahlgren 2009, p. 74–76). The Internet works as an alternative way to gain access to political information and expression when information from traditional media is inaccessible or limited, hence, allowing citizens to engage in civic participation. In non-democratic countries, particularly, citizens who suspect the available information has been censored or manipulated by the government may try to obtain information from external sources of social media (Mou, Atkin et al. 2011, p. 345). Therefore, the investigation of the different influences of traditional media and SNSs is helpful to my analysis of the different effects of media platforms. In the study of political discussion in a censored virtual environment in China, Mou, Atkin et al. (2011, p. 349–350) demonstrated that different influences indeed exist. Trust in the Chinese traditional media (believed to be controlled and censored by the Government) is negatively associated with online political expression; whereas trust on the Internet can increase online political discussion.

H12d: Trust on SNSs is positively related to online political expression.

SNSs and Political Efficacy

Efficacy has been demonstrated to be related to political actions in political and civic participation (Pinkleton, Austin et al. 1998, p. 44, Johnson and Kaye 2003, p. 19, Kenski and Stroud 2006, p. 173, Zhang, Johnson et al. 2010, p. 86, Gil de Zúñiga, Jung et al. 2012, p. 329). Conclusively, political efficacy is an important factor influencing political expression (Craig, Niemi et al. 1990, p. 292–294, Pinkleton and Austin 2001, p. 321). Political efficacy refers to "the feeling that political and social change is possible, and that the individual citizen can play a part in bringing about this change" (Campbell, Gurin et al. 1954, p. 187). This feeling can be categorized into two components: *internal efficacy* and *external efficacy. Internal efficacy* refers to "beliefs about one's own competence to understand, and to participate effectively in, politics"; while *external efficacy* refers to "beliefs about the responsiveness of government authorities and institutions to citizen demands" (Niemi, Craig et al. 1991, p. 1407–1408). A person with high political internal or external efficacy expects benefits through the expression of personal political opinion by means of influencing politics. Internal and external political efficacies are perceived to be reciprocal behaviors for political expression. Before taking action, an individual judges the costs and benefits of expression. Only after he or she has perceived the outcome to induce more benefits than the initial costs is any action performed (Bandura 1999, p. 26–30).

These two components influence political expression on different levels. Internal efficacy highlights the influence of personal abilities, such as educational background and social status; whereas external efficacy is generally based on certain social and political system. The boundary between "the private" and "the public" is the affectation of a set of behavior influenced by one's social environment. By this, I mean that the internal efficacy operates on a personal level and differs according to each person; external efficacy, on the other hand, varies in different social and political systems among countries, and is linked to opinion expression and discussion (Finkel 1985, p. 891–893). Hence, I focus on both internal and external political efficacies as separate entities in my examination of social influence in this dissertation. More details about cross-national comparison have been discussed in Chapter IV.

For decades, many studies have indicated that a greater political efficacy increases participatory behavior (Almond 1989, p. 188–196, Karp and Banducci 2008, p. 311). However, the strength of political efficacy and its influence on political participation remains questionable and unclear. Kenski and Stroud (2006, p. 173) insist that although the influence of political efficacy on political participation is "statistically significant", the correlation is still insignificant[25]. On the other hand, a recent study by Chan and Guo (2013, p. 460) suggests that political efficacy has an significant and negative effect on participation. Thus, I conflate internal and external political efficacies into a singular type (political efficacy) and examine its effect on political expression on SNSs:

H10: Political efficacy is related to opinion expression on SNSs.

Comparing other traditional communication channels, different platforms on the Internet, such as discussion forums, Blogs and SNSs, have provided a relatively easier way for users to engage in acts of political expression that may potentially facilitate increased political efficacy by providing users with access to politically active social groups (Lee 2006, p. 415). Efficacy is also positively associated with political opinion expression in non-democratic countries like China (Mou, Atkin et al. 2011, p. 352). Instead of expressing themselves on FtFC, Chinese citizens prefer to express political opinions using CMC (Wu 2013). Shen, Wang et al. (2009,

25 Kenski and Stroud did not mention the conditions under which this political efficacy becomes quite small.

p. 464) studied the online forum and found that Chinese Internet users demonstrated "an optimistic view toward new technologies and regard the internet as a tool for communicating ideas to the government" (2009, p. 464). As such, higher Internet efficacy leads to more online expression. In order to compare the different effects of political and SNSs efficacy, and examine how SNSs efficacy influences political expression, I come up with the following hypothesis:

H11: SNSs efficacy is related to the expression of opinion on SNSs.

Perceived Anonymity

In light of the pseudo- anonymity in the online communication environment, the environment on the Internet may be different as that in an offline space (McKenna and Bargh 2000, p. 57). Individuals can choose to register on SNSs with their real names or with a virtual handle which has almost no relation with the person in the real world and thus, the user is not easily identified. When the opinion of an anonymous individual differs from that of the online majority, he experiences less social pressure and remains more willing to express his thoughts (Ho and McLeod 2008, p. 198–199). The promised anonymity offered by the internet reduces the risk of being marginalized for revealing political opinions that differ vastly from the norm. As such, anonymity may contribute to an increase in the expression of opinion. Studies demonstrate that anonymity is related to "more critical and solution-questioning comments" (Lee and Nass 2002, p. 352), as well as resistance to "pre-established group norms" (Lea and Spears 1991, p. 296). However, a recent survey by Wu (2013, p. 12) demonstrates that anonymity does exert a negative influence on the willingness of an individual to speak out on cyberspace. In other words, anonymous users demonstrate higher scores of willingness to express than those who register using their real names. Whereas experiments conducted on selective posts on Internet forums also reveal the non-salient quality in the difference in willingness to speak out between the "real names" and anonymous registrations (Woong Yun and Park 2011, p. 213). Two questions arise here: 1) What is the relationship between anonymity and political expression? 2) Is the willingness to speak out different from the expressive behavior itself? To examine the influence of perceived anonymity on SNSs political expression, an additional hypothesis is proposed:

H13: Perceived anonymity on SNSs is related to political expression.

5.3 Self-disclosure and Political Expression under a Cross-Cultural Context

In Chapter 3.3, SET explains that people of different cultures usually observe different standards of reciprocity such that they perceive different levels of benefits. In addition, CPMT suggests that culture is one of the five factors that formulate normative privacy rules. Reviews on Chapter IV also reveal some differences between German and Chinese societies, in addition to several similarities that are brought about by globalization and ICTs. Germany and China are different in terms of media freedom and system, economic development and cultural value. The Chinese social reformation and the globalizing process in both countries account for the similarities in terms of commercialization of media, diffusion of ICTs, opened media market and individualization. Based on these diversities and similarities, this cross-national comparison examines the frameworks of sociability in China and Germany, in an attempt to compare the differences in their respective boundaries between "the private" and "the public". These similarities and differences are contextualized as consequences of globalization and attributed to the different ways in which SNSs are used in both societies. Therefore, two hypotheses about the boundary between "the private" and "the public" will be examined in this dissertation.

H14: SNSs users in Germany have a higher score of self-disclosure than those in China.

H15: SNSs users in Germany have a higher score of political expression than those in China.

VI. Research Method

The former five chapters are the theoretical parts of this dissertation. I performed a historical comparison of the different notions of "the private" and "the public" and introduced five frameworks to aid in the distinction between them. After comparing the advantages and disadvantages of each framework, the framework of sociability emerged as the most suitable one to facilitate my analysis of the boundary between "the private" and "the public" on SNSs. In collaboration with the framework of sociability, three sets of theory – the Social Exchange Theory (SET), the Social Penetration Theory (SPT) and the Communication Privacy Management Theory (CPMT) – were introduced to explain the motivation behind people's acts of self-disclosure and the behavioral aspects of political expression, both of which account for the transfer of personal information and political opinion from a private to a public space on SNSs. After proposing two models for the boundary between "the private" and "the public" on SNSs, I also contextualize these two models cross-culturally to examine the possible digital differences and similarities in a globalized Germany and China. Based on these theoretical backgrounds, this chapter introduces the research method that I undertake, including the ways in which samples in Germany and China are selected and variables are measured. This dissertation utilizes the results of an online survey and interview to investigate the location of a boundary between online private and public spaces, as well as to determine the differences and similarities of this division in a comparative study of Germany and China.

6.1 Combining Quantitative Questionnaires and Qualitative Interviews

Chapter III introduces the mechanism of the boundary management, and Chapter V constructs two models according to the framework of sociability to examine how self-disclosure and political expression are influenced by SNSs use, social norms and influences, social benefits and costs/risks. Conducting experiments that are similar to Woong Yun and Park's (2011, p. 209) study, analyzing quantitative data in a way similar to Wu and Lu's (2013, p. 103) research, and making use of quantitative questionnaires like Cheung's, Lee et al. (2015, p. 283–284), are primary tools for testing the causal relationships between perceived cost, perceived benefits, social influence, anonymity and self-disclosure and political expression on the Internet. Each of the above method has its own strengths and weakness.

Although a controlled experiment can affordably and effectively isolate the impact of the experimental variables over, the constructed simulation is always a problem. As Babbie (2015) points out, "Social processes that occur in a laboratory setting might not necessarily occur in nature social settings" (Babbie 2015, p. 249–250). This may cause internal and external invalidity of research results.

To alleviate the problems of the above methods, content analysis is performed. The advantage of content analysis is mainly economic, enabling the research to extend over a long period of time (Babbie 2015, p. 344). In addition, content analysis may make random samples for online study possible. Wu and Lu (2013, p. 103) made use of the search bar of Facebook to select random samples. However, the greatest handicap of content analysis on SNSs is the unpredictability of the random user's privacy settings. While some of the random samples may not be protected, others may have implemented a high degree of protective mechanism. In other words, the privacy settings of individual users stand between the researchers and the contents of self-disclosure. In addition to the inconvenience, this inaccessibility also poses a problem for content analysis on SNSs. Besides, it's always a controversial question of ethics when it involves an unknown researcher delving into the personal information of someone's online account. Therefore, content analysis is not a suitable method for studying SNSs behaviors.

The quantitative questionnaire is one of the most popular survey methods to examine proposed models (Young and Quan-Haase 2009, p. 267, Mou, Atkin et al. 2011, p. 346, Gil de Zúñiga, Jung et al. 2012, p. 323, Dienlin and Trepte 2014, Taddicken 2014, p. 256). It has been proven to be an effective means of studying the behaviors, attitudes, preferences, opinions and intentions of the respondents as the quantitative questionnaire provides both subjective (e.g., SNSs users' estimation of trust among the users and their network friends and the perceived risks of revealing personal information, etc.) and objective (e.g., demographic information, frequency and visibility of self-disclosure and political expression) results with regards to the management of private/public boundary on SNSs.

With the help of the Internet, the convenience of using an online quantitative questionnaire proves to be extremely advantageous. Surveys that are performed with the assistance of software and the Internet reduce the costs of operation. In a face-to-face environment, it would take considerably longer to reach an equivalent number of respondents, and then to input the data into the statistic software. Also, mistakes can easily happen when data are input manually. In addition, an online questionnaire allows research material to reach people across any geographical distance, and this is more convenient for cross-national research like my study, which is conducted in Germany and China. As compared to the paper-and-pencil questionnaire, the online questionnaire is more efficient in the collection of data and the comparison of results. Furthermore, the statistical analysis of survey results can quantify and enrich the basic concepts of boundary between "the private" and "the public". Respondents can fill out the questionnaire quickly by selecting the corresponding scales of variable-measurement. This means that respondents are able to answer many questions rapidly, allowing the scope of the research to expand and the occurrence of an anomaly to minimize. Data can therefore be easily collected and the proposed models can be more accurately tested. Moreover, the online questionnaire has been demonstrated to be more attractive among young people and would probably obtain a higher response rate as compared to the paper-and-pencil survey (Beebe, Mika et al. 1997, p. 167). Majority of the SNSs users are members of the younger generation who are mostly under 30 years old (BITKOM 2013b, CNNIC 2014). As most of these young adults have a smart phone, a mobile version of the online questionnaire has been developed and widely used. SNSs users find it convenient to take part in the research as the questionaire is accessible by either clicking on the URL link on a computer or scanning the QR code with a smart phone.

The choice of using an online quantitative questionnaire does not mean that this method is perfect. On the contrary, the results of this sampling can end up rather problematic. Generally, online questionnaires are sent within an online community and people in the same community usually exhibit certain homogeneities (Wright 2005). One of the major limitations of online survey is the self-selection bias (Stanton 1998, p. 712, Thompson, Surface et al. 2003, p. 218). There are always some people who are more willing to complete the online questionnaire than others. Consequently, the results of the online survey can only represent the group of people who respond to the questionnaire while little is known about the group who ignore the online survey. It leads to a systematic bias such that these samples become non-probability samples; which means, these results will not be adequate for the estimation of the population parameters.

Admittedly, there are advantages and disadvantages to the use of an online questionnaire. Taking into consideration the accessibility, economic advantage, outreach potential, rapid response, low error tolerance, efficiency, and preference of our reasearch targets, the research in this disseration was conducted through an online questionnaire. However, the online questionnaire is not the only method my research appropriates in the study of the boundary between "the private" and "the public" on SNSs. As with most of the studies formerly conducted, a quantitative questionnaire strengthens the operationalization of variables, the profiling of dimensions, the trending process of relationships, the formalization of comparisons and the use of large (and perhaps representative) samples (Punch 2013, p. 236–240). The quantitative questionnaire has been proven to be "good for finding probabilistic relationships among variables in a large population" but it experienced "difficulties with the causal" (Clark and Badiee 2010, p. 293). Additionally, as compared to a face-to-face questionnaire, whereby the relationship between the respondents and the researchers is fairly stable, the online questionnaire struggles with issues of basic trust, causing researchers to fail in obtaining real-time interaction with respondents. This may increase the error concession. Therefore, besides quantitative questionnaires, qualitative interviews were conducted to better understand the question of "why" behind the statistics of the empirical results. This is good for contributing different insights into what accounts for the data, especially towards the various reasons why users consider SNSs as either a private or a public space. The interaction between respondents and researcher during the interviews helped to instill a basic level of trust and produce results that are based on real-time response.

The main purpose of a qualitative interview is to explore the following aspects:

1) To what extent do users wish to preserve their privacy on SNSs?
2) How has the user's behavior on SNSs changed over an extended period of usage?
3) Do users consider SNSs a private or public space?
4) Does the consideration of SNSs as a private/public space affect the user's self-disclosure and political expression behaviors?

* A detailed form of the interview guide is presented in the Appendix.

6.2 The Procedure of Data Collection and Data Quality

I recruited university students between the age of 18–35, who are users of SNSs and who live in the capital cities of Germany and China (Berlin and Beijing), to participate in the survey. This survey took the form of an open-ended online questionnaire on Unipark (www.unipark.com) and ran from November to December 2014. The original questionnaire is in English but has been translated into German and Chinese. We sent out Emails via the institution mailing list systems of both countries to invite students to fill out the questionnaire. In an effort to conduct a more comprehensive research, students from the faculties of Sociology, Politics, Communication and Media studies were invited to participate. The URL link of the online questionnaire was provided in the email so that students could simply click on the link to access the questionnaire. In order to keep the cross-cultural comparison valid, only respondents who are German natives and Chinese natives were invited to participate. The final sample consists of 393 responses. 201(51.1%) from Germany and 192 (48.9%) from China, with an average age of 23.36 (range 17–34). 31% were male and 69% were female.

The valid respondents were 153 Bachelor-Students (38.9% of total sample. 101 in Germany and 52 in China), 198 Master-Students (50.4% of total sample. 60 in Germany and 138 in China), 9 Diplom-Students[26] (2.3% of total sample), and 33 Ph.D. Students (8.4 of total sample. 31 in Germany and 2 in China, see table 3. The gender distribution is very similar in Germany and China: male participants comprised one third of the total group.

Table 3: Respondents in Germany and China

		Country			
		German	Chinese	Total	Valid Percent
Semester	Bachelor-Student	101	52	153	38.9
	Master-Student	60	138	198	50.4
	Diplom-Student	9	0	9	2.3
	Ph.D. student	31	2	33	8.4
Gender	Male	61	61	122	31.0
	Female	140	131	271	69.0
Total		201	192	393	100.0

Although Facebook and Google+ are both popular SNSs in Germany (BITKOM 2013a), the survey reflected that many of the respondents (N=200, 50.9% of the total sample) use Facebook but only one student uses Google+. In China, I selected Renren, Qzone and Sina Weibo, all of which are wildly popular SNSs in China currently (Millward 2013). The most popular Chinese mobile application, WeChat, is not considered as SNSs.[27] In total 126 (31.8% of the total sample)

26 Diplom is a special academic degree in Germany.

27 WeChat is an "instant message software" that connects users through telephone numbers or QQ numbers. Although the "monument" of WeChat has a function of social networking, it is a network of people who already know one another. On contrary to platforms like Renren. QZone and Weibo, WeChat does not use a public profile. Unlike other social network sites, users of WeChat aren't required to provide much personal information, such as gender, region and personal status. Strangers also could not view someone's personal information directly after searching a private user name. According to Ellison's and Boyd's (2013. p. 151) widely-used definition of SNSs, SNSs can publicly articulate connections that could be viewed and traversed by others. WeChat therefore doesn't belong to SNSs. Thus, I only investigate Renren, Qzone and Sina Weibo in China.

of the respondents used Sina Weibo. Qzone and Renren users only constituted 12.5% and 4.6% (see table 4). All data was analyzed with SPSS.

Table 4: SNS That Are Used Mostly in Germany and China

		Frequency	Percent
Germany	Facebook	200	50.9
	Google+	1	.3
China	Renren	18	4.6
	Qzone	49	12.5
	Sina Weibo	125	31.8

To supplement the online questionnaire, interviews with respondents who filled out the questionnaire were conducted in a further attempt to understand the statistical results and cross-cultural differences. At the end of the questionnaire, the respondents were invited to participate in an interview, in which case if they were agreeable, they should provide their contact information. I then selected 20 respondents (10 for each country) who displayed low, moderate and high scores of self-disclosure and political expression on SNSs and interviewed them. These interviews took place from Jan. 3rd to Feb. 7th 2015 over Skype, WeChat, Email, QQ and Facebook, with each session lasting approximately 50 minutes. A total of 9 male users and 11 female users, all aged between 18 to 28 years old, across education levels of Bachelor, Masters and Ph.D., participated.

Table 5: Self-disclosure and Political Discussion of Interviewees

Name	Self-disclosure frequency	Self-disclosure visibility	Political expression frequency	Political expression visibility
German Interviewees				
Anna	1	3	0	0
Iwo	1.4	6	1.6	6
Nell	1.5	6	2	6
Denny	1.6	4	2.4	4
Kai	1	0	3	0
Julchen	1.2	6	1	6
John	2	6	2	6
Ansgarb	1	0	1.4	2.4

Name	**Self-disclosure frequency**	**Self-disclosure visibility**	**Political expression frequency**	**Political expression visibility**
Eramthgin	1.4	2.8	1.4	3.2
Fabian	1.8	3	2.4	3.6
All German Samples				
Mean	1.3	3.5	1.8	4.5
Median	1.3	3.5	1.6	5.8
Chinese Interviewees				
Juan	2.4	5.7	2	6
Mickey	2.2	5.6	1.8	5
Tang	2	7	1.2	2.2
Potter	2	5	2	5
Lulu	2.4	4.8	3	7
Alice	2.4	7	3	7
IND	2.4	7	2	7
Tao	2	6	2.6	6
Xu	1.6	4	1	1
Ting	2.2	7	2	7
All Chinese Samples				
Mean	2.2	4.8	2.1	5.1
Median	2.2	5.1	2.0	6.0

Note: The range of self-disclosure frequency and political expression frequency is from 1 to 6. The range of self-disclosure visibility and political discussion visibility is from 1 to 7.

As with every study, this dissertation faced some limitations. The first restriction is the method of data sampling. The data of this dissertation was collected through online surveys (carried out by means of the mass-mailing system) and interviews (conducted through Skype) with university students. Although mass-mailing is a rapid and efficient way to invite as many research subjects as possible to take part in the survey, it makes the random selection of samples nearly impossible. This is because there is no way of obtaining a clear profile of each respondent to ensure an even distribution of results across ages, education levels, and faculties. Additionally, the faculties that I was able to reach out to imposed a limit on the collection of data by virtue of the gender composition in these subject majors. More than two thirds of the respondents are female, which is typical of the gender distribution of students in the departments of Sociology, Politics, Communication and Media studies. Therefore, the results could be biased towards female SNSs users. Also, many of the respondents were Masters-students, resulting in a possible bias towards Masters-students. Moreover, there is a considerable disparaity between the percentages of Bachelor, Master and Ph.D. students in Germany and China. This may cause the comparison between these two countries to become biased. Finally, due to the limited time and finances, I could not organize a panel study to observe the boundary management for an extended period of time. The results of how SNSs users change their self-disclosure behaviors and political expressions are based solely on their reports in the interviews. Consequently, it is impossible to construct a diagram that describes the trend of boundary changes in proportion to the time spent on SNSs. Instead, I can only provide some rough descriptions according to their responses. As such, the results of this questionnaire can only represent the boundary management on SNSs during the last two months of 2014.

Two other limitations of our samples are the range of age of the respondents and the fields of their majors. The results represent the boundary management on SNSs of university students who are between the age of 18–35 and who are studying in the institutes of Sociology, Politics, Communication and Media studies during November and December 2014. These samples can also only represent a portion of SNSs users in Germany and China.

6.3 Variables and Measurements

Self-disclosure and political expression are two important components of information transfer from a private to a public space. By controlling the revealing and concealing of personal information and political opinion, SNSs users are able to manage the boundary between "the private" and "the public". Many former studies focused on the calculation of the frequency to disclose and users' willingness or agreement of different items of self-disclosure and political expression on social media (Leung 2002, p. 245, Qian and Scott 2007, p. 1434, Trepte and Reinecke 2012, p. 1106). SNSs provide a function that allows users to select the audience for their posts and personal information. Take Facebook for example, its privacy settings currently comprise of 17 different operations, making it hard to objectively judge the privacy of any individual profile. One of the most important settings on SNSs is the function of 'audience selection'. This means that when users post an entry, they can control the visibility of the post by applying the audience selector. This permits the users to control the receiver of their information.

The function to control visibility increases the complexity in examining how users manage the boundary on SNSs. To construct a clear framework for an exploration of how users protect their private information on Facebook, Minkus and Memon (2014, p.) suggested a novel and holistic measure (sensitivity and visibility) for the privacy settings. They make use of sensitivity to measure how private or embarrassing the information in question may be, and then make use of visibility to measure how public the information will become in the situation of a breach. The results indicate that every individual has different levels of sensibility and visibility for different types of content posted on Facebook. This highlights the function of visibility in the privacy settings. In this dissertation, visibility is also an important operative in the management of the boundary between "the private" and "the public" on SNSs. Hence, I will attempt to quantify it in my analysis. However, I am not going to address the sensibility issue. Instead, I will pay more attention to the behavior of boundary management, which informs the location of the boundary between "the private" and "the public" according to the framework of sociability. To measure the behavior of boundary management on SNSs, we introduce another measure – frequency – to examine how often users post personal information on SNSs. Frequency and visibility are two key features of self-disclosure.

Much like the studies of self-disclosure, many former studies of political expression also neglect the function of visibility, and simply measure the willingness to express (Salmon and Neuwirth 1990, p. 573, Shen and Liang 2014, p. 6) or the frequency of discussions (Brundidge and Rice 2009, p. 153, Gil de Zúñiga, Jung et al. 2012, p. 323). However, as mentioned in the discussions above, the function of visibility is important to the management of boundary. The boundary contains both *spatial* and *informational* characters so that users can control the information they share and the accessibility of information channel (Thompson 2011, p. 61). Therefore, behaviors of self-disclosure and political expression are determined by two key features, namely, frequency and visibility. *Frequency* is the measurement of how often personal information and political expression is updated and posted on SNSs while *Visibility* is the measurement of the number of people on SNSs who can see these posts and updates. In an act of setting up a boundary between "the private" and "the public", SNSs users can choose whether to post their political opinions or not. Or, if already posted, users can choose to whom they want to make it visible.

The study of self-disclosure has been ongoing for more than forty years and various methods have been used in an effort to measure it. In recent years, the Self-disclosure Scales (Wheeless and Grotz 1976, p. 344, Wheeless 1978, p. 147), which includes factors such as intentions, amount, positivity, depth, honesty/accuracy, are used to measure an individual's online disclosure behavior (Gibbs, Ellison et al. 2006, p. 163, Posey, Lowry et al. 2010, p. 187). The Self-disclosure Scales provide an insight into a number of important dimensions of self-disclosure, but it not suitable for our study due to the complexity of such measurements. This dissertation needs to focus on the *frequency* and *visibility* of disclosure behavior. As such, a measurement of the contents of self-disclosure is required so that the frequency and visibility of each item can be measured and the boundary between "the private" and "the public" can be established. In Chapter 3.2.1, self-disclosure is defined as an act of presenting private information, such as personal feelings, opinions and judgments, about the self to an external audience. According to these items, the index of self-disclosure (Miller, Berg et al. 1983, p. 1235), which lists the detailed content of disclosure behavior, will be used to evaluate the act of revealing personal information. The Self-disclosure Index includes ten items: [1] My personal habits; [2] Things I have done which I feel guilty about; [3] Things I wouldn't do in public; [4] My deepest feelings; [5] What I like and dislike about myself; [6] What is important to me in life; [7] What makes me the person I am; [8] My worst fears things; [9] I have done which I am proud of; and [10] My close relationships with other people.

The score of self-disclosure is measured by *sd(i)*. Here, *i* refers to the above ten items of self-disclosure, which is adapted to SNSs. The measurement of each item of self-disclosure is expressed as follows:

$$Sd\ (i) = frequency\ (i) * visibility\ (i)$$

The total score of individual *x*'s self-disclosure is calculated as:

$$\mathrm{S}\ (\mathrm{x}) = \frac{\Sigma_{i=1}^{n}\ frequency(i)}{n} * \frac{\Sigma_{i=1}^{n}\ visibility(i)}{n}$$

The Cronbach's alpha reliability for the items of frequency of self-disclosure is .932 and for items of visibility, .941, indicating an acceptable internal consistency.

The second dependent variable, *political expression*, is measured according to different behaviors of posting and updating as related to politics on SNSs. We summarized five items, which are political content posted on SNSs, to evaluate users' expression behaviors: [1] Posting personal experiences related to politics or campaigning; [2] Sharing a public profile of political news, political advocate or politician; [3] Posting or sharing thoughts about politics; [4] Posting or sharing photos, videos, or audio files about politics; and [5] Forwarding someone else's political commentary to other people. In a similar method of calculation, political expression is measured by *Pe (j)*, *j* refers to different items of political expression. Therefore, the score of each item of political expression is:

$$Pe\ (j) = frequency\ (j) * visibility\ (j)$$

The total score of individual *z*'s political expression is calculated as:

$$\mathrm{P(z)} = \frac{\Sigma_{j=1}^{n} frequency(j)}{n} * \frac{\Sigma_{j=1}^{n} visibility(j)}{n}$$

The Cronbach's alpha reliability for items of the frequency of political expression is .912 and for items of the visibility, .934. Both indicate that the internal consistency of items of political expression is acceptable.

SNSs users were asked to select their answers to the question "how often do you update or post" among 6 scales: [1] never; [2] rarely; [3] several days a month; [4] several days a week; [5] once a day; [6] many times a day, in order to evaluate the frequency of their acts of self-disclosure and political expression.

In Chapter 2.3.2, I introduced six different levels of social circles on SNSs, through which people can manage the extent of visibility in relation to shared information. Incorporating these six social circles into the control function of "who can see your postings" on SNSs, I designed corresponding the items of visibility. Visibility of both dependent variables is measured on a scale of 7, including: [1] never update or post; [2] only me; [3] family; [4] friend; [5] colleague/classmate; [6] friend on SNSs (also including friends of friends); [7] public (also includes the situation that "you publicize your information to all on SNSs except for family").

Table 6: Descriptive Statistics of Independent Variables

Dependent Variables	Mean	Std. Deviation	Composite reliability
Self-disclosure frequency	1.761	.734	.932
Self-disclosure visibility	2.113	.931	.942
Political expression frequency	1.928	.841	.912
Political expression visibility	2.419	1.042	.934

To measure the independent variables, I designed 5 Likert scales to assess different items, ranging from [1] "strongly disagree" to [5] "strongly agree". First, the regularity of *SNSs use* is established through these 4 options: "SNSs is part of my everyday activity"; "I use SNSs several times a day"; "I feel out of touch when I haven't logged onto SNSs for a while" and "I don't feel like I belong to the SNSs community (RE)" (α=.634). The 4 combined items measure more dimensions of SNSs use than just asking "how many minutes do you use SNSs every day". Although the Cronbach's alpha reliability is not high, the internal consistency is still acceptable.

Two independent variables were designed to evaluate the influence of social interaction: 1) *Social influence to disclosure* – this was measured by three items, including "when I see others post personal information on SNSs, I believe that they expect me to do the same"; "other SNSs users trust me to return the favor of sharing personal information"; and "I know that other users post information about themselves on SNSs, so it is only fair to do the same" (α=.816); 2) *Social influence to use SNSs* – this variable was measured by widely utilized items suggested by Hsu and Lin (2008, p. 70) and Venkatesh, Morris et al. (2003, p. 458), and includes "people who are important to me think that I should participate on SNSs"; "people who influence my behavior encourage me to participate on SNSs" and "I use SNSs because a significant proportion of my friends use them". Due to the low reliability (.539), however, the last item was deleted and the Cronbach's alpha subsequently increased to .827.

Perceived trust was assessed by asking SNSs users to select the extent of their agreement or disagreement with the following statements adapted to the SNSs context. "Trust" is a tricky word. In the context of SNSs, the object of trust could be the SNSs platform or the company who provides the service, or people on SNSs, or even information that have been provided by the mass media or users. As this dissertation mainly focuses on interpersonal trust, we use the items provided by Hsu and Lin (2008, p. 70) to measure perceived trust: "overall, people in my friend list of SNSs are NOT trustworthy (reversed)"; "people in my friend list of SNSs usually considerate of one another's feelings"; "generally, people in my friend list of SNSs are friendly" and I can rely on those with whom I disclose personal information to in my SNSs" (α=.713).

The measurement of the *perceived risk beliefs* of SNSs users, an item that is comparable to trust, varies according to different acts, including the revealing of personal bank information and the provision of personal telephone number on Facebook. According to our definition of perceived risk beliefs, 4 items suggested by Malhotra, Kim et al. (2004, p. 344) were introduced. These 4 items include "in general, it is risky to post my personal information on SNSs"; "there is a high potential for loss associated with posting my personal information on SNSs"; "Something uncertain may happen when posting my personal information on SNSs"; "providing others with my personal information on SNSs involves many unexpected problems" and "I feel safe giving my personal information to others on SNSs (reversed)", and are used to examine the privacy concern of the information on the Internet and then developed by Posey, Lowry et al. (2010, p. 188–189) into a SNSs context. As compared to other former measurements of risk, such as "to achieve something in life, one has to take risks" of the Risk Averseness scale from Pan and Zinkhan (2006, p. 333), these 4 items focus on the risks undertaken by SNSs users during the disclosure of personal information on SNSs, and are therefore suitable measurements for the perceived risk in our dissertation. The Cronbach's alpha for the above was .769, which is an acceptable internal consistency.

Reciprocity is one of the influential factors of self-disclosure and is initially discussed in the early works of Altman (1973, p. 257). In Chapter 5.1, I discussed different concepts about reciprocity, such as the development of reciprocal relationship. This dissertation focuses on the SNSs users' perception, explicitly with regards to how they experience pleasure when using SNSs. Thus, the measurement of *perceived reciprocity* was obtained using 3 items related to perception suggested by Hsu and Lin (2008, p. 70) that were adapted to suit the SNSs context. SNSs users were asked to evaluate the following items: "while participating on SNSs, I experienced pleasure"; "the process of participating on SNSs is enjoyable" and "I have fun using SNSs" (α=.861).

To calculate the score of the last independent variable for self-disclosure, *perceived anonymity*, a scale of 1 (totally anonymous) to 5 (totally identifiable) was created to answer the question "to what extent do you think you are anonymous on your SNSs".

The independent variables of political expression were also evaluated according to 5 Likert scales, ranging from 1 "strongly disagree" to 5 "strongly agree". At first, instead of measuring the degree of "fear of isolation" (more discussion see Chapter 5.2), Hayes, Glynn et al. (2005, p. 306) constructed *self-censorship* to explore the reasons behind expressions of opinion. They also proposed 8 items of self-censorship and examine this measurement in different social contexts and countries (Hayes, Glynn et al. 2005, p. 298, Hayes 2007, p. 795, Hayes, Matthes et al. 2011, p. 15–18, Matthes, Hayes et al. 2012, p. 287). As this method has been proven to be reliable in a few countries, it serves as a useful research tool for the investigation of opinion expression and political participation. Consequently, 8 items of self-censorship were introduced to evaluate how expression of opinions can be influenced by others. These 8 items include "it's difficult for me to express my opinion if I think others won't agree with what I say"; "there have been many times when I have thought others around me were wrong but I didn't let them know"; "when I disagree with others, I'd rather go along with them than argue about it"; "it's easy for me to express my opinion around others who I think will disagree with me (reversed)"; "I'd feel uncomfortable if someone asked my opinion and I knew that he or she wouldn't agree with me"; "I tend to voice my opinion only around friends or other people I trust"; "it's safer to keep quiet than publicly expressing an opinion that you know the majority doesn't share" and "if I disagree with others, I have no problem letting them know (reversed)" (α=.819).

I categorized political efficacy into external and internal. There are various methods to measure political efficacy (Finkel 1985, p. 895, Craig, Niemi et al. 1990, p. 291–292, Chan and Guo 2013, p. 461). Some of them fail to distinguish between internal and external political efficacies, but I must emphasize the importance of treating them as two separate dimensions that make up political efficacy. Some others focus on the comparison of effects and calculate internal and external political efficacies using different standards of measurement (Craig, Niemi et al. 1990, p. 290). However, the purpose of examining political efficacy here is not to compare the internal and external effects but rather, to compare the different influence of political efficacy and SNSs efficacy. Therefore, a measurement technique that applies to both of these dimensions must be used in order to ensure the same standard of calculation. Items adopted from Stroud (Kenski and Stroud 2006, p. 179) are used to measure the two aspects of *political efficacy*, namely: "people like me don't have any say about what the government does"; and "sometimes politics and government seem so complicated that a person like me can't really understand what's going on" (α=.530). The first item measured external efficacy and the second item internal efficacy.

In accordance with the definition of SNSs efficacy in Chapter 5.2, SNSs users were invited to evaluate three items proposed by Bandura (1986, p. 208–211) and Shen, Wang et al. (2009, p. 460), which were adapted to the context of SNSs as follows: "SNSs can help people have a say about politics"; "political discussion on SNSs CANNOT influence the government (reversed)" and "SNSs can help people to be better informed about political affairs". The reliability (α=.446) of my research is relatively low. Even if items 2 and 3 were deleted, the reliability will not increase too much (see Table 7). However, studies by Shen, Wang et al. (2009, p. 460) show that the reliability of the three items mentioned above were .717, .711, .621 respectively for data collected in 2003, 2005 and 2007; these were acceptable. More importantly, these three items represented the real situation of SNSs usage pertaining to political expression as described by the SNSs users whom I interviewed. Therefore, I maintain the use of these three items in my measurement of the efficacy of SNSs.

Table 7: Item-Total Statistics of SNSs Efficacy

	Scale Mean if Item Deleted	Scale Variance if Item Deleted	Corrected Item-Total Correlation	Squared Multiple Correlation	Cronbach's Alpha if Item Deleted
SNSs can help people have a say about politics	6.60	2.241	.409	.168	.062
Political discussion on SNSs can NOT influence the government	7.00	3.355	.229	.092	.434
SNSs can help people be better informed about political affairs	6.10	3.816	.212	.088	.455

To measure *political interest,* respondents answered the question of "how interested are you in government and political affairs?" according to a 5-point Likert scale (1 = very uninterested to 5 = very interested).

I also designed three items to measure *trusts of different media platforms* through items from the studies. To evaluate trust on different media platforms like the press, public or state TV, private TV and SNSs, respondents awarded scores to the following items: "I trust the information from press /public or state TV/ private TV/ SNSs"; "I believe that news from press /public or state TV/ private TV/ SNSs is reliable"; and "I believe the news from press /public or state TV/ private TV/ SNSs is skewed in general (reversed)". The Cronbach's alpha reliability for items relating to the press, public/state TV, private TV were .559, .628 and .686, indicating an acceptable internal consistency. However, the reliability of trust on SNSs is relatively lower. After item three was deleted, the final Cronbach's alpha was .581.

Table 8: Descriptive Statistics and Composite Reliability of Independent Variables

	Mean	Std. Deviation	Composite reliability
SNSs use	3.60	.870	.634
Social influence to disclose	1.86	.901	.816
Social influence to use SNSs	2.32	1.045	.829
Perceives trust	3.61	.750	.713
Perceived risk believes	3.86	.751	.769
Perceived reciprocity	3.57	.830	.861
Perceived anonymity	3.55	1.022	.819
Self-censorship	2.78	.756	.446
SNSs efficacy	3.27	1.306	.530
Political efficacy	2.60	1.005	.559
Trust on press	3.12	.778	.628
Trust on public TV	3.25	.762	.686
Trust on private TV	2.80	.804	.819
Trust on SNSs	2.76	.732	.446

VII. Results

7.1 Results of Online Questionnaire

7.1.1 Description of Survey Respondents

35.6% of SNSs users provided only partial real names while 34.4% provided their full real names on their SNSs profile. By "partial real names", I include entities such as an authentic first or last name, a nickname that the user responds to, and initials. Meanwhile, 24.7% of SNSs users used obvious pseudonyms while another 4.8% used non-obvious pseudonyms. In Germany, Facebook requires people to provide the name which they use in real life, so that the users always know who they are in contact with. It helps to keep the online community reasonably safe even though users can still change their name or add another name (e.g., nickname, maiden name) to their accounts (once every 60 days). Some limitations restrict the users in this aspect, however. For instance, the names provided cannot include: (a) symbols, numbers, unusual capitalization, repeating characters or punctuation; (b) a mixture of characters from multiple languages; (c) titles of any kind (ex: professional, religious); (4) words, phrases or nicknames in place of a middle name; and finally (d) offensive or suggestive words of any kind (Facebook 2014). Unlike Facebook, users of Google+, Sina Weibo and Qzone can chose to use any names they like. Renren, the Chinese version of Facebook, also requires people to provide their real names. However, this requirement is offset by Renren's system's inability to detect the difference between a real name and a pseudonym. Therefore, users can essentially provide any "names" they prefer on their profiles.

Figure 8 represents the percentage distribution of the names used on different SNSs platforms. Results show that "full real name" and "partial real name" are used most frequently. The distribution also shows the different types of name that different SNSs platforms require upon registration. Among all the respondents, only 0.5% (2 users) of SNSs users refrain from using their full real names and instead, employ aliases such as a real surname combined with a fake family name, or a pet's name.

Figure 8: Distribution of the Types of Name Used on SNSs (N=393)

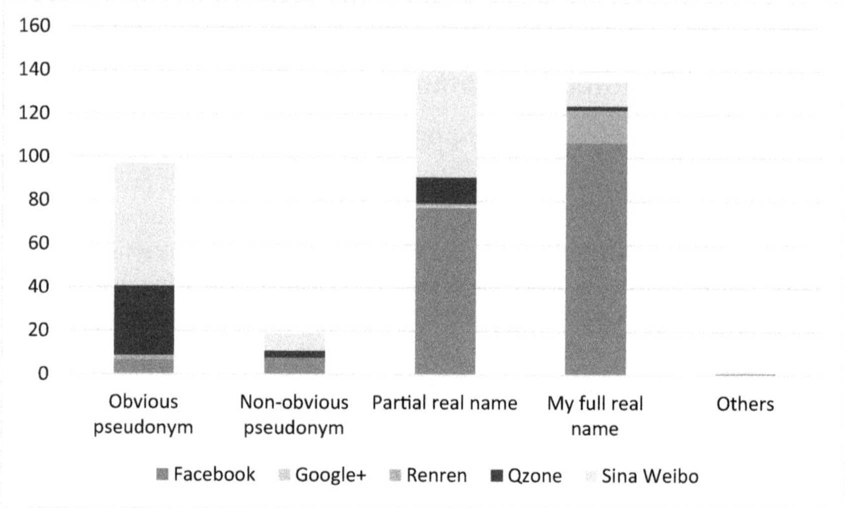

36.1% of SNSs users use borrowed pictures of celebrities, landscape, cartoon characters or animals, in the representations of themselves while 35.1% used real pictures of themselves. 16.8% of the respondents use photographs that reveal only partial images of their faces. Only 7.4% use actual photographs of themselves with family members and 3.3% completely do not use any photographs on their profiles. Additionally, 0.8% of SNSs users used images of logos, self-designed collages without any identifiable person, or even a plain colored wall, as profile photos. The reasons for not using a photograph of oneself are numerous, out of which, the dominant one could be a conscious act of privacy protection.

Users on different SNSs platforms also express different preferences when it comes to choosing profile photos (see Figure 8). Facebook and Renren require users to provide genuine personal information and profile pictures, which probably accounts for why most users use authentic photographs. On the other hand, due to different and less stringent requirements, Sina Weibo and Qzone users mostly provide borrowed pictures in place of real photographs. Other than to fulfill the requirements of SNSs, a genuine photograph allows other users to recognize a "friend" and establish contact with the right person, which is pretty much the whole point of SNSs. In terms of such user-friendliness, the role of a profile picture is similar to that of a real name. Functions aside, factors that influence a user's decision to provide genuine data about himself/herself are aplenty, out of which, peer-pressure is possibly the greatest. When a user realizes that friends and others are providing actual genuine information about themselves, he/she succumbs to peer-pressure and follows this trend of self-disclosure. As long as the disclosed photograph does not reveal any physical flaws, users admit that they usually have no issues with publishing it.

Figure 9: Types of Profile Pictures Used on Online Profile of SNSs (N=393)

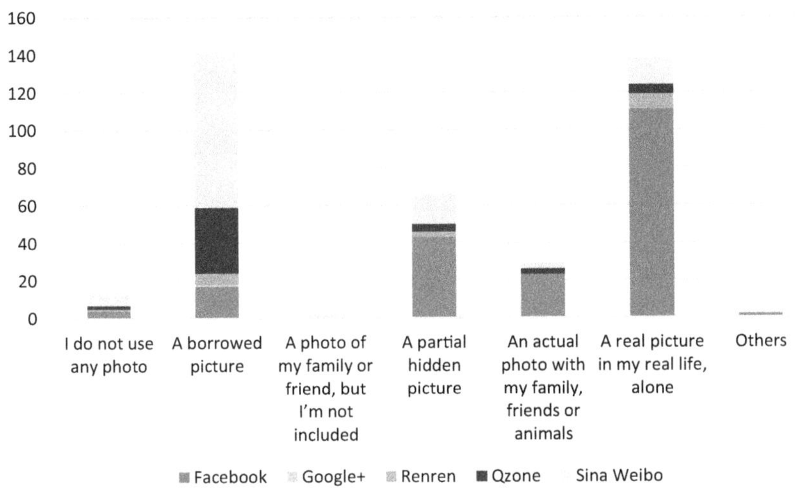

SNSs users also provide some personal information about themselves on their profiles. Gender (90.3%), birthday (87%), local residence (76.8%), school/ university (74.3%), photos of oneself alone (75.3%) and photos with friend (77.1%) are some of the common data that most SNSs users have no problems revealing to others. On the contrary, employer (50.6%), relationship status (42.5%), contact Information (43%) and photographs with family members (45.8%) are things that people feel uncomfortable with disclosing on SNSs. Let's consider the following diagram and the data it provides.

Figure 10: Visibility of SNSs Profile Information (Median, N=393)

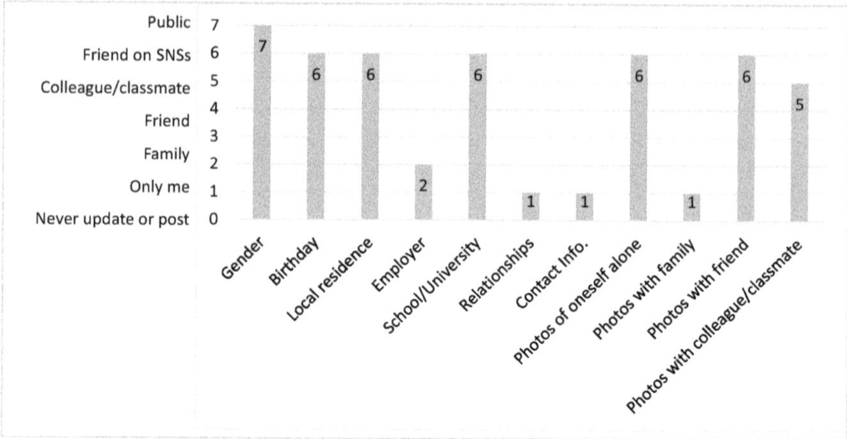

As mentioned previously, many SNSs users publish photographs on their platforms. However, the visibility of these photographs differs according to many factors (such as intimacy level of relationships, prevention of parental censure, discomfort with extensive disclosure, etc.). In Figure 10, the median of each item indicates to whom users prefer to disclose each type of information. Many users demonstrated no reticence about sharing information such as gender, birthday, local residence, school/university and photographs of oneself alone or with friends. Information of these types is made visible to all of the user's SNSs friends, and sometimes, even the public. Conversely, many users opt to hide information pertaining to their jobs (such as company of employment, or job position) from other users.

Obviously, the types of information that are visible on the user's profile are data that the users do not mind revealing to their friends and/or the public. After all, SNSs are created to forge and foster relationships between the users and their friends so a certain degree of transparency is fundamental. Unfortunately, as the size of a user's friend-list expand, the information visible on the user's personal profile will become more inaccessible.

Figure 11: Percentage Distribution of SNSs User's "Friend-list" (N=393)

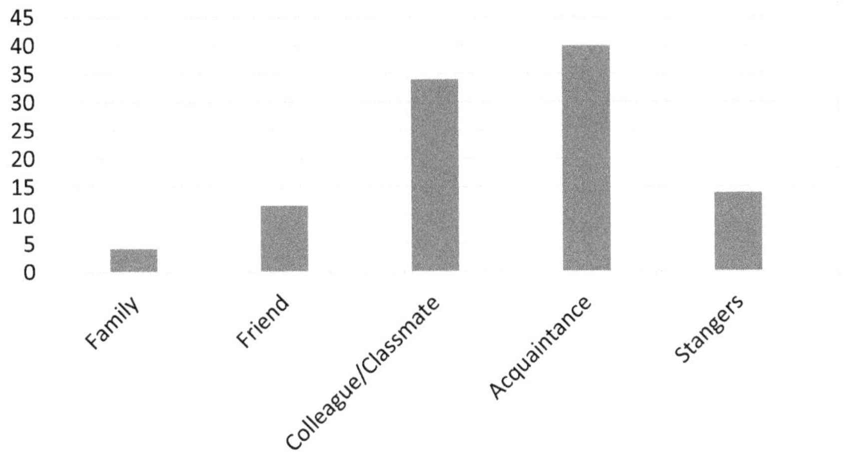

In the survey, SNSs users were asked to estimate the number of family members, friends (incl. a romantic partner), colleagues/classmates, acquaintances and strangers (incl. people whom the user met on SNSs but have never met offline) on their lists of friends. The percentage of each category of relationship was then calculated. Acquaintances (39.9%) and colleagues/classmates (34.0%) accounted for most of the people on an average SNSs friend-list. Family members and friends, who supposedly engage in relatively close relationships with the users, comprised of only 4.2% and 11.7% respectively. Strangers also made up a small part of the surveyed friend-lists (13.9%). From the above distribution, it can be concluded that SNSs are social connecting platforms for people like colleagues/classmates and acquaintances, rather than a space for people who are involved in close relationships.

7.1.2 Self-disclosure and Model Testing

Boundary of Self-disclosure between "the Private" and "the Public"

Among the items of self-disclosure, SNSs users disclose "my personal habits" (M=2.03, SD=1.168), "what is important to me in life" (M=1.95, SD=.923), "what makes me the person I am" (M=1.90, SD=1.001) and "I have done which I am proud of" (M=2.01, SD=.859) most frequently (see Table 9). While they disclose considerably less frequently about "things I have done which I feel guilty about" (M=1.52, SD=.836), "things I wouldn't do in public" (M=1.45, SD=.831) and "My worst fears things" (M=1.53, SD=.848).

Table 9: Frequency of Self-disclosure on SNSs (based on a score between 1–5, N=393)

	Mean	Median	Std. Deviation
My personal habits	2.03	2.00	1.168
Things I have done which I feel guilty about	1.52	1.00	.824
Things I wouldn't do in public	1.46	1.00	.798
My deepest feelings	1.85	1.00	1.119
What I like and dislike about myself	1.60	1.00	.890
What is important to me in life	1.95	2.00	.923
What makes me the person I am	1.90	2.00	1.001
My worst fears things	1.54	1.00	.829
I have done which I am proud of	2.01	2.00	.859
My close relationships with other people	1.82	2.00	.864

In common situations, SNSs users reveal their personal information, thoughts, deepest feelings and attitudes only with friends and colleagues/classmates. In other words, content of such personal sorts can be viewed by only those who are closely related and not by strangers. Figure 12 displays the extent of visibility applied by SNSs users across the different types of content that they share on SNSs. "My personal habits", "what is important to me in my life", "what makes me the person I am" and "I have done which I am proud of" are things that users want to make visible to more people, while "things I have done which I feel guilty about", "things I wouldn't do in public" and "my worst fear things" are material that SNSs users would like to share only with people who are closely related to them.

The distribution in Figure 12 indicates that information users frequently share on SNSs are the same information that users want friends to see. In other words, the regularity of certain types of self-disclosure coincides with the desire to make such information visible. Based on this result, let's examine further the relationship between the frequency and the visibility of self-disclosure. As presupposed, the frequency of self-disclosure is a positive predictor of the visibility of self-disclosure (β=.581, t=14.101, p<0.001).

Figure 12: Visibility of The Items of Self-disclosure (N=393)

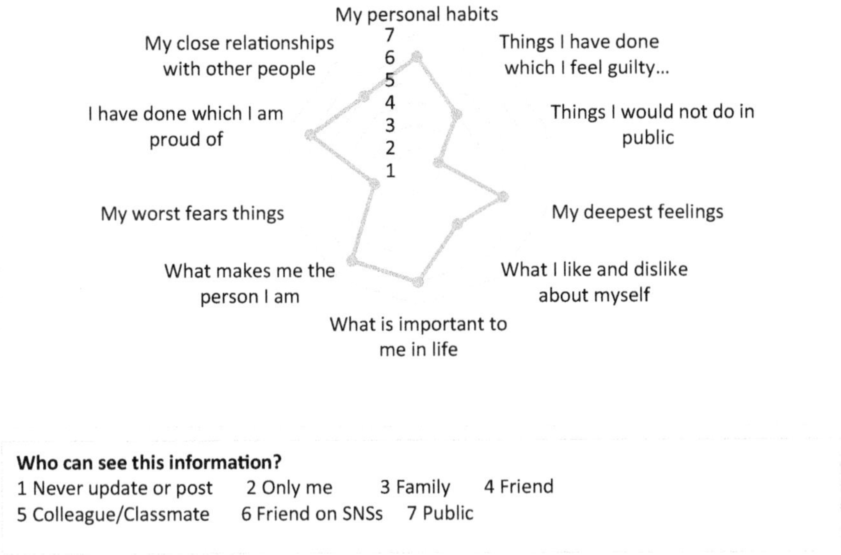

Note: The boundary was measured by the median of visibility of Self-disclosure on SNSs.

Model Testing of Self-disclosure

In Chapter V, a model of self-disclosure is constructed according to SET, SPT and CPMT. The dependent variable self-disclosure is measured by frequency*visibility, as discussed earlier in chapter VI. Since the frequency and the visibility of self-disclosure are not normally distributed, the data is first ranked and then a multiple linear regression is conducted. As shown in Table 11, the data presented by my model is statistically significant ($F=10.486$, $p<0.001$). The results predicted that the use of SNSs is positively related to self-disclosure ($B=.118$, $t=2.139$, $P<.01$), as hypothesized in H1a. However, the number of people on a friend-list had no effect on self-disclosure ($B=.015$, $t=.695$, ns) (H1b).

Table 10: Multiple Regression Analysis on Self-disclosure on SNSs

	Self-disclosure B(t statistic)
Hypothesis	
SNSs use	.118 (2.139)*
SNSs size	.015 (.695)
Social influence to use SNSs	.078 (1.573)
Social influence to disclose	.235 (3.938)***
Perceived reciprocity	.126 (2.145)*
Perceived risk believes	-.118 (-2.032)*
Perceived trust	-.170 (-2.680)**
Perceived anonymity	.031 (.687)
Covariates	
Age	-.035 (-2.674)**
Gender	.094 (.975)
Friend list	
Percentage of family	-.116 (-1.715)
Percentage of friend	.049 (1.423)
Percentage of colleague/classmate	.051 (2.583)*
Percentage of acquaintance	-.015 (-.783)
Percentage of strangers	.057 (2.286)*
Adjusted R^2	.266
N	393

Note. Entries are standardized final regression coefficients
All variables are entered as grouped entities
*p<.05, **p<.01, ***p<.001

Although several former studies have indicated that the size[28] of SNSs is positively associated with self-disclosure (Lampe, Ellison et al. 2007, p. 440), the different categories of "friends" on a friend-list may produce totally different effects on a user's acts of self-disclosure. For example, the number of actual friends, *not* the

28 SNSs size here refers to the number of people on SNSs friends list. See Chapter 5.1 for more details.

number of people on one's friend-list, influences social capital and further affects self-disclosure (Ellison, Steinfield et al. 2011, p. 10).

The size of SNSs exerts no influence on the disclosure behavior as there are many different kinds of people on a user's friend-list who, in their own rights and ways, affects the user's self-disclosure decisions. In an exploration of the effects that different categories of "friends" on one's friend-list potentially induce, investigations must be performed on the relationship between self-disclosure and the number of family members, friends, colleagues/classmates, acquaintances and strangers on a user's friend-list. Results indicated that the percentage of colleagues/classmates (B=.051, t=2.583, P<.01) and strangers (B=.057, t=2.286, P<.01) are positive predictors of self-disclosure.

I also examined the possibility that the social pressure on an individual to use SNSs and to disclose are both related to the individual's choice of self-disclosure. The results failed to prove the relationship between the social pressure to use SNSs and self-disclosure (B=.078, t=1.573, ns) (H2a), but revealed that the social pressure to disclose is a positive predictor of self-disclosure (B=.235, t=3.938, P<.001) (H2b). The more information shared by a user's SNSs friends, the more likely he or she would do the same. Moreover, perceived reciprocity was discovered to be positively related to self-disclosure (B=.126, t=2.145, P<.05) (H3). When users perceived more benefits from using SNSs, they automatically disclose more information to their friends. Conversely, the higher the risk is perceived by users, the less they disclosed (B=-.118, t=-2.032, P<.05). This proves my hypothesis H4.

There is a negative relationship between perceived trust and self-disclosure (B=-.170, t=-2.680, P<.01) (H5). Although some former studies indicated a positive relationship between trust and self-disclosure (Sheldon 2009, Posey, Lowry et al. 2010, p. 186), reasons such as the sharing of hobbies on SNSs and the illusion of anonymity, may account for a negative relationship in the test model.

As discussed in Chapter 2.1, ICTs change the communication environment so that the relationship between trust and self-disclosure is changed as well. Self-disclosure on SNSs takes place in an online context, which means it takes place on an online platform where there is a lack of social cues. As such, the act of self-disclosure may happen between anonymous users or strangers who do not know each other. Here, it becomes important to acknowledge that in addition to connecting people with friends, SNSs platforms are also used to exchange ideas and information of personal interests and hobbies. In other words, on any given site of a specific sort, users may not know or trust the members with whom they share information pertaining to a common interest. This could be one reason for the negative relationship between perceived trust and self-disclosure on SNSs. Another reason for this could be the illusion of anonymity on SNSs. In Chapter 3.3 I concluded that anonymity reduces the risks of disclosure in that people feel more comfortable with disclosing more when they think that their identities are safely hidden. Trust is defined as the degree to which an individual believes in the reliability of his or her SNSs friends with information that makes the individual vulnerable (Mayer, Davis et al. 1995, p. 714, Posey, Lowry et al. 2010, p. 186). This definition emphasizes the vulnerability of the individual with respect to the disclosed information. Although some of the information are classified as benign (non-threatening to an individual), others may be classified as vulnerable (potentially threatening to the individual). As this dissertation focuses on the boundary between "the private and "the public", I will not investigate the different ways in which perceived trust influences the depth (the levels of inner personality) and the width (the range of contents) of self-disclosure.

The result of H6 revealed that perceived anonymity is not related to self-disclosure (B=.031, t=.687, ns). This result aligns with the studies of Knoll and Bronstein (2014, p. 175), as well as Qian's and Scott's (2007, p. 1428). In Qian and Scott (2007, p. 1440–1441) discussion, they explained that the target audience is related to how anonymous people perceived themselves. If the audience include people they knew offline, users would feel more identifiable. Since it is true that the target audience influences the way users share information on the blog, it could be equally important for users to keep themselves anonymous if the target audience includes strangers. This behavior corroborates with my findings. Firstly, most of the names used on SNSs are identifiable because platforms such as Facebook and Renren require users to register with their real names. Even if users employ fake names, our survey respondents revealed during the interviews that their friends and family can still recognize them. In other words, they remain identifiable on SNSs despite using aliases. Secondly, due to the mixed context of SNSs, it can be hard to tell who the target audiences really are. Studies revealed that most of the "friends" on an actual friend-list are actually colleagues/classmates and acquaintances; in short, people who engaged in relatively loose social relations with the users.

According to the model, age is a negative predictor of self-disclosure on SNSs (B=-.035, t=-2.674, P<.05) while gender has little or no effect on self-disclosure (B=.094, t=.975, ns).

Figure 13: Regression and Path of Self-disclosure (N=393)

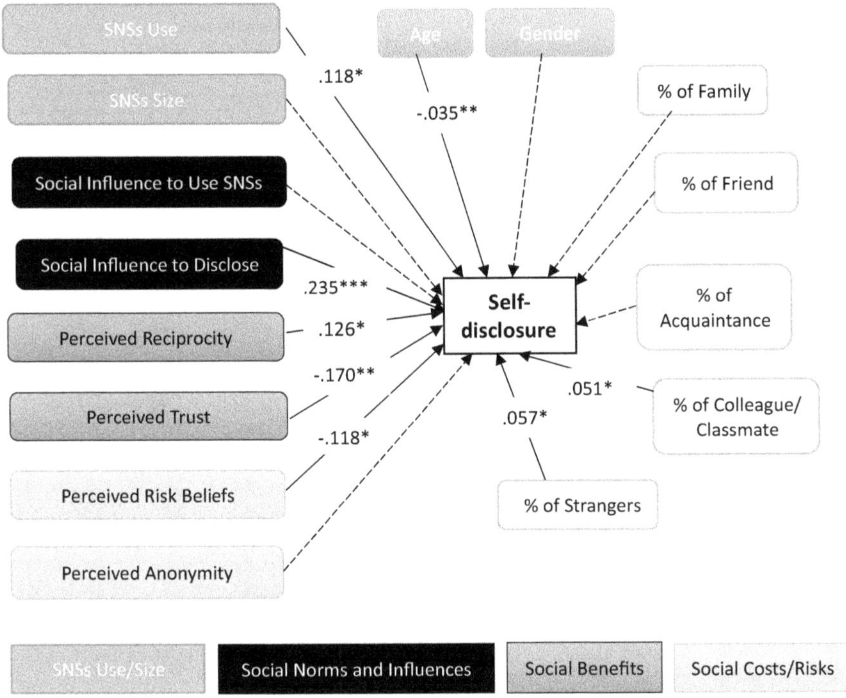

Note. Dashed lines represent insignificant paths while solid lines represent significant paths.

As frequency and visibility are two key features of self-disclosure, it is imperative that I examine the application of the model with close reference to each key feature (multiple linear regression). As shown in Table 11, both models are statistically significant. Independent variables such as the social influence to disclose and perceived reciprocity are all influencing factors of the frequency and visibility of self-disclosure. Furthermore, the more colleagues or classmates there are in the friend-list, the more frequently and openly SNSs users share personal information. While the regularity with which people disclose about themselves on SNSs is influenced by the frequency of SNSs usage, perceived risk beliefs, perceived trust and age affect, the percentage of strangers merely signals a positive influence on the visibility of self-disclosure. In other words, when people connect with more strangers on SNSs, they tend to allow more people to see the information they share.

Table 11: Multiple Regression Analysis of Two Components of Self-disclosure

	Self-discourse B (t statistic) *(df=392)*	
	Frequency (F=15.465, p<0.001)	**Visibility (F=5.559, p<0.001)**
SNSs use	.146 (2.891)**	.080 (1.386)
SNSs size	-.002 (-.116)	.029 (1.251)
Social influence to use SNSs	.082 (1.796)	.041 (.789)
Social influence to disclose	.250 (4.551)***	.174 (2.771)**
Perceived reciprocity	.132 (2.446)*	.130 (2.105)*
Perceived risk believes	-.141 (-2.641)**	-.046 (-.753)
Perceived trust	-.235 (-4.038)***	-.070 (-1.059)
Perceived anonymity	-.015 (-.358)	.066 (1.407)
Covariates		
Age	-.038 (-3.137)**	-.027 (-1.945)
Gender	.121 (1.368)	.113 (1.123)
Friend list		
Percentage of family	-.109 (-1.745)	-.082 (-1.159)
Percentage of friend	.028 (.881)	.051 (1.425)
Percentage of colleague/classmate	.049(2.733)**	.052 (2.537)*
Percentage of acquaintance	-.022 (-1.266)	-.008 (-.428)
Percentage of strangers	.044 (1.923)	.068 (2.591)*
Adjusted R^2	.356	.149

Note. Entries are standardized final regression coefficients
All variables are entered as grouped entities
*p<.05, **p<.01, ***p<.001

As evident from the results, independent variables have different effects on the frequency and visibility of self-disclosure. There are two ways in which SNSs users can manage their self-disclosure: 1) to control the frequency of their posting actions, and 2) to apply different levels of visibility on each post. Users can share all the information they want on SNSs, but they may not want to make all this information visible to everybody. This could be one possible reason for the different treatments of frequency and visibility of self-disclosure. Although there is no valid evidence to support this hypothesis, based on the fact that former studies have never examined the effect of influential factors on the visibility of self-disclosure, this explanation becomes rather plausible.

7.1.3 Political Expression and Model Testing

Boundary of Political Expression between "The Private" and "The Public"

SNSs users were asked how frequently they express their political opinions on SNSs and to whom are these posts visible. The results in Table 12 indicate that SNSs users express themselves politically rather irregularly, and the frequency of each item of political expression was similar. SNSs users shared personal experiences related to politics or campaigns (Mean=1.98, Median=2.00, SD=.987), as well as thoughts about politics (Mean=1.97, Median=2.00, SD=1.010) relatively more often as compared to reposting official information about politics. This reveals that many SNSs users think of their online space as an outlet for voicing out their personal sentiments towards political affairs.

Table 12: Descriptive Statistics: Frequency of Political Expression (based on a score between 1–5, N=393)

	Mean	Median	Std. Deviation
Posting personal experiences related to politics or campaigning	1.98	2.00	.987
Sharing a public profile of political news, political advocate or politician	1.90	2.00	.999
Posting or sharing thoughts about politics	1.97	2.00	1.010
Posting or sharing photos, videos, or audio files about politics	1.90	2.00	.898
Forwarding someone else's political commentary to other people	1.92	2.00	.992

As evident in Figure 14, SNSs users share political expressions with their online friends, excluding strangers. Instead of making political expressions visible for the public, SNSs users limit the visibility of this information to their SNSs friends. Of course, the default visibility setting on some SNSs platforms may also be responsible for the limited audience of political expression. Renren and Qzone, for instance, automatically make posts visible for the user's SNSs friends. However, Facebook, Google+ and Sina Weibo, set the posts as "visible to public" by default. As such, the reasons that account for the limited visibility of political expression on SNSs can be either by choice or by default. In order to find out which accounts for the majority, more details must be gathered from the SNSs users during the interviews (see Chapter 7.2.5).

Figure 14: Visibility of Political Expression items on SNSs (N=393)

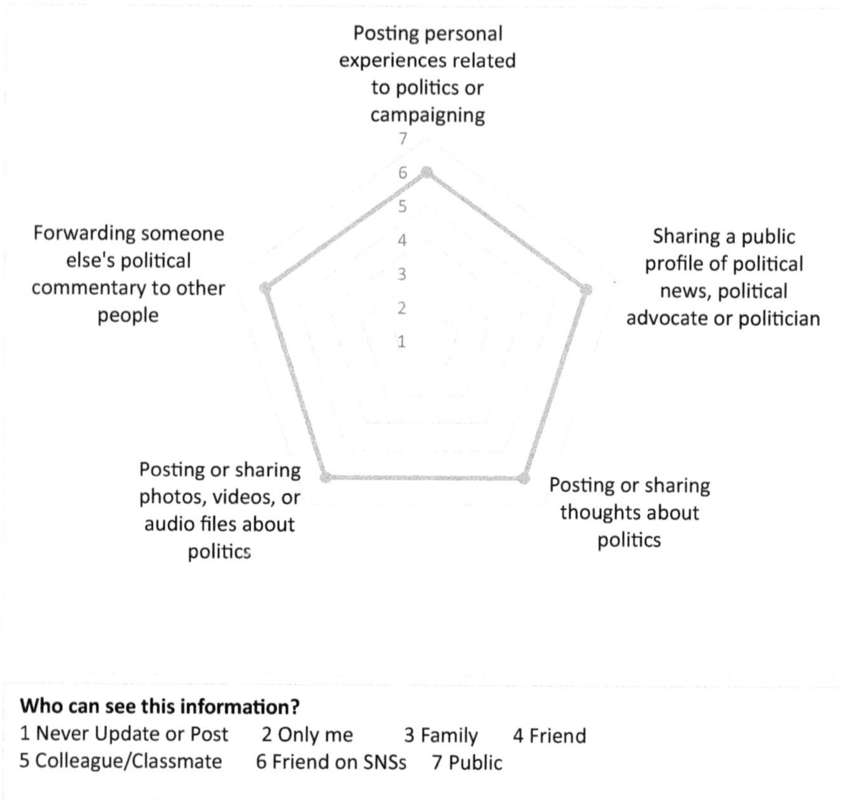

Note: The boundary was measured by the median of visibility of political expression on SNSs.

Model Testing of Political Expression

Based on the theoretical model in Chapter V, I examine how SNSs use, SNS size, self-censorship, political interest, SNSs efficacy, political efficacy, trust in press, trust in public TV, trust in private TV, trust in SNSs, as well as perceived anonymity affect political expression on SNSs ($F=4.755$, $p<.001$). Since the frequency and the visibility of political expression are not normally distributed, the data is first ranked and then a multiple linear regression is conducted. As shown in Table 13, no matter how many friends the user adds on SNSs (H7b), how much he censors his opinions (H8), how high the political efficacy is (H11), how much he trusts the press (H12a), private TV(H12c) and SNSs (H12d), and how anonymous he is on SNSs (H13), these bear no effect on his acts of political expression. However, SNSs use (β=.156, P<.01) (H7a), political interest (β=.171, P<.001) (H9), and SNSs efficacy (β=.219, p<.01) (H10) are positive predictors for political expression on SNSs. Trust on public TV (β=-.341, p<.001) (H12b) and gender (β=-.214, P<.05) are negative predictors. Additionally, the percentage of colleagues/classmates is positively related to political expression (β=.045, p<.05). Therefore, my hypotheses H7a, H9, H10 and H12b have been duly proven by the model.

Table 13: Multiple Regression Analysis on Political Expression on SNSs

	Political Expression B (t statistic)
SNSs use	.156 (2.784)**
SNSs size	.012 (.502)
Self-censorship	.019 (.272)
Political interest	.171 (3.538)***
Political efficacy	-.047 (-.941)
SNSs efficacy	.219 (3.371)**
Trust in press	.064 (.777)
Trust in public/state TV	-.341 (-4.041)***
Trust in private TV	.064 (.908)
Trust on SNSs	.053 (.741)
Perceived anonymity	.003 (.063)
Covariates	
Age	.004 (.303)
Gender	-.214 (-2.121)*
Friend list	
Percentage of family	-.052 (-.725)
Percentage of friend	.069 (1.908)
Percentage of colleague/classmate	.045 (2.147)*

	Political Expression B (t statistic)
Percentage of acquaintance	.021 (1.080)
Percentage of strangers	.039 (1.489)
Adjusted R^2	.147
N	393

Note. Entries are standardized final regression coefficients
All variables are entered as grouped entities
*p<.05, **p<.01, ***p<.001

Figure 15: Regression and Path of Political Expression (N=393)

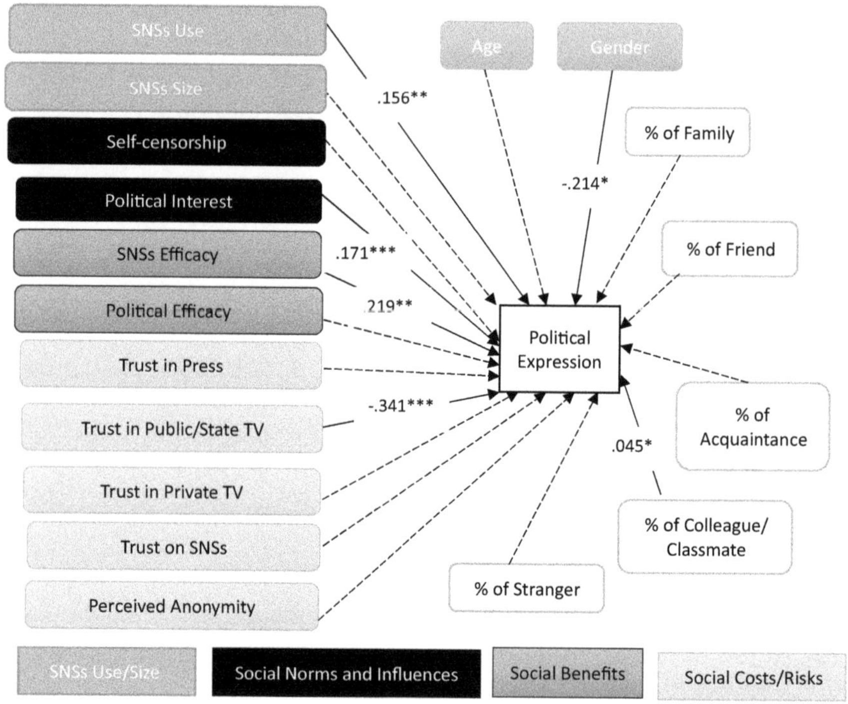

Note: The dashed lines represent insignificant paths while solid lines represent significant paths.

The comparisons of models of frequency and of visibility in Table 14 predicted different influences of independent variables. SNSs usage and political interest only influenced the frequency of political expression on SNSs, while the percentage of colleagues/classmates and strangers affect the visibility of online political expression. SNSs efficacy and trust in public TV are positively related to both frequency and visibility of political expression.

Table 14: Multiple Regression Analysis of Two Components of Political Expression on SNSs

	Political Expression B (t statistic) (*df*=392)	
	Frequency (F=4.051, p<.001)	**Visibility (F=3.492, p<.001)**
SNSs use	.151 (2.724)**	.091 (1.701)
SNs size	.014 (.621)	-.006 (-.289)
Self-censorship	.018 (.265)	.021 (.327)
Political interest	.178 (3.732)***	.065 (1.409)
Political efficacy	-.054 (-1.090)	-.007 (-.157)
SNSs efficacy	.163 (2.532)*	.242 (3.913)***
Trust in press	.054 (.653)	.123 (1.547)
Trust in public/state TV	-.319 (-3.812)***	-.272 (-3.385)**
Trust in private TV	.068 (.970)	.038 (.572)
Trust on SNSs	.089 (1.259)	-.012 (-.173)
Perceived anonymity	-.051 (-1.071)	.046 (1.005)
Covariates		
Age	.006 (.408)	.011 (.825)
Gender	-.197 (-1.965)	-.098 (-1.022)
Friend list		
Percentage of family	-.034 (-.474)	-.058 (-.841)
Percentage of friend	.056 (1.581)	.054 (1.586)
Percentage of colleague/classmate	.031 (1.477)	.063 (3.106)**
Percentage of acquaintance	.014 (.714)	.028 (1.496)
Percentage of strangers	.015 (.565)	.071 (2.873)**
Adjusted R^2	.123	.103

Note. Entries are standardized final regression coefficients
All variables are entered as grouped entities
*p<.05, **p<.01, ***P<.001

7.1.4 Cross-cultural Differences of the Boundary between "The Private" and "The Public"

Differences in Self-disclosure

German and Chinese exhibit various differences in self-discosure. As shown in Table 15, German and Chinese users prefer to disclose different types of information. German users typically disclose "what is important to me in life" (M=1.66, SD=.749), "I have done which I am proud of" (M=1.80, SD=.719) and "my close relationships with other people" (M=1.51, SD=.659) most frequently; while Chinese users usually disclose data pertaining to "my personal habits" (M=2.69, SD=1.248), "my deepest feelings" (M=2.66, SD=1.097) and "what makes me the person I am" (M=2.35, SD=1.089). In addition, German users share less about "things I have done which I feel guilty about" (M=1.07, SD=.249), "my deepest feelings" (M=1.09, SD=.307) and "what I like and dislike about" (M=.326); while Chinese users reveal less about "things I have done which I feel guilty about" (M=2.00, SD=.938), "things I wouldn't do in public" (M=1.84, SD=.954) and "My worst fears things things" (M=1.98, SD=.935). Both German and Chinese users display a reluctance to disclose things they have done which they feel guilty about. Interestingly, information about "my deepest feelings" is least disclosed by German users but most frequently shared by Chinese users.

Table 15: Comparison of Frequency of Self-disclosure in Germany and China (based on a score between 1–5)

	Germany (N=201)			China (N=192)		
	Mean	**Median**	**Std. Deviation**	**Mean**	**Median**	**Std. Deviation**
My personal habits	1.39	1.00	.609	2.69	2.00	1.248
Things I have done which I feel guilty about	1.07	1.00	.249	2.00	2.00	.938
Things I wouldn't do in public	1.11	1.00	.342	1.84	2.00	.954
My deepest feelings	1.09	1.00	.307	2.66	3.00	1.097
What I like and dislike about myself	1.09	1.00	.326	2.14	2.00	.977
What is important to me in life	1.66	2.00	.749	2.23	2.00	1.004
What makes me the person I am	1.46	1.00	.682	2.35	2.00	1.089

	Germany (N=201)			China (N=192)		
	Mean	Median	Std. Deviation	Mean	Median	Std. Deviation
My worst fears things	1.12	1.00	.387	1.98	2.00	.935
I have done which I am proud of	1.80	2.00	.719	2.23	2.00	.946
My close relationships with other people	1.51	1.00	.659	2.15	2.00	.938

German and Chinese SNSs users also manage the visibility of self-disclosure differently (see Figure 16). Generally, Chinese users are more open than German users when it comes to making disclosed information visible to other users. SNSs users in Germany limit the audience of "things I have done which I feel guilty about", "things I wouldn't do in public", "my deepest feelings", "what I like and dislike about myself" and "my worst feelings" to only themselves, but users in China make them visible to SNSs friends or colleagues/classmates. However, both sets of users make "I have done which I am proud of" visible to SNSs friends.

Figure 16: Different Visibility of Self-disclosure in Germany and China (N=393)

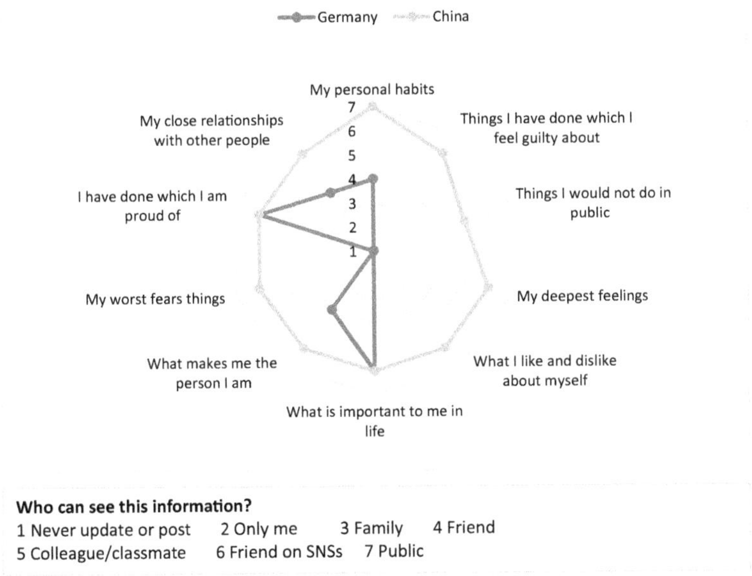

Note: The boundary was measured by the median of visibility of Self-disclosure on SNSs.

As shown in Table 16, German SNSs users demonstrated a higher level of perceived trust and perceived anonymity than the Chinese users. However, Chinese users displayed higher levels of SNSs usage, social influence to use SNSs and to disclose, as well as perceived reciprocity. Cross-cultural studies suggest that the tendency towards cultural value collectivism exerts a positive influence on whether a person is inclined to be socially influenced and to reciprocate in self-disclosure (Posey, Lowry et al. 2010, p. 191). People who are more collectivistic orientated are also more cohesive and integrated with other people in their interactions, more likely to define themselves in terms of group membership and place great value on its welfare, and they could feel "duty to the in-group" (Oyserman, Coon et al. 2002, p. 3). Conversely, people who display individualistic inclination have much looser social ties, and are more unique and independent in interpersonal interactions (Husted and Allen 2008, p. 295, Posey, Lowry et al. 2010, p. 187). The differences of cultural value in Germany and China explain the difference in behaviors of SNSs users. The Chinese are collectivistic orientated. They place great emphasis on group interests and interactional relationships. Therefore, in terms of SNSs use and disclosure, the Chinese are more easily influenced by others during social interaction. Similarly, they experience a higher level of reciprocity and comfort from social interaction on SNSs.

Table 16: A Comparison of German and Chinese Independent Variables of Self-disclosure

	Mean		**F**
	German	**Chinese**	
SNSs use	13.71	15.17	.336***
Social influence to use SNSs	1.8483	2.8047	1.902***
Social influence to disclose	1.3930	2.4219	44.320***
Perceives trust	3.9129	3.2878	2.589***
Perceived risk believes	3.9204	3.7844	1.743
Perceived reciprocity	3.4892	3.6545	2.675*
Perceived anonymity	3.73	3.37	2.078***
N	201	192	

Note. Sig. (2-tailed) Equal variances not assumed
* p<.05, **p<.01, ***p<.001

In order to compare how these models apply to the German and Chinese users, they are tested separately in both countries. Because the data is not normally distributed, its log value is calculated and then a multiple linear regression is conducted. The respective results indicate that only the model in Germany is significant (p=.003) while the model in China is not. The interaction between two independent variables could account for the non-significance of the model. However, the p (p=.055) level of the Chinese model is still reasonably close to the mark of significance. As such, the model of self-disclosure can be considered befitting for both German and Chinese societies. As the models were tested separately, the sample size for each country was reduced by half. This would, in turn, influence the significance quite considerably. Based on the results of regression, we can compare which independent variables have effects on the German society and which on the Chinese one. Clearly, the social influence to use SNSs and perceived reciprocity only influenced self-disclosure in Germany; while the Chinese model suggests that SNSs use is the only factor that influences self-disclosure. These differences suggested that there could be highly salient differences affecting the behaviors of self-disclosure between German and Chinese SNSs users.

Table 17: Comparison of German and Chinese Models of Self-disclosure

	Self-discourse B (t statistic)	
	Germany (F=3.002, p<.005)	**China (F=1.954, ns)**
SNSs use	.010 (.592)	.036 (2.255)*
SNSs size	.015 (.590)	.000 (1.613)
Social influence to use SNSs	.131 (2.399)*	-.052 (-.770)
Social influence to disclose	-.030 (-.348)	.070 (.991)
Perceived reciprocity	.142 (2.116)*	.056 (.717)
Perceived risk believes	-.043 (-.687)	-.092 (-1.169)
Perceived trust	-.073 (-1.044)	.025 (.272)
Perceived anonymity	.082 (1.550)	.032 (.596)
Adjusted R^2	.074	.038
N	201	192

Note. Entries are standardized final regression coefficients
All variables are entered as grouped entities
*p<.05, **p<.01, ***p <.001

Differences in Political Expression

I also compared the frequency of the five items of political expression among the German and Chinese users. Table 18 shows the huge disparity between the online political expressions of German and Chinese users. German users most frequently post personal experiences related to politics or campaigning (M=1.84, SD=.905), while Chinese users merely forward someone else's political commentary to others (M=2.20, SD=1.025). "Sharing a public profile of political news, political advocate or politician" (M=1.64, SD=.864) and "forwarding someone else's political commentary to other people" (M=1.64, SD=.890) are acts that German users less frequently perform on SNSs, while Chinese users infrequently post or share photos, videos, or audio files about politics (M=1.99, SD=1.025). "Forwarding someone else's political commentary to other people" happens more frequently on Chinese SNSs platforms and less on German's.

Table 18: Comparison of Frequency of Political Expression in Germany and China (based on a score between 1–5)

	Germany (N=201)			China (N=192)		
	Mean	**Median**	**Std. Deviation**	**Mean**	**Median**	**Std. Deviation**
Posting personal experiences related to politics or campaigning	1.84	2.00	.905	2.13	2.00	1.061
Sharing a public profile of political news, political advocate or politician	1.64	1.00	.864	2.16	2.00	1.076
Posting or sharing thoughts about politics	1.82	2.00	.933	2.14	2.00	1.070
Posting or sharing photos, videos, or audio files about politics	1.82	2.00	.865	1.99	2.00	.935
Forwarding someone else's political commentary to other people	1.64	1.00	.890	2.20	2.00	1.025

German and Chinese users exhibit only a few differences in how they manage the visibility of political expression (see Figure 17). German users make "forwarding someone else's political commentary to other people" only visible to colleagues/classmates, but Chinese users make it visible to all.

Figure 17: Different Visibility of Political Expression in Germany and China (N=393)

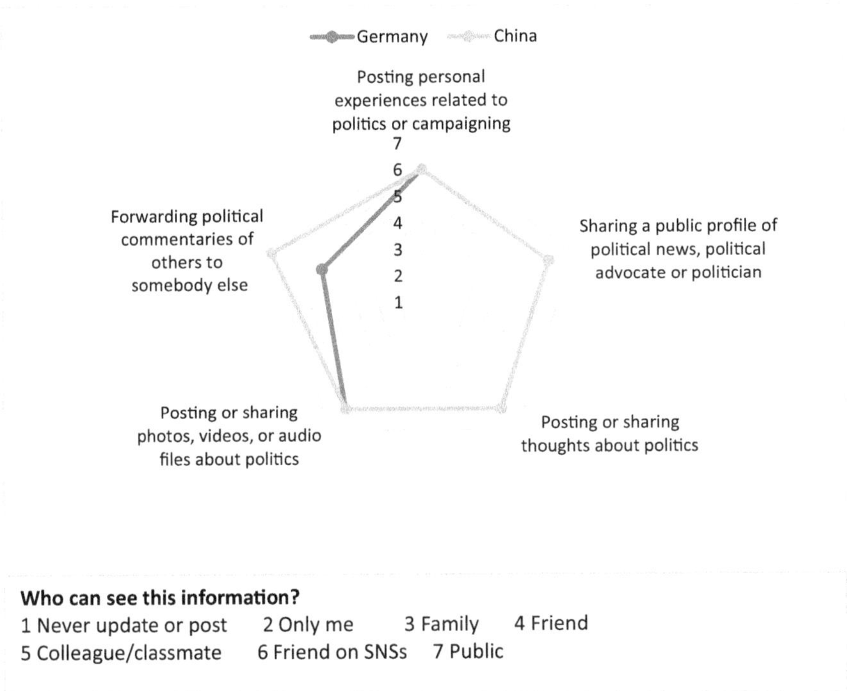

Note: The boundary was measured by the median of visibility of political expression on SNSs.

The model of political expression was also separately tested in Germany and China respectively. Because the data is not normally distributed, its log value is calculated and then a multiple linear regression is conducted. Similar to the model of self-disclosure, only the model for German SNSs users is significant while the model for Chinese users is not. The models for German and Chinese users reflect totally different influential factors for political expression on SNSs. The German model shows that political interest, SNSs efficacy and trust on public TV are related to SNSs political expression. Whereas in China, only trust on public TV negatively influences political expression on SNSs. Additionally, trust on public TV demonstrates a stronger effect on German SNSs users than on Chinese users.

Table 19: Comparison of German and Chinese Model of Political Expression

	Political Expression Beta (t statistic)	
	Germany (F=5.992, p<.001)	**China (F=1.652, ns)**
SNSs use	.012 (1.352)	.015 (1.570)
SNSs size	.014 (.944)	2.240E-5 (.194)
Self-censorship	.024 (.629)	-.051 (-.868)
Political interest	.136 (4.708)***	.059 (1.650)
Political Efficacy	-.016 (-.500)	-.032 (-.943)
SNSs Efficacy	.124 (3.471)**	.017 (.316)
Trust in Press	-.003 (-.047)	.096 (1.848)
Trust in Public TV	-.135 (-.2.585)**	-.160 (-2.562)*
Trust in Private TV	-.026 (-.661)	.062 (.993)
Trust on SNSs	.003 (.063)	-.049 (-.858)
Perceived anonymity	.029 (.960)	-.002 (-.065)
Adjusted R^2	.215	.036
N	201	192

Note. Entries are standardized final regression coefficients
All variables are entered as grouped entities
*p<.05, **p<.01, ***p<.001

The proposed model works well in the German context, but is not significant for Chinese SNSs users. Due to the cultural differences, different political and media systems, the influential factors which work in German possibly become ineffectual in China. A cross-cultural study conducted by Matthes, Hayes et al. (2012, p. 301) compared 9 countries and districts, and discovered that the model of "willingness to express" applied to all districts expect China. This suggests that the willingness to express might be driven by contextual factors in strongly authoritarian and collectivistic societies, such as a limited freedom of opinion expression. Additionally, China has a different media system (as discussed in Chapter 4.3), and this may result in a different impact of trust of media with respect to political expression. These factors contribute to an insignificant result of the regressing Chinese model.

German users exhibit a higher level of interest in politics than their Chinese counterparts. When the independent variables of political expression are compared, users in Germany exhibited a higher level of trust in public TV, perceived anonymity and political interest than those in China. Meanwhile, Chinese SNSs users displayed a higher level of self-censorship, SNSs efficacy, trust in private TV and SNSs. However, the levels of political efficacy and trust in press are similar in Germany and China.

Table 20: Comparing German and Chinese Independent Variables Affecting Political Expression

	Mean		**F**
	German	**Chinese**	
Self-censorship	2.4241	3.1615	18.062***
SNSs efficacy	3.1542	3.4323	7.396***
Political efficacy	2.6020	2.6849	1.455
Trust in press	3.1891	3.0660	.378
Trust in public/state TV	3.3648	3.1250	8.299**
Trust in private TV	2.4660	3.1406	23.537***
Trust on SNSs	2.4975	3.0417	15.250***
Perceived anonymity	3.73	3.37	2.078***
Political interest	3.96	3.29	.034***
N	201	192	

Note. Sig. (2-tailed) Equal variances not assumed
*p<.05, **p<.01, ***p<.001

Different cultural values, as well as different political and media systems, account for these differences between Germany and China. In accordance with the culture of collectivism, people in the Chinese society pay more attention to the social group they belong to and are more easily influenced by others during interpersonal interaction. They experience a higher pressure of the "quasi-statistical sense"[29] and withhold their opinions when they perceive that their opinions coincide with the

29 Quasi-statistical sense is "an innate ability" gauge public opinion, by which people assume they can sense and figure out what others are thinking Scheufele, D. (2007). Opinion Climates, Spirals of Silence and Biotechnology: Public Opinion as A Heuristic for Scientific Decision-making. The Media, the Public and Agricultural Biotechnology. D. Brossard, J. Shanahan and T. Nesbitt. Oxon and Cambridge, CAB International: 231–244.

minority, in order to maintain collective harmony (Huang 2005, p. 324). Thus, self-censorship has a stronger impact on Chinese SNSs users, who observe a collectivistic culture, than on German users, who observe an individualistic culture.

Besides, more Chinese users than German ones believe that SNSs are effective in influencing their society. As discussed in Chapter 4.3, the Chinese media is under strict governmental control, causing a lack of public platforms for political expression and discussion. However, ICTs changed the Chinese media environment by providing more channels for public discussion, transforming the Chinese public sphere, and influencing dominant values in the Chinese society. Discussions on SNSs in China are more effective than those in Germany, where people exert more influence on politics through the act of voting and demonstrations. Also, the Chinese people believe that the Internet empowers them politically (Shen, Wang et al. 2009, p. 456).

Another difference brought about by the difference in media systems between Germany and China is the trust in TV. Clearly, the Germans trust the news disseminated by public TV more while the Chinese trust news broadcasted by private TV more. Due to the dual media system in Germany, the public TV industry is sponsored by public funding and aims to serve the democratic, social, and cultural needs of the people. The commercial interests of and advertisements on such TV programs are therefore limited. Every bit of effort made by the German public TV is to increase the quality of the programs and provide cultural contributions, according to the German Interstate Treaty on Broadcasting and Telemedia (Interstate Broadcasting Treaty)[30]. The responsibility and objectives of the public TV sector make it more trustworthy as compared to the private TV sector which only focuses on commercial profits. However, the situation in China is different. State-owned TV is under the complete control of the Chinese government. Therefore, sources for political news appear homogenous. On the other hand, the private TV sector provides alternative news sources and perspectives as this sector is not as "controlled" by the government as the state-owned TV is. Take Chinese Phoenix TV as example, people consider it an important substitute of the official news

---

30 The Interstate Treaty on Broadcasting and Telemedia/Interstate Broadcasting Treaty (Staatsvertrag für Rundfunk und Telemedien/Rundfunkstaatsvertrag) is the most important part of the Interstate Treaty on Broadcasting in Unified Germany (Staatsvertrag über den Rundfunk im vereinten Deutschland) since August 31st, 1991. It has been amended several times and the most recent amendment is the 12th Interstate Treaty for Amending the Interstate Treaties with Regard to Broadcasting Law (12. Staatsvertrag zur Änderung rundfunkrechtlicher Staastverträge/12. Rundfunkänderungsstaatsvertrag), which is published on December 18th, 2008 and is enforced since June 1st, 2009.

channel, especially when important political issues are being censored on the state-owned TV. For the same reason, Chinese SNSs users trust the SNSs platforms more than Germans do.

Interestingly, although most Germans provide their real names on SNSs, a higher level of anonymity is associated with their online personas. The Chinese, meanwhile, maintain less anonymity although they use pseudonyms liberally and extensively.

Differences in the Boundary between "The Private" and "The Public"

Upon further comparison of the dependent variables, self-disclosure and political expression between the German and Chinese cyber societies, I discovered that users from both countries demonstrate completely different understanding of the boundary dividing "the private" and "the public". As the distribution of these dependent variables is abnormal, the Mann-Whitney U test was used to compare the German users with the Chinese ones. As shown in Table 21, the results support my hypothesis H14. Chinese SNSs users displayed a higher frequency and visibility of self-disclosure, as compared to the German users. However, on contrary to H15, Chinese users share political expressions more often and make it more visible to others. As such, they facilitate a higher level of political expression on SNSs than the German users do.

Table 21: Comparison of the Boundary between "The Private" and "The Public" on SNSs in Germany and China

	Mean Rank		**Z**
	German	**Chinese**	
Self-disclosure frequency	122.42	275.08	-13.353***
Self-disclosure visibility	155.35	240.60	-7.449***
Political expression frequency	172.56	222.58	-4.408***
Political expression visibility	174.38	220.68	-4.120***
Self-disclosure	134.04	262.91	-11.244***
Political expression	170.73	224.51	-4.703***
N	201	192	

Note. Asymp. Sig. (2-tailed)
*p<.05, **p<.01, ***P<.001

Due to the globalization process, economic development, opened media market and the diffusion of ICTs, China is becoming more similar to Germany in terms of cyber social affairs and behavioral trends. Nevertheless, the differences in the boundary between "the private" and "the public" on German and Chinese SNSs suggest that there are actually more differences than similarities. Globalization and social media increase the sense of individualism and privacy concerns of Chinese SNSs users. Yet, they remain deeply influenced by traditional culture and therefore feel comfortable with and inclined towards self-disclosure, as supposed in Chapter 4.3.3. Although German SNSs users are subscribers of the individualistic culture and also have the freedom to express more personal political opinions than the Chinese, the media and political systems that they use to express political opinions create results that are contrary to expectations. It is the Chinese SNSs users, rather than the German ones, who express more political opinions that are also more publicly visible on SNSs. I have discussed the use of SNSs for political expression in both countries in Chapter 4.1.2 and 4.2.2. In Germany, there are more ways to express political opinions, such as voting and demonstration, or discussion on press and TV. SNSs, therefore, are not as important as in China. The situation in China, however, is totally different. The media faces strict censorship and is under complete control of the government; the people have almost no chance to be involved in democratic voting. SNSs, with its mask of anonymity and uncontrollable character that eludes governmental control, change the disadvantageous situation into one that is more advantageous for the citizens in terms of political expression.

An additional reason for a higher political expression in China could be the huge impact of political expression on Chinese SNSs. SNSs is a special platform used to attract the attention of the masses and has the power to make a name famous due to its expanse of network. Take the Chinese platform Sina Weibo for example, some famous characters like Jack Ma[31] opened an account using the title "V-user" (registered with real name) and gained a vast number of followers and social influence, so that they can further influence public opinion. These "celebrities" are active on Sina Weibo: they post comments and create topics for discussion. Even an unknown person can attract a large amount of attention by posting controversial or alluring topics.

Differences in the Various SNSs Platforms

As the data is an abnormal distribution, I conducted a Kruskal Wallis Test on self-disclosure and political expression to see how they differ across various SNSs

---

31 Jack Ma, also known as Ma Yun, is the founder of the Ailibaba Group. He is the most famous Chinese manager for Internet-based business in the world. He is also the only Chinese entrepreneur who graced the cover of Forbes.

platforms. As shown in Table 22, the frequency and visibility of self-disclosure, as well as of political expression, are noticeably different on each SNSs platform. Users of Qzone demonstrate the highest frequency of self-disclosure, while users of Renren make their posts most publicly visible. Additionally, users on Sina Weibo post information more frequently and visibly.

Table 22: Kruskal Wallis Test of Self-disclosure and Political Expression (Frequency and Visibility)

	Mean Rank					**Chi-Square (df=4)**
	Germany		**China**			
	Facebook	**Google+**	**Renren**	**Qzone**	**Sina Weibo**	
Self-disclosure frequency	122.90	26.50	268.53	284.22	272.44	179.471***
Self-disclosure visibility	154.89	247.50	249.81	226.98	244.62	57.133***
Political expression frequency	172.93	98.50	212.47	213.09	227.76	20.627***
Political expression visibility	174.37	177.00	196.56	194.20	234.53	22.528***
N	200	1	18	49	125	

Note. Asymp. Sig.
*p<.05, **p<.01, ***p<.001

7.2 Results of Qualitative Interview

The results of the online questionnaire established the location of the boundary between "the private" and "the public" on SNSs, and reveal how influencing factors operate in the models. However, the results of the questionnaire based on empirical surveys merely describe the phenomenon but do not explain the reason behind why users consider SNSs a public or a private space. The results also do not account for the ways in which users manage the boundary, nor do the results explain the choice behind certain extent of visibility on some posts. Further, the results also do not address users' preference of political expression both on SNSs and in reality. As such, interviews with some of the SNSs users are conducted to find the answers to the above uncertainties.

7.2.1 Name, Photo and Profile Information

Many interviewees prefer to use a partially real name than a full one. They explained that the partially real names reveal their identities sufficiently for friends to recognize them while at the same time, serve to protect their privacy from strangers. Some users include their nicknames on Facebook to further allow friends and family members to distinguish them from other users with similar names. A partially real name is also presumed to protect people from suffering the repercussions when they share sensitive personal political opinions. Fabo, a 22-year-old Bachelor student, uses a partially real name on Facebook. He has been using Facebook to share his political beliefs with his friends for a long time:

> *"When I started to publish some political images publicly (like my actual banner or profile picture), I changed my name to prevent that anybody I don't know could make a conclusion between my political standpoint and my name. Because someone browsing my profile without being my friend gets to know my face and partly my political beliefs, but only my first name. Giving my full name on Facebook would be dangerous. I could end up on some lists of neo-Nazis or just don't get the job I want because the employer looks me up on Facebook and doesn't like my political views."*

Some of our interviewees also had concerns about that their future employers may find their SNSs profiles and see their personal information. As such, they provide only a partially real name. Nevertheless, SNSs are platforms that establish connections among friends, classmates and colleagues; hence, some users prefer to use a real and full name so that they can be easily found by people they know. A case in point would be Facebook in Germany, which is an international communication network. Before 2011, StudiVZ, the German version of Facebook, was more popular. Although some students already registered for a Facebook account, they did so while they were in other countries. After returning to Germany, these users continued to use Facebook to remain in connect with their foreign friends. For such purposes, they needed to use their full real names on Facebook so that they can be identified by friends. Later, after Facebook became more popular in societies all over the world, users who provide full and real names could be easily found by fellow students and coworkers, not just friends. In fact, the pressure to use full and real name is a result of social influence. Iwo, Kai, Julchen, Ansgarb and Tang revealed in the interviews that the main reason for their use of real names was because their friends on SNSs were also doing so. These users experienced peer pressure to conform to social norms, coupled with the SNSs contractual term that stipulates the use of a real name as a prerequisite. Naturally, because of the use of real and full names, SNSs users harbor privacy concerns on these platforms and refrain from sharing too much personal information. Information posted on SNSs was irrelevant and inconsequential. When sharing too much, they would change their names.

People also used pseudonyms to protect themselves from being stalked by strangers. Especially on Sina Weibo, the Chinese microblog, on which users could be followed by any strangers without permission. Therefore, pseudonyms became a precautionary measure undertaken by most interviewees for self-protection.

Lulu, a 23-year-old Masters student never ever provides real personal information on Sina Weibo; both her name and her profile photo are not genuine. For her, Weibo is a public space and she would never post private and personal information there. She thinks of Sina Weibo as different from Wechat, the latter is an instant message mobile application that functions like a social network. All of the people on her Wechat are people she knows in real life; hence, she has no qualms about sharing personal information there. On the other hand, she considers Sina Weibo a public domain in which she needs to be careful about privacy. Admittedly, a pseudonym does not guarantee total anonymity as even a personal symbol can be identifiable to friends who are familiar with the users. Ermathgin, a 22-year-old bachelor student, uses the name of a street in London that sounds like his actual name, but was spelt differently, on Facebook. He also uses the street sign as his Profile picture. "I want people to recognize me when I add them, but I don't want people to be able to find me without me knowing."

Additionally, users create a pseudonym to present an ideal self. The SNSs platforms are virtual spaces in which users can construct an ideal world that is different from reality. A Chinese Weibo user named herself "Potter", the same family name of Harry Potter, and posted Harry Potter's portrait on her profile. She wanted to create a name for her virtual world, where she needed neither to maintain the complicated social relationships nor do things that she did not like to do in the real world. On her Sina Weibo profile, she filled her gender as male so that male strangers would not disturb her. Naturally, she never posted anything related to herself, and instead, only read information shared by others. She accepted strangers because for her, Sina Weibo is a public platform that also functions as an imaginary world that is divorced from her reality.

For the same reason – to allow friends to recognize them and to protect themselves from strangers – the partially obscured profile picture is used prevalently on SNSs platforms. This serves two functions as SNSs users would also prefer to remain anonymous on SNSs so that their data will not be abused by commercial organizations or third parties. Especially since the security of Facebook has been repeatedly challenged and compromised in recent years. To protect themselves as best as possible, users use borrowed pictures as their profile photographs. Something connected to the user, such as one's own brand, can also be posted on Facebook as a profile picture. Of course, sometimes SNSs users want their profile photos to be completely unassociated with them and so, they simply use normal images that can be downloaded off any websites. Tang, a female 24-year-old Masters student hides both her real name and portrait on Qzone. As she thought that her profile picture on SNSs was public and everyone could see and download it, she simply used a borrowed image so that strangers would not disturb her. She found that as a woman, it is easy to be watched by strangers on QQ and Qzone. "The security on SNSs for me is more psychological than financial or something else."

Many interviewees also find using genuine photographs a little bit strange as most of their friends use borrowed pictures. This situation happens very often on Chinese SNSs like Qzone and Sina Weibo. A borrowed picture allows the user to mask his/her own identities and offer some semblance of security when interacting with strangers on SNSs. Sometimes, women users use pictures of men or cartoons to create an online persona to avoid potential disturbance from male strangers.

SNSs users share a routine behavior with regards to the visibility of photographs on online platforms. Ana and Fabian never ever post photographs publicly on SNSs and believed that it is inappropriate to post others' photographs without permission. "If I post photos with friends, it's only visible to friends. This is because I don't want to be found. My friends already know those things, or can ask me if they want to." As Ana said, the only type of photographs that is always public on SNSs is the profile photo. The remaining information, whether graphic or linguistic, can be restricted from the public. In the earlier years of SNSs usage, people might have been eager to present themselves on their profiles in a bid to attract more friends and so, may make profile items more publicly visible. Later, they realize the danger of privacy breaches and begin to implement some form of control over their posts. Subsequently, users start to change the settings of their posts from "public" to "friends only" and also, exercise greater discretion over accepting friend requests from strangers, to the extent of deleting those already on their friend-lists. Denny has been using Facebook for 8 years now. During these 8 years, there have been some changes in his user-behavior. He used to be a little more opened about the information that he shared on Renren, but as more people joined his friend-list, he began to filter the information that he published and even started to moderate the visibility setting on his account. He found that this change in attitude "is a steady process."

Tao was a Renren user. After some online strangers brought to his attention the issues of privacy concerns, he developed a strategy to manage his friend list:

"Because it's possible to check and delete people from my friend list, if I find that this person is unsuitable to be my SNSs friend, then I delete him or her. In the beginning, my friend circle on SNSs was expanding and I didn't think too much about adding strangers. But later, when the circle of friends developed steadily, I begin to check the background of people in my friend-list. Especially those shared no common things with me, I delete them."

A 22-year-old Sina Weibo user, Ting, also deleted most of the personal information and posts two weeks before our interview. She had seen the news reports on scores of people who were trampled to death during 2015 New Year's Eve celebration in Shanghai. Several journalists had found some personal photographs and posts on a victim's SNSs profile and had presented those findings in their reports. She was so astonished about the journalist's behavior and the breach in privacy that she decided to delete her personal photographs from Sina Weibo. "I think that Weibo is a public space but not suitable to place private things."

Instead of a space of contact for people who share close relationships, SNSs are platforms for interactions with colleagues/classmates and acquaintances. Fabian's Facebook friend-list contains very few friends. Most of his FB friends are either classmates or acquaintances. For him, Facebook is a practical way to stay in contact with casual friends and to keep up to date with what they are doing. He enjoys sharing information with his FB friends and wants to know that they are reading his posts. In corroboration with former studies (Ellison, Steinfield et al. 2007, p. 1146, Lampe, Ellison et al. 2008, p. 724, Gilbert and Karahalios 2009, p. 211), Fabian's and other users' friend-lists reveal the kinds of weak social relationships that are prevalent on SNSs. Each SNSs platform has its target users. Therefore, users may utilize different SNSs platforms to communicate with different groups of people. Tang uses Qzone to communicate with classmates and prefers to use instant-messaging software like QQ to send short messages (SMS) to closer friends. Qzone, for her, is a platform to share recent information with acquaintances and classmate. If she needs to discuss anything with her classmate or friends, she would make a call. Our interviewees hardly ever accept friend requests from strangers. They typically check out the sender's personal information to establish identification before accepting any friend requests. Users will also ignore the request if the sender does not answer any questions that they asked. However, there are also some users who will accept the friend requests first and *then* delete the person after finding out who they are. In general, it is not uncommon for SNSs users to establish contact with acquaintances with whom they may not be familiar. In other words, most interviewees accept friend requests from people whom they have met at least once. Naturally, requests from family members, friends and colleagues/classmates are almost always accepted. Some users are insistent on adding strangers who share similar backgrounds and interests with them, because they think that SNSs are created to widen one's social circle and to help individuals meet new people. Even so, the number of strangers on an average friend-list remains very limited.

In a SNSs user-survey with American teens, Boyd (2014, p. 35–36) discovered that teenagers like to keep their SNSs contact list devoid of family members. This is mainly because they understand the social context of SNSs as one that is related to friends, classmates and acquaintances, instead of close familial relationships. Of course, there is also a privacy concern here in that some teenagers may divulge information that they consider confidential from their family members. Many adamantly insist that the day their parents infiltrate their SNSs page would be the day they abandon their accounts. In contrast, University students do not exhibit the same concerned about family members being privy to their personal information or posts. As these University users explained, although students establish a connect with their parents over SNSs, these parents are mostly very busy with work and have no time to keep themselves up to date with their children's posts. It is a different story, however, with cousins, siblings, and other relatives of similar age groups. These same-generation users are treated as any other SNSs friends with whom users share secrets, hobbies and personal information. Users also try to manage the contents which their family members could see and so they publish information that is not too personal. By doing so, users manage to include their parents in their SNSs social circle and yet retain a certain element of secrecy with the implemented control over privacy of entries.

For Fabian, it was not an easy decision to include family member in his friend-list. "But as long if what I'm posting doesn't annoy them, it's okay for me. I needed longer to include my parents in the list, and I think my use of Facebook made them more clear some of my ways of thinking." He also chats with family members on Facebook and shares interesting and funny articles. However, Fabian draws the line at political discussions. He refuses to discuss politics with family members in real life and therefore, also refrains from making explicit political expressions online. Facebook provides a platform on which he could have more conversational topics that help in his communication with family.

Mickey, a 22-year-old Masters student, also communicates with her parents on SNSs. When she was younger, she avoided her parents on SNSs, but as she grew older, she began to make information she shares on SNSs visible to her parents. Interestingly, this trend of parental exclusion does not seem to extend to other relatives like cousins, brothers and sisters. Many interviewees added cousins and siblings as friend on SNSs and exhibited no reservations about information that can be seen by them. A possible explanation for this reservation could be the user's reluctance to allow parents access into their "private" domains. They resist the idea that their lives on SNSs could be observed by their parents. In China, this generation of parents faces some difficulties in navigating the forms of new media; as such, despite many of them having SNSs accounts, they find it hard to connect with their children's profiles.

It is not uncommon for SNSs users to provide only pieces of information that they feel comfortable with and leave all other blanks unfilled. The most common types of data that users feel comfortable with revealing are gender, birthday, local residence and school/university. These pieces of information normally suffice in the search for friends as people are generally able to make intelligent guesses at the identities of their request recipients based on this data. Hence, users find it necessary to display this information on their profiles. As majority of the SNSs users try to stay anonymous so as to avoid catching the attention of strangers, they refrain from posting any contact information. Ansgarb, a 25-year-old master student, has no strangers on his Facebook friend-list and he never reveals contact information online. He believes that friends should know how to contact him when the need arises and believes that "if they want it (contact info.), they should ask."

As a precautionary measure, many SNSs users are very careful about divulging information related to their workplace or school/university. Unlike other professional career-development platforms (such as LinkedIn and Xing) that regard user profiles as business cards, Facebook is more for the sharing of personal information. As such, Facebook profiles typically reveal a side of the user that differs greatly from professional expectations. Since many interviewees do not want their personal lives to be accessible to their future bosses, they exercise more discretion with such SNSs accounts. During the interview, Eramthgin, a Bachelor student, revealed his professional concerns even before his career life begins. Eramthgin did not want people to associate any information that he posted on Facebook with his 'role' in the office; as such, he filled in only information about his education history.

When Mark Zuckerberg founded Facebook in 2004, his objective was to utilize this social networking site to enhance the quality of varsity social interaction and to help students build relationships with one another. Therefore, there was a special portion detailing one's "relationship" status on the profile. Based on this data, singles can find partners accordingly. Later, this function became prevalently used by almost every following social network site. As a relationship status is highly personal, many users balk at the thought of making it visible to the public. The results of my interviews show that users either leave the relationship field blank in order to protect their own privacy, or make their single status visible in order to encourage potential suitors. In the case of the former, users who are in a relationship point out that it is an extremely private affair that would not benefit from exposure. Besides, real-life friends would already be privy to their relationship status and so, it is not necessary to declare such information on SNSs. In the case of the latter, however, users take advantage of the relationship status to announce their availability and to create opportunities for potential suitors.

7.2.2 The Parameters for Personal Information

SNSs are also platforms where people can join groups formed by like-minded people who share similar interests to get to know one another and to exchange information and ideas among fellow hobbyists. This is especially useful for people who are looking to expand their social circles and link up with more friends who share common interests and background. In order to achieve this aim, users would need to present information about their interests and hobbies, and sometimes also physical appearance, personal characters and habits, so as to attract people of a specific type to their profiles. Also included are information segments about favorite books and films that they have read and watched recently. Xu, a Masters student, uses Sina Weibo to read information posted by others and to share his personal habits. However, he seldom talks about personal interests with his offline friends as he finds that online communication differs greatly from offline communication. To put it more clearly, Xu posts information on Sina Weibo for public eyes and not for a specific person. He shares his personal interests and book reviews with his friends in that cyber domain and if someone is interested in the information that he has shared, they can initiate a chat. However, Xu never shares feelings on SNSs because he believes this exposes him to potential danger. After all, any random stranger on Sina Weibo (other than his friends) may chance upon his posts. If he really wants to express some personal information, he makes use of the privacy settings to limit the visibility of that information to "only friends".

Unlike Xu, there are others who delight in being able to share important events that they are proud of on SNSs. To these users, SNSs provide opportunities for the development of social relationships, albeit of a weaker kind, with people whom they do not associate with in real life or people whom they have not contacted for a very long time. These platforms allow people to keep track of their friends' recent situations. Things posited in the deeper layers of personality (such as mistakes that people feel guilty about, things they wouldn't do in public, or their worst fears) are disclosed less due to privacy concerns and personal security. For many Interviewees, interaction on SNSs is more of a public kind as compared to the offline communication with friends. As information posted on SNSs can be diffused and perpetuated through online social networks, users would rather discuss personal affairs with friends face-to-face or through instant message software such as SMS.

Additionally, the boundary between "the private" and "the public" has been evolving. After using SNSs for a few years, majority of the users exhibit a trend of reduction in the frequency of posts they make and its attached visibility. Such users may still use SNSs, but they assume a passive role as recipients of information instead of active perpetuators. In other words, these users only read information shared by others to stay in touch with friends and keep up to date on the happenings in the lives of their friends. Privacy concerns also contributed to the reduction of posting actions. After users have stayed on SNSs for several years, they begin to grow concerned about what would happen if they were to post their whole life story online. This concern stops them from future sharing of personal information and reduces them to the passive roles of commentators, in which they only leave comments on others' posts or merely click the "like" icon. Ana, who has 68% acquaintance and only 1% strangers on her Facebook, expresses a deep concern about the security of her posts and tries not to share too much personal information on her Facebook. She guessed (correctly) that some people are able to work their ways around the cyber security of Facebook and so, her only form of self-protection is to limit her self-disclosure acts. Although Ana dislikes this lack of security, she is unable to change anything. During the interview, she pointed out the conflict in this situation: on one hand, she refrains from sharing too much information for security's sake; on the other hand, she needs Facebook as a means to contact friends and people at the university.

Sometimes, users may find themselves bored with certain SNSs platforms and so, they switch to another platform. Another likely scenario could be the overactivity of SNSs advertisements that interrupts usage and causes users so much frustration that they decide to move to another domain. SNSs have no problem with wooing new members. The question is *how* SNSs can make profits while keeping their users happy. No matter F-commerce[32] or online advertisements, both evoke negativity and dissuade users from using SNSs. In addition, new SNSs platforms like WeChat, Line, WhatsApp pose great challenges for the older ones.

As an analogy, Facebook is very much like a hotel that you can check out of anytime you want, but you can never actually leave. Once registered, the account

32 F-commerce is a strategy that focuses on developing or designing ecommerce content on Facebook.

cannot be deleted and all individual's traces will be kept online. Denny tried to wipe out his personal information on Facebook but failed.

> *"I think I used to share more personal information back then than I do now, because I wasn't aware of how hard it actually is to erase something from the Internet, that you once shared but don't want to be there anymore. I also found it rather appalling how personal the Ads I got, as Facebook seems to know so much about me and my interests, more than I'm comfortable with. I wanted to delete my account once, and had the hardest time trying to do so. Then, when I logged back in months later, everything was still there."*

However, this phenomenon only exists on Facebook. Users of Renren, Qzone, Weibo and Google+ still have the option of deleting their accounts and erasing personal information off cyberspace. However, these SNSs platforms demonstrate similar privacy concerns as Facebook. Tao had shared some personal information about his life on Weibo. He did not want people who knew him in real life to see what he had posted, so he regularly checked his posts on Weibo and periodically deleted them. Most of the entries he deleted, Tao admitted, were related to his personal life.

All the respondents in the survey were university students who explained that they used SNSs in the first year of varsity life to establish connections with new friends, share photographs and record details of their daily life. They also presented their new lives to family members and old friends through SNSs. After some time, however, they reduced the frequency of their posts until their final year in university, when they shared the least information. Mickey enjoyed sharing her life on Renren when she was a freshman and found many things novel and interesting. She did not mind sharing personal information such as diary entries and photographs, during her first three years of varsity life. In retrospect, however, she feels that she was too naive and ignorant about privacy issues at that time. She spent the whole day at university and frequently contacted classmates on Renren. "Renren is just like another space of our university." However, life during her final year was overwhelmed by thesis-writing, internships and job searches. Like many of her peers who no longer had time for SNSs, Mickey updated less frequently as well. Meanwhile, as they get older, they begin to be concerned with privacy and lose interest in conversing with strangers.

In addition to the reduction of posts on SNSs, users are also becoming more aware of the contents and exercising more stringent control over the visibility of these entries. In the beginning, they might share a lot about themselves on their profiles in order to get to know more friends, but after some time, this interest fades and privacy concern takes over. Boyd (2014, p. 32) survey results reveal the main reason for the general unwillingness of teenagers to allow open access to their profiles. It turns out that these teenagers are mostly interested in interacting with like-minded people and not the general public. Restricting the accessibility of their profiles allow them to act on this desire. The situation is the same for our research targets – the university students. After using SNSs for a few years, most people change the visibility of their profiles from being accessible to the public to being accessible only to SNSs friends. They know that strangers exist on SNSs, so they manage their posts in manners that keep their private information away from unknown people.

The implementation of control settings proves extremely useful in the reduction of users' privacy concerns. However, users are not completely confident of the effectiveness. During the interview, Ana expressed her worries about this function to control visibility of her posts, "I saw it, I use it. I sure hope it works." To some extent, the control function that limits visibility on information does prevent strangers from accessing one's personal information, albeit remaining susceptible to hacks and skillful cyber meandering. A recent survey by Minkus and Memon (2014, p. 5) agrees with the idea that the effectiveness of visibility control is an important part of users' privacy settings on Facebook. In my survey, many interviewees still harbor doubts about the effectiveness of this security measure as commercial organizations or companies still retain access to and abuse their personal data. Thus, many users prefer to omit their personal information rather than risk this breach of privacy. Eramthgin does not provide much personal information on Facebook; those data that he does provide, he restricts the visibility to "friends only". He believes that privacy is not a problem for him as his privacy setting is high. On the other hand, some Facebook users are still concerned over information leaks. For them, keeping published information impersonal and infrequent will offer a better peace of mind.

The results of the online questionnaire also revealed that the percentage of colleagues/classmates and strangers on users' SNSs acounts is positively related to self-disclosure behavior. To explore these reasons further, some users provide explanations for this relationship in the interviews. As all of our interviewees were university students, they used SNSs mainly for communication purposes with classmates and schoolmates, especially in the early stages of their varsity life. The percentage of classmates/colleagues naturally plays an important role in influencing their SNSs behaviors. Additionally, many of the interviewees revealed that they do not mind accepting friend requests and disclosing information about themselves to people they do not know in real life, as long as these strangers share similar hobbies and interests as them. One reason for this is that they hope to learn something interesting from new sources of information; another reason is the desire to engage in discussions with like-minded folks about a similar interest or hobby. Therefore, the presence of strangers on a friend-list implicitly encourages users to share and disclose information on SNSs while the presence of family members, friends and acquaintances demonstrate little or no influence at all. As SNSs users explained, they prefer to make a telephone call to contact friends, or speak with them directly face-to-face. University students seldom use SNSs to communicate with family members, as such, family members comprise only a small part of their friend-lists. As for acquaintances, although they take up a huge portion of a user's friend-list, their roles remain peripheral as people of weak social ties often do, and hence, they exert no influence on self-disclosure.

7.2.3 Trust on SNSs

When I asked the respondents whether they trust their friends on Facebook, several of them answered "it depends". Denny has almost 400 friends on Facebook, some of who are his closest friends while others are just people he had met on holidays. He specifies that he trusts only his friends and has reservations about the rest whom he does not really know. Ansgarb also trusts only a selected few on his SNSs friend-list, with whom he shares personal information (e.g. photos). Eramthgin, meanwhile, trusts no one on his Facebook friend-list and barely talks to any of them because he considers them as strangers. Clearly, he also refrains from sharing personal information with them. Sina Weibo user, Potter, expressed that she does not trust every one of her followers. She even tried to analyze the people who followed her Weibo and discovered that a surprising 30% of them are strangers.

SNSs users who do not trust the people on their friend-lists can set up a virtual wall that prevents strangers from seeing their personal information. Even if some users trust a large percentage of their SNSs social circle, the question of trust remains a sensitive and complex issue. Trusting the people on their SNSs friend-lists does not automatically mean that users also trust the SNSs platforms per se. In the interviews, many users revealed that it is not their SNSs friends whom they distrust but rather, the SNSs platform security. Many raised doubts about the limitations of cyber security systems as they worry that third party organizations can get hold of their private information. They also expressed worry over the trail of information that could be traced back to them that might potentially jeopardize their career prospects or cause a political repercussion. Therefore, they are very careful about the information they share and some even deleted their words on hindsight. This is one of the most important reasons that accounts for why perceived trust relates negatively to self-disclosure. Future studies should consider the distribution of different types of relationships on an individual's friend-list and its influence on trust.

7.2.4 Target Audience on SNSs

In Chapter 2.3.1, I introduced the model of *Mediated Social Communication*. The model suggests that SNSs users consider not only their perceived audience, but also their target communication partners, when deciding which information to share. This means that users may choose to manage the visibility of their posts if they decide that the information they share should remain within a certain social boundary. Some users on Sina Weibo (a microblog that is more public) have no target audience in mind; they simply publish information that is public to their Weibo followers. As for Facebook, Renren and Qzone, the disclosure behavior of users depends on the subject of that particular post. I talked to Denny and Mickey, who both made friends the target audiences of their published entries, while keeping classmates and strangers as target audience for posts pertaining to politics and public activities.

> *"Depends on the topic, I guess. If it's personal, I only share it with a very close group of friends (those are people I know for years and am also close with offline). When it comes to politics and News, I mostly share it either with people from university or university-related. I almost never share anything with people from my party, although I probably should."*
> *"If it's about my mood, then I would like to only let my friends see; if it's about some activities, I hope I can share it with people who also participated."*

If they really want someone to see their posts, they will leave a message directly instead of sharing it with the general public. Eramthgin prefers to write a message to specific friends whom he wants to talk to. Also, SNSs users can make use of the "tag" function to address their target audience directly. Ansgarb pointed out that the act of posting information on his profile means that the information is meant for public consumption; otherwise, the posting action defeats its own purpose. Conversely, if he wants to address a specific group of friends, he would make use of the tag function.

During our interview, Xu, a 23-year-old Sina Weibo user, explained why he enjoys posting on Weibo frequently and why he makes his posts widely visible. Although all of his friends on Weibo can see his posts, he only chats with people who share common interests as him and who initiate conversations about his posts. However, he is careful to keep conversational topics impersonal so as to protect his privacy. His explanation suggests that microblog is more of a public platform than a private one, although SNSs offer functions such as visibility control. From this aspect, Sina Weibo differs from Facebook, Google+, Renren and Qzone, where private and personal communication takes place more prevalently.

7.2.5 The Boundary of Political Expression

I asked some of the respondents about their preferences and attitudes towards political discussions. On contrary to expectations, our interviewees actually disagree that SNSs are public spaces that provide convenient environments conducive for political expressions. In fact, the interviewees actually expressed less political opinions on SNSs. They prefer to discuss politics with people in real life because it is easier and more effective to communicate verbally face-to-face than virtually about such sensitive issues. They also found it difficult to express opinions clearly through typed words on SNSs, especially since there is usually a limit for words on such platforms.

Alice, a 24-year-old Masters student, focuses more on entertainment contents on Sina Weibo, such as film and design. She also receives most of her political information from Sina Weibo. However, she restricts her role on Sina Weibo to that of a passive reader because she feels that that she is too powerless to change anything and her voice is too weak to be heard. Alice prefers to discuss current affairs in an offline environment because of that. She majors in journalism and media studies so she participates actively in class discussions whenever her professor broaches political topics. Additionally, she and her roommates talk about public affairs a lot. Somehow, this political engagement and expression is not carried over into the cyber world.

Like Alice, Eramthgin expresses more personal political opinion offline while he sometimes shares articles (from traditional media sources such as newspapers and magazines) that his SNSs friends might be interested in. Yet, he never expresses his own opinions on SNSs as he believes such expressions to be useless. However, he still maintains that opinions or articles that are circulated on SNSs attract attention. One of the interviewees, Julchen, also seldom discussed politics on Facebook. According to her, discussing or sharing political information on FB is just a way to start a conversation with friends instead of influencing politics. In her opinion, there are many people who gather on the discussion boards of SNSs to engage in superficial political discussions that unfortunately will never lead to appropriate deliberation or any kind of influence on politics. Julchen expresses no interest in participating in such pointless commentary. Therefore, her political involvement, even within personal contacts, is very limited.

Another interviewee, Denny, is a member of a political party. He actively participates in the perpetuation of political news and articles, but he draws the line at expressing personal political opinions on Facebook. In the rare cases that he does, he restricts the information within a very tight circle of "friends".

> *"I have FB-friends whom I don't know personally. Some people I've only met once or twice, so they are not really friends. I have no problem discussing politics with friends online (although I only do it on a few occasions per year), because those are people I have known for years. Since I trust them and I know them well, this is okay. When it comes to other people that I don't know as well, I fear that it could become a situation like comments on a news site (which are so terrible that they are the best argument for print)."*

Many interviewees share Denny's opinion. They only trust people whom they know very well. This causes them to restrict the visibility of their political expressions and personal information. By extension, the boundary between "the private" and "the public" is redefined by the users' implementation of control over the visibility of shared information on SNSs platforms.

7.2.6 The Use of SNSs Increases Political Expression

I asked the respondents to share their opinions on how the use of SNSs increases an individual's political expression in general. Although the answers differ greatly from one another, several users agree with the results of the model test that suggest the use of SNSs is a positive predictor for political expression on SNSs.

Interestingly, many respondents of the interview expressed that the use of SNSs did not increase their political expressions. In fact, any political information they shared on these platforms was purely by chance. In fact, they became rather tired of seeing such posts flood their newsfeed. Instead, they would rather write an article or speak at a convention to express political opinions. Ansgarb has been using Facebook for six years. Yet, he discusses politics only in an offline context. He finds it tiring when people re-post the same information repeatedly and he is forced to scroll through the same news repeatedly. Consequently, he decided that he will not become one of these "spammers" who constantly repost information of no concrete value. Often, Ansgarb only receives political information on Facebook but never reposts it. His explanation reveals another category of SNSs users – the passive receiver. Passive receivers are users who use SNSs platforms as sources of political news, yet they do not engage personally in discussions or any forms of political expressions.

However, some users believe that SNSs do somewhat increase their interest in political expressions. Lulu, a 23-year-old Masters student, has been using Sina Weibo for about four years. During this period of time, she found that the regular use of SNSs did increase her political expression, both online and offline. Tao, her classmate, explained that the regular use of Sina Weibo has significantly increase his information sources as he could access various discussions shared by different friends, hence, resulting in a heightened awareness of political affairs. Ting, a 22-year-old female Masters student, used to have zero interest in politics. This changed when she started using Sina Weibo. A similar change happened to Alice as well. She felt that her interest in politics and current affairs increased after using Sina Weibo and being more aware of public affairs and political topics. "This is because there is a great deal of information on Sina Weibo. You can get different opinions and learn the various facets of an event. I really enjoy reading these opinions and if I have personal thoughts or opinions, I can post or comment." All these examples prove that the use of SNSs has an exponential relationship with political expressions.

Although the use of SNSs affects political expression positively, this effect is admittedly limited. Besides offering alternative sources of political news, SNSs provide users with alternative platforms on which they can express personal opinions. I must point out, though, that these functions of SNSs may not necessarily be better. As a student, Eramthgin discusses politics on Facebook with his online friends. He believes that Facebook has the power to increase political expression "because it's a platform where you can reach millions of people at once." However, he does not use Facebook frequently and so, does not increase his political discussions much.

John, on the other hand, feels that Facebook did fuel his political expressions as he had not been an active participant in offline discussions. The cyber environment and its networking methods present him with opportunities to engage in political discourse with others. Besides the extensive outreach potential, John also feels that the convenience of online political activity would need less effort and possibly reduce the repercussions of such expression. Of course, this preference is solely subjected to personal habits and is not a fair general assumption. In short, SNSs are not considered an ideal space for political expression since such platforms generally lack effectiveness and influence. Political discussion on SNSs remains only a supplement for offline political expression.

7.2.7 Self-censorship on SNSs

The results of regression indicate that self-censorship is not a predictor of political expression on SNSs. In Chapter 5.2, I introduced the "spiral of silence" theory and the development of self-censorship, which presupposes that expressions of opinion happen in a hostile context and that individuals perceive a disagreement with others. This theory examines offline hostile situations, such as conflicts between two people on board a train or an airplane, or at a party, where individuals are able to profess opinions directly.

However, when the individuals moved from an offline situation into an online virtual sphere, the hostile context has been changed. Schulz and Roessler (2012, p. 352–354) summarize three prototypical section patterns that can possibly take place in an Internet environment. The first one, the *subjective-consonant selection* of information, describes the shift of individuals' attention to information supporting their own position based on personal interests, favorites, and needs, such that they avoid dissonant content. The second, the *subjective-pluralistic selection* of information, assumes that Internet users act more rationally and process both consonant and dissonant information. In an online context, it's not always possible to avoid dissonant information. A Facebook friend could sometimes post a hostile opinion. Therefore, users face information of both consonant and dissonant types. The last one is the *dissonant selection* of information, that assumes that individuals might search for or read arguments challenging their own views. These three patterns happen in an online environment. A recent Pew Research Internet project "social media and the 'spiral silence'" (Hampton, Lee et al. 2014, p. 5) proves that previous findings of the 'spiral of silence' theory (such as people's willingness to speak out in various settings) also apply to social media users. People are more willing to share their opinions if they think that there is a high chance of their followers or friends agreeing with them. Considering the situation on SNSs, it is clear that users connect with more friends who share similar interests, hobbies and backgrounds with them (Prommer, Brücks et al. 2009, p. 29–30). Hence, we can safely assume that it helps to construct a friendlier and more homogeneous opinion climate, instead of a hostile one like that in the "spiral of silence" theory. Additionally, users may selectively expose themselves to a consonant media environment.

During the interviews, SNSs users also revealed that they experienced less pressure when expressing a different opinion on SNSs as compared to a face-to-face situation. The anonymity of an online environment offers a certain degree of protection from being recognized by the public. This makes users more courageous in voicing out opinions. Unlike offline situations, the online discussions do not demand a spontaneous feedback. This gives people more time to think over their words and responses. Moreover, the environment on SNSs is believed to be more tolerant as irrational and aggressive expressions are abhorred. McDevitt, Kiousis et al. (2003, p. 463) suggest that people in the computer-mediated setting find it easier to express themselves in a moderate manner than in a face-to-face setting, no matter the kind of opinions they held. This empirical study also suggests that the decreased social cues (due to anonymity and the absence of nonverbal communication) may lead to the perception of more moderate opinions even if the person who is posting information intended to express an extreme view. To sum up, we can assume that the moderate rather than hostile situation of opinion climate on SNSs result in the ineffectual influence of self-censorship on political expression.

7.2.8 Political Efficacy vs. SNSs Efficacy on SNSs

Interestingly, it is not political efficacy, but rather, SNSs efficacy, that influences the political expressions of SNSs users. Since the 1950's, many former studies suggested vastly differing results on the relationship of political efficacy to participatory behavior and political expression (Craig, Niemi et al. 1990, p. 292–294, Pinkleton, Austin et al. 1998, p. 44, Johnson and Kaye 2003, p. 19, Kenski and Stroud 2006, p. 173, Zhang, Johnson et al. 2010, p. 86, Gil de Zúñiga, Jung et al. 2012, p. 329). Especially after the diffusion of ICTs, the effect of efficacy on political participants is destabilized. My measurement of political efficacy is based on Kenski and Stroud (2006, p. 173–179) studies, in which their result suggested only a very slight significant relationship between political efficacy and participation. In the model, we suppose that political and SNSs efficacies may reflect different influences and that the ensuing results suggest that SNSs efficacy affects political expression more than its political counterpart.

In my study, the relationship between political efficacy and expression is insignificant. On the contrary, SNSs efficacy is related to political expression. In order to examine what SNSs users think about SNSs efficacy, the respondents were asked to share their ideas on the ways in which SNSs give people a political voice. Many of them believed that SNSs did facilitate political discussion to some extent but expressed concerns over the rationality and efficiency of such online discussions. Juan, a 27-year old Masters student, disclosed that she likes to express political opinions on Weibo because of the likelihood of more people seeing the information. This, she thought, could be helpful towards encouraging a diversity of opinions. Of course, not all the topics on SNSs attract good attention; some topics are easily forgotten. In addition, not everyone on SNSs is interested in politics.

Tao, a 25-year- old Masters student, also revealed that political expression on SNSs, especially on Sina Weibo in China, is more efficient because more people can participate in political discussions. When a Weibo account attracts enough followers, it becomes the equivalent of a media platform in itself. This means that this specific Weibo account exerts an influence over others. From BBS to SNSs, Tao believes that technology provides more platforms for political discussion.

Kai, a Masters student the same age as Tao, also believed that Facebook is better for political expression as there is more equality and a potential of forging better relationship between politicians and citizens. For Facebook to become an effective platform, the quality of discussions that take place on it must be consistently high. The presence of small groups compounded the effectiveness of political cohesion on Facebook. Kai himself joined several of these small political/social groups on Facebook.

Users also find SNSs platforms useful towards promoting civic participation. Denny is a student of political science and he believes that Facebook is able to rally people very easily, although he doubts its ability to transform the current political climate much.

> *"I think that expressing your opinion on Facebook does not lead to political change. It is a great tool to be network and to organize, but online protest, so to say, is very easy to ignore. Thus, people could try to comment on the FB-page of a government Institution but that won't change anything, because they can be blocked. But if FB is used to bring lots of people to a Demonstration, then it is a great tool, but nothing more. You couldn't ignore thousands of people in front of the Bundeskanzleramt, but thousands of FB-comments can easily be ignored.... Because a demonstration is more visible, is more immediate and brings more people directly together. Sure, voting is a great democratic advantage. And we should preserve its influence. But you're only allowed to vote very four-five years. In the meantime, citizens have to use different means to have their opinions considered."*

In addition, the networks of SNSs connect more people than that of FtFC. This is another advantage of political expression on SNSs. John, a 24-year-old Masters student, thought that Facebook could help to connect people directly as users can publicize information that cannot be changed by other users or a system moderator. John felt that Newspapers may be under the influence of certain affluent parties and so, only publish particular types of information. When asked if he was worried about the irrational political expressions on Facebook, he expressed optimism for the future of cyber politics instead. To John, even if his friends disagree with his political sentiments, he prefers to share perspectives so that both parties are aware of the alternatives and can then agree to disagree. He believes in giving political discourse a chance to take place and prefers discussions of this sort to take place on a channel where opinions remain unmediated. "Everything can be shared all over the world. Not just at a specific place. People can post war videos of Syria or wherever..."

Iwo, a 27-year-old Ph. D. student, was not as optimistic as John about the role of SNSs in political expression. She maintained that while SNSs can be somewhat helpful, there are too many problems that must be taken into consideration. In her opinion, politics is a complex subject that is hardly ever objective, transparent, or straight forward. Therefore, she refuses to influence another's political views. Eramthgin, another respondent, also argued that the effectiveness of political expression on SNSs depends on what people want. In his opinion, if the user wants to share personal opinions with other people, then the political expression is effective in this aim; or, if the user wants to engage in a thorough and insightful debate on a particular subject, then the political expression also effectively achieves this aim. Although, it should be acknowledged that Facebook rarely allows for a nuanced and detailed discussion.

Fabian, a young Bachelor student, also supported Eramthgin's beliefs and commented that personal expression on Facebook is more effective on the individual front. After all, SNSs are platforms for personal instead of public communication. Therefore, the effectiveness of political expressions depends on the purpose of that given expression: It is effective in representing pluralistic ideas, but less effective if taken to be a means of deliberation.

Ting, a Chinese Sina Weibo user, explained that because a typical discussion on SNSs only lasts for a short period, the SNSs efficacy is extremely limited. Even worse, after using SNSs for a few years, users begin to leave the platforms, resulting in a declining social media influence. Ting recalled having experienced the powerful influence of Weibo on public opinion during the Wenzhou train collision in China. On 23 July 2011, two travelling high-speed trains collided on a viaduct in the suburbs of Wenzhou, Zhejiang Province, China. Officials responded to the accident with slow rescue actions and even buried the train. These actions incurred public wrath and gave rise to strong criticism from the Chinese media and online communities. The government restricted mass media coverage, and even state-owned media tried but failed to find out the truth. 10 minutes after the accident on July 23, micro blogger with the name of "sheep circle" released the first microblog about the latest situation of train via a smart phone. In the next 10 hours, this microblog was forwarded more than 100,000 times. Some Chinese officials also follow the updates on this accident via Weibo. At 4 o'clock on the July 24, police officers began to leave Wenzhou and it was announced that "there is no sign of life". Later, the front and scattered parts of the train were buried. However, the public believed there was still life on the train and many rallied for rescue actions to be carried out. The mass public made use of the microblog and together with the mainstream Chinese media, questioned the Chinese government. Topics and attitudes of the reports from mainstream media were decided by Weibo users when criticism, anger and discussion reached an all-time high. The negative public opinion disseminated via Weibo affected the forms of mainstream media and shaped the ways that journalists covered that incident.

The train collision accident demonstrated how cyber opinions on SNSs influence public opinion and media effectively. However, only a few years later, the number of users on Sina Weibo decreased heavily, reducing its influence greatly. Just as Ting expressed, the efficacy of Weibo is decreasing. She joined some Weibo group activities, such as birds and environment protection, but the efficacy of this platform remained very limited. Ting finds that if a topic on SNSs involves only a few people or is only related to a certain social group, it is hard to attract public attention. Recently, Weibo has evolved into a discussion platform for entertainment topics. Its value as an efficient SNS platform hit rock bottom. Consequently, it is now difficult to raise effective and meaningful public discussions on Weibo.

In conclusion, the expression of opinions on SNSs is considered more effective than in offline political activities. This accounts for why SNSs efficacy, instead of political efficacy, influences political expression on SNSs. However, researchers must be clear about the limitations of SNSs efficacy. Firstly, as users generally keep in contact with people they already know in real life, the communication on SNSs is regarded as personal instead of public. This is one reason for the limitation of political expression on SNSs. Moreover, the turnover rate of discussion topics on SNSs is very rapid, making it hard for users to maintain interest in one topic for an extended duration. Even as users post an updated expression, it can quickly become obscured by the influx of new topics. Therefore, political expression remains fleeting in its appearance and influence. Finally, as compared to other political engagements such as voting and demonstration, cyber political expression is a less effective way to express personal opinions. Although, it must be acknowledged that online expression *can* help to promote more involvement from users. SNSs serve as substantial platforms for political expression, especially in countries with non-democratic systems and where traditional media and public opinion are being controlled.

7.2.9 Trust in Public/State TV or Private TV

In the testing process of my model, the results revealed people's trust in public TV to be negatively associated with political expression on SNSs, while people's trust in the press, private TV and even SNSs proved to have no impact. During the interview, I asked users if they trusted the aforementioned forms of media. As it turns out, SNSs users only trust the mainstream and social-qualified newspapers and magazines, such as Frankfurter Allgemeiner Zeitung, the Zeit, the Spiegel and Neon in Germany, and South Weekend, Chinese News Journal in China. One respondent, Nell, an 18-year-old Bachelor student, professed to distrust tabloidizational newspaper such as Bild Zeitung, and to trust mainstream newspapers and magazines. Even when news articles of such traditional mainstream periodicals are disseminated via Facebook, he still trusts the news source. Denny agrees with Nell. He also thinks that information from the Bild Zeitung is not trustworthy. However, he trusts news reports written by qualified journalists, who mostly work for the mainstream media.

As for news propagated via TV, regardless of public/state or private TV stations, SNSs users could not agree on whether they trust or distrust them. When it comes to news reports broadcasted on public or state media, SNSs users reported a high level of trust. Eramthgin does not watch TV, but if he has to pick one, he would trust public TV more because the source of information is gathered from the public and not dependent on the audience's support to boost TV ratings. A Chinese SNSs user, Potter, revealed that although she watches entertainment programs televised by private TV, she only trusts news reports shown on Chinese state TV because "they are making news more carefully and seriously". As for commercialized private TV, the broadcasted programs mainly aim to sell advertisements and make profits, as such, SNSs users demonstrated a deep distrust of it. Nell seldom watches TV but she clearly harbors different levels of trust towards different sectors of TV. If the news has anything to do with money, war and Russia, she discounts the televised reports. However, if it is news about the PEGIDA, something unrelated to money and important to the German society, then she trusts it.

As a member of the younger generation who grew up with access to the Internet, Denny does not like to watch TV. When it comes to private TV stations, he often feels that their TV programs serve a certain commercial interest, which comes into conflict with the integrity of news-making. There is an obvious clash of interests between objective news-reporting and/or data protection and commercial investors. However, he trusts public TV stations a little more. He believes that citizens-funded TV stations have some sense of social responsibility towards the paying party. "Take Tagesschau and RTL News, for example. Tagesschau is something I like to watch very much and I have a lot of trust in the journalistic integrity of their journalists. With RTL News, not so much."

People's decision to trust SNSs-disseminated news differs according to the sources of such information. If the post comes from mainstream or social – qualified press, such as official sites like Spiegel online, Focus online, David Bowie official, naturally this particular post garners viewer's trust. On the other hand, if the news is reported by tabloidizational newspaper, then it is deemed untrustworthy. Denny believed that the information on Facebook and TV programs should share the same purpose:

"You can make lots of money with product placement on Facebook, so I'd be somewhat reluctant to believe everything that is up there, especially when profit-oriented companies are involved. But Tagesschau on Facebook is great."

This trust issue can actually be easily resolved. SNSs users simply have to exercise more discretion by finding out the source of the news, in order to determine its trustworthiness. If the newsmaker is trustworthy, then the news report is the same; and vice versa.

7.2.10 SNSs as Private and Public Spaces

In chapter III, I have discussed the private and public characters of SNSs platforms. To understand how users conceptualize SNSs as either a private or a public space, I invited them to participate in a real-time interview over skype. During the interview, users revealed that SNSs is actually a combination of both private and public spaces to them. They further elaborated that the context of "private" and "public" is actually decided by how and why people use these platforms. This context is mediated by the function of "accessibility-control", that allows users to customize the privacy settings of individual pieces of information. Although users are unsure whether their personal data will be abused, at least they could control who could see their posts by using the function "to whom it is visible".

Anna thinks of her Facebook as both private and public spaces. When communicating with friends, her Facebook performs a private function, but when contacting certain groups, such as school mates, her Facebook becomes public. This shift between "private" and "public" is performed through the adjustment of communication audience. Ansgarb and Eramthgin pointed out that the transformation of Facebook from a public to a private space is easily done:

"Public to a certain extent, because although I know all the people that are in my FB, I indiscriminately publish some information about me (be it only one picture) to people who may not be as related as people I would normally talk to in private; private because some of the information, I wouldn't share it to anyone."
"It is only private in that you can choose who gets to see what, but it's public in that Facebook uses all your information anyway."

Denny also used privacy settings to manage the audience of his posts. He considered Facebook a public space because people are able to view unprotected user profiles. Therefore, he is reluctant to reveal personal information on Facebook. However, Denny also believes that Facebook can be, to a certain extent, a private space, in that users are able to engage in private text-conversations.

Admittedly, the compromise of privacy on SNSs platforms arise out of a commercial factor. Since the inauguration of SNSs, many companies have jumped onto the bandwagon and taken advantage of these social pages as a way of reaching potential customers. As SNSs are also channels of commercialization, for the sake of profits, these platforms cooperate with enterprises. As such, many SNSs users feel uneasy about revealing personal data online. In an effort to overcome such negativity, SNSs platforms create special spaces for business, such as F-commerce, on which companies can advertise and run promotions for their products. In the wake of such creations, Facebook, for Iwo at least, is no longer a private space. According to him, Facebook is private "if you will take just your private connections with your friends in consideration; but [it] could be used as a marketing tool for business, therefore it was public."

Additionally, many public figures and politician create public pages on SNSs, which they use to communicate with members of the public and to attract attention and woo public support; such pages are considered public. Kai viewed Facebook as both a private and a public space.

> *"Chat, for instance, is very private. Angela Merkel's fan page is very public. I don't know. For me, it's both. I sometimes use it sometimes for private purposes and other times for public purposes. I liked some newspapers, media and artists on Facebook, that I like to follow. Sometimes I liked their new song or an article."*

Sometimes, users make their SNSs profiles and posts public because they need to attract more attention for one reason or another. Juan, for instance, once used her Qzone to collect money to help people. She accomplished that feat by making her appeals visible to the public. Within three days, more than 1000 people viewed her post and that surprised her a lot. However, she was very careful not to reveal any personal information in the posts that appeal for money. That way, she managed to fulfill her agenda yet maintain her privacy. Juan also uses different platforms like Qzone, Renren and Sina Weibo to communicate with different groups of people. She uses Qzone and Renren to contact friends and classmates, and Sina Weibo to keep track of political information and discussions. The different groups of people whom she communicated with determine that Qzone and Renren are mostly private spaces to her while Sina Weibo is more public.

The Chinese SNSs market is more competitive than the German one. No matter in which country, nevertheless, each SNSs platform needs to create its niche on the market. Although Chinese users use SNSs for both private and public reasons, their user-behaviors differ according to each SNSs platforms. Mickey uses mainly Renren, although she also has accounts with Sina Weibo and Qzone. For Mickey, Weibo is a public space. She accesses public information pertaining to her interest on Weibo and maintains the passive role of a reader on this platform. Renren, however, she considers a private platform. This is because she uses Renren to keep up to date with her family members and friends.

Whether SNSs platforms are considered private or public spaces depends solely on the userly contexts. Different people utilize different platforms for different purposes. These functions determine a private/public context that is subjective and differs from user to user. With the rapid development of SNSs performativity, these platforms can change their characters and main functions fluidly.

VIII. Conclusions and Discussion

As the final part of this dissertation, Chapter VIII describes the research goals and summarizes the main results of my study. I will conclude with a discussion on the limitations of this research and offer some suggestions for further studies.

8.1 Summary of Research Goals

This dissertation concentrates on the exploration of the boundary between "the private" and "the public" on SNSs based on the *sociability framework*. Analyses and investigation of the roles of social norms and influences, benefits, and risks/costs, on the behaviors of SNSs users had been conducted through an examination of models that were constructed on the basis of SET, SPT and CPMT. In tracing the social traditions that have influenced the historical definitions of *private* and *public*, this dissertation is especially interested in the ways new communication technologies influence the subjective experiences of the division between "the private" and "the public"; particularly how this boundary differs, or is similar, across countries. In my quest for a satisfactory answer, I constructed several representative models of the German and Chinese societies, and used them to perform a comparative study on the digital differences and similarities in the contexts of globalization and mediatization. My study deals with three specific objectives:

1) To select a suitable type of framework that would aid in my analysis of the division between what is "private" and what is "public". To accomplish this, six theoretical frameworks applicable to the study of the boundary between "the private" and "the public" were first constructed. After reviewing each of these frameworks according to different social aspects and procedures, I finally decided on the framework of *sociability* by virtue of its focus on contextual social behaviors and interpersonal interaction. Using this framework, I extended my study into analyzing a chosen sample of SNSs users who determine their subjective views of the SNSs as a private or public space, based on their target communication partners. Whereas other former studies have addressed either the private or the public territory as independent entities, I seek to conflate both of these spaces into one. I contend that the concepts of "private" and "public" are no longer separated because SNSs have blurred the distinction between them. However, it is undoubted that there exists a boundary that distinguishes private affairs from public issues. The question is no longer *if* this boundary exists, but rather, *where* an individual draws this subjective dividing line.

2) To extend theoretical discussions into practicality. A lot has been said about the shifting boundary between "the private" and "the public". However, very little has been done. To rectify this situation, I first proposed two models (based on CET, CPT and CPMT) of self-disclosure and political expression on SNSs and then conducted research to determine which factors influence, and how do they affect, the frequency and visibility of these dependent variables. My study pointed out that frequency and visibility are two key features (informational and spatial) that control the disclosure and withdrawal of personal information and political opinions. The measurements of these influencing factors further clarify the relationship between them and an individual's boundary management behavior. The result became the foundation on which I explained the redefinition procedure of "private" and "public". To provide an overview of the test model, although some independent variables are not significant in this model, other variables in the categories of SNSs use, social norms/influence, social benefits and social costs/risks – affect the boundary. The result resonates with our theoretical framework in Chapter 3.3.4.

3) To perform a comparative study of the German and Chinese private/public boundaries. In the earlier chapters, I summarized the historical and social differences between ancient German and Chinese understandings of "the private" and "the public". I chose these two countries for my comparative study on account of their cultural and social incompatibilities. However, evolving economic developments and the process of globalization has done much to redefine these differences. I acknowledged the impact of new communication technology and the ensuing transformations, and used these factors to analyze them as cyber contemporaries. Thereafter, I introduced Elias's framework of *Kultur* and *Civilization* to supplement Hofstede's cultural value, so as to interpret the differences and similarities in a globalized world. Using online questionnaires and individual interviews as data collection methods, I computed my findings and then expounded them. This cross-national comparison was designed to examine the ways in which online network technologies influence different societies. These differences resonate with the discussion about *Kultur*, which emphasizes the special identity of a group and its differences with other groups. Meanwhile, the results of the interviews also reveal that both German and Chinese SNSs users share similar concepts of privacy and feel that SNSs extends a space for public discussion. This demonstrates the influence of *Civilization* in the forms of economic development, international cooperation and diffusion of media technology.

My work is contributive towards further research pertaining to SNSs. The results of the empirical study provide a deeper inspection of the influences of

ICT and offer valuable insights into how to improve online privacy protection, development of SNSs privacy settings, and international privacy policies. A clear boundary between "the private" and "the public" can help researchers to understand the psychology behind users' implementation of privacy measures. Meanwhile, users' control over the visibility of their profiles can offer precious suggestions towards the improvement of privacy systems. I would like to emphasize especially the value of my cross-national comparison. It has been supposed that globalization and the emergence of new communication technology bridge the differences and create more similarities. On contrary to this belief, my research results prove that digital differences and diversities still exist. These results provide valuable evidence against digital utopian and cosmopolitan.

8.2 Review of Research Findings

8.2.1 The Boundary between "The Private" and "The Public" on SNS

SNSs have both private and public characters. On contrary to the formers findings of Meyrowitz (1985, p. 71)[33], Thompson (2011, p. 120–125)[34], and Habermas (2004)[35], the results of my study contends that there is a boundary on SNSs. The

33 Meyrowitz argues that the idea of "the public" is becoming ambiguous due to the emergence of electronic media. According to him, the electronic media accounts for the shifting cultural and social barriers between children and adults, men and women, and even humanizing and demystifying the powerful.

34 Thompson believes that the public and the private spheres are reconstituted as spheres of information and symbolic content, which are largely detached from physical locales and increasingly interwoven with evolving technologies of communication and information flow. The existence of a boundary is not related to any point in time, but contestable and subject to constant negotiation and struggle.

35 In a Commemorative Lecture in Kyoto on 11th Nov. 2004, Habermas offers a general remark that the line between public and private spheres does not become blurred; the two complement each other instead. In the current media society, the public is supposed to serve people who present themselves. The price for these people to be presented in mass media is to accept the conflation of their private and their public lives. On the contrary, according to the function of public sphere, the intention behind political participation, literary and scholarly debates is totally different. Instead of presenting themselves to others, the public is a space for the contributions of speakers and addresses with several of opinions and discussions. So the *people* presented in the media are actually not the focus of the public, while the exchange of reasons and opinions is. Since talking about themselves is not needed in discourses that focus on a shared subject, the participants turn their backs on their private lives.

sociability framework helps in the differentiation of *private* and *public* by relating particular sets of social behaviors to corresponding situations. As mentioned previously, "the private" is associated with the "territories of the self", where people remain as separate individuals and withhold information that potentially makes them vulnerable. On the contrary, "the public" refers to a collection of people and the visibility of information. As I have proven, the contextualization of a situation as either "private" or "public" is based on the target partner in communication. Using a range of social distances from "close" to "distant", the target partner is categorized into the private (family and friends), between the private and the public (colleagues/classmates), and the public (acquaintances and stranger). The segregation of people into these classes makes it easier to impose a systematic measurement of the social distance between each category of relationships and the self. These measurements become one way to define private/public spaces by virtue of the kinds of information an individual chooses to share with each group. In other words, by controlling the visibility of a particular piece of information, the private or public status of this information can be determined by the target audience to whom it is made visible.

Based on the *sociability framework*, this dissertation also proposed two models that explore the influencing factors of boundary implementation, namely: the use of SNSs, social norms and influences, social benefits and social costs/risks. A closer inspection of SNSs revealed that the prevalent use of such platforms challenges the once-defined boundary between "the private" and "the public". The conflation of the virtual world with the real has made it difficult to pinpoint the defining criteria for "public" or "private". In fact, a piece of political comment may be released from the extremely private location of a toilet. Clearly, concepts such as privacy or publicity are no longer definable through traditional understandings of pre-internet times. By extension, one possible way of redressing such complexity may be performed by subjecting a piece of information to a systematic analysis of its target audience and motivation. This is where the influencing factors of social norms and influences, social benefits, and social costs/risks, come into play. These factors influence an individual's behavior towards self-disclosure and political expression, which in turn affects how an individual perceives privacy and publicity on SNSs.

Naturally, other factors, such as age or privacy concerns, also affect the stability of defining "the public" and "the private" by such means. The user's personal objective in publishing certain pieces of information also complicates this division. For example, a young user who hopes to increase his social capital would likely make personal information visible to a more public audience that includes colleagues/classmates and strangers in order to elicit a satisfactory desired response. Consequently, the number of colleagues/classmates and strangers on his friend-list affects his disclosure behavior, as well as his perception of the private/public boundary on SNSs. Conversely, an older user who is more aware of the privacy concerns attached to the use of SNSs would likely express reluctance in disclosing information about the self, and even more so regard personal opinion and data as highly private entities. This exemplifies the fluidity of the partition between "the private" and "the public", and reveals how factors such as age and motivation affect the location of this boundary. Of course, privacy concerns are right in raising alarms about the ease of transgression across this dividing line. Through social interaction in the forms of reposting and unintentional sharing, private information may be disseminated beyond the intended audience. This breach of privacy exposes the frailty of the boundary between "the private" and "the public" on SNSs.

I have also mentioned the role of SNSs in facilitating political discussions and the expression of political opinions (see Chapter 7.1.3). In some non-democratic countries where the channel to discuss is still limited or even impossible, SNSs redraws the boundary between private and public spaces by problematizing the traditional notion of "private' and "public", and allowing the articulation of personal opinions on public platforms. The delocalization of a standard information source spells new possibilities for the political future of many countries, although SNSs as political platforms still have a long way to grow. The transfer of political opinion from a private to a public space is a result of social interaction. However, as majority of the population still considers SNSs as private spaces, political expressions on these platforms are seldom as effective as public demonstrations and voting procedures, especially in democratic countries. Non-democratic countries, on the other hand, rely more on SNSs to provide a kind of "public" space for political discussions and deliberation. Also, SNSs use, political interest, beliefs in SNSs efficacy and trust on public/state TV, all have an effect on the expression behaviors of SNSs users and are all culpable to some extent for the indistinctive line dividing "the private" from "the public".

The type of SNS platform that a user utilizes is also responsible for the way in which he perceives the divider between "the private" and "the public" (see chapter 7.1.5). Users of different SNSs platforms behave differently. QZone users post information most frequently, Renren users share personal information most publicly, whereas Sina Weibo is a special place for political expression where the frequency and visibility are on the highest level. Such results further expose the subjectivity of the boundary between "the private" and "the public" on SNSs.

The boundary between "the private" and "the public" is the result of social interaction and balance between social costs/risks and benefits. This is a contested division that is also subjective and extremely fluid. The characteristics of SNSs defy a clear-cut classification of such platforms as either "private" or "public" spaces. Instead, I argue that "the private" and "the public" on SNSs are actually two sides of the same coin. As such, they should not and cannot be analyzed separately. Regardless of personal information or political expression that originated from the private "territories of the self", once this data is articulated, it is transferred into a public space. The problem herein lies with how the individual perceives the new status of this information. Is it still a private property? Or has it morphed into a public asset? Here, the *sociability framework* becomes the key that makes the analysis of the conflated private and public space possible.

8.2.2 Differences and Similarities in a Globalized Germany and China

Germany and China have their own historical definitions of "private" and "public". Since the rise of the Internet, the German and Chinese concepts of privacy began to evolve; especially in China, where the modern definitions of "private" and "public" only emerged at the beginning of the 20th century. By the turn of the 20th century, economic development and globalization had started to trend behaviors and social norms that were more or less similar across many different countries. A global Internet culture has taken the world by storm, resulting in an almost universal attitude towards cyber freedom of expression and privacy. For this reason, I performed a comparative study on two of the most contrasting nations in the history of man.

Germany and China, in spite of their cultural differences, dissimilar political and media systems, and uneven social and economic developments, are both experiencing the influences of globalization and digitization in terms of social impact and traditions. The media of both countries has been commercialized and embroiled in the rivalry of market economics. National audiences in both countries are also consuming international televised and broadcasted programs off Internet sources such as social media and instant message software. These trends appear to increase digital similarities in German and Chinese societies such that users of either nationality begin to view the cyber community as one large global society. Consequently, their understanding of *private* and *public* take on a common shift towards unity. However, based on the results of this dissertation, I must argue for the existing differences in the ways the Germans and the Chinese perceive the private/public boundary. This is in spite of the illusion of similar perceptions towards privacy concerns and extended public space on SNSs. This difference that I am positing for is evidenced by the higher level of self-disclosure and political expression that Chinese SNSs users demonstrate, as compared to their German counterparts. This result confirms the differences in cultural values and media systems in Germany and China.

The behavioral aspects of self-disclosure have been proven to be related to cultural factors. The Germans live in an individualistic culture and demonstrate a stronger desire and sense of privacy. Consequently, they disclose less as they are more careful about posting personal information on SNSs. The results of my study confirm that cultural dimensions indeed influence users' inclination to reciprocate. Meanwhile, the collectivistic culture observed by the Chinese emphasizes on group interest. Chinese SNSs users are thus more willing to reciprocate and are more easily influenced by others. Many of the Chinese respondents confirmed this trend.

On contrary to the expectation based on the above paragraph, SNSs users in collectivistic China express more political opinions on SNSs than German users (see Chapter 7.1.4). Although former studies suggested that users in Germany have more freedom to express political opinions (Hofstede, Hofstede et al. 1997, p. 81–83, Shen and Liang 2014, p. 10), because of the individualistic social culture and democracy, it is surprising that Chinese users who live in a collectivistic society actually express more politically. As mentioned in previous chapters, the lack of communication channels for political expression creates a low expectancy rate for the Chinese to express political ideas. Interestingly, though, it is precisely this lack that compels them to turn to SNSs as an alternative form for political expression. Although the control and censorship on these platforms are high, Chinese users are willing to negotiate these difficulties so as to garner a space for public discussion. Many of the Chinese respondents believe that SNSs provide an alternative platform for political discussion and the diversity of opinions. Conversely, the German users maintain that political expression on SNSs is not as effective as actions in real life. As such, their influence is not strong as in China. Although Chinese users might limit their political expression out of consideration for the censorship or fear of possible punishment, it cannot be denied that SNSs do provide a greatly expanded space for effective public discussions. Given this comparison, it becomes obvious that the role of SNSs as alternative political platforms is only important in non-democratic countries. Admittedly, in cross-cultural comparisons such as this, the actual social and political situations are more meaningful than the theoretical expectations.

Beyond the differences of the German and Chinese boundaries between "the private" and "the public", I would like to underscore the different levels of development and divide of SNSs platforms in the national media market. These influence the diversity of SNSs in each country. Facebook dominates the German SNSs market while Google+ and other SNSs have almost no influence there. Within the Chinese digital market, Renren, Qzone and Weibo are rivals. Each of these platforms has its own character. Renren leans towards a more private function (our respondents mainly use this to communicate with classmates); Qzone gears towards the private and the familial (many users communicate with family members here); and Sina Weibo is considered a more public space (that is mainly used to exchange information with strangers). Recently, a new platform, Wechat, combines the role of an instant messenger and social network site, and becomes the more welcomed option with users. This causes the previous three SNSs platforms to decline. The Chinese SNSs market is more competitive and diverse than the German one. Naturally, the situation of the private/public boundary becomes more complicated in correspondence.

Beyond the cultural differences, Elias and Gong's concepts of *civilization* provide a clear explanation of why the Western or European centered values became the universal principle. On one hand, Internet users from various countries exercise a similar freedom of cyber speech and display a similar concern about privacy protection. On the other hand, as proven by my findings, there are cross-cultural differences in the dividing boundary between "the private" and "the public". The framework of *sociability* analyzes the boundary on SNSs and translates the distinction between "the private" and "the public" into social behaviors under the restriction of cultural conventions and differences. The behavior of self-disclosure and political expression is based on a national, social and political culture, and is distinctive in different countries. Incidentally, this means that global homogeneity and heterogeneity remain very much a controversial topic of study.

8.3 Limitations, Discussions and Suggestions for Further Research

Due to the qualitative aspects of this study, a bias was inevitable in the samples (see Chapter 6.2). In order to obtain the samples quickly and affordably, I conducted my research through online questionnaires that were disseminated by the mailing lists of selected academic institutions. This confined my research to the faculties of Political Science, Communication, and Sociology, which in turn limited the diversity of the data collected as the gender distribution of these faculties are typically 70% females. The collection of data relied solely on the initiative of the respondents, who could decide whether or not to participate in the survey. This meant that the diversity of the data collected was out of my control. Future research studies should consider a more feasible approach to obtain random and widely diverse samples.

Conducting research based on Internet surveys also causes limitation in sample validity. Although respondents were presupposed to have access to the Internet and are SNSs users, they were not distributed equally across different social groups. In addition, these respondents were selected from universities located in the capital cities of Germany and China, where the diffusion of ICTs is naturally higher than in any other cities. Factor in the fact that residents of the capital city tend to have higher chances of coming into contact with governmental bodies due to their location at the heart of political actions. This naturally creates more opportunities for them to obtain political information. Therefore, the samples were inevitably restricted a unique group of SNSs users who also reside in the capital cities. I recommend that future researchers transcend the limitations of my study and extend the parameters of their samples to obtain a more diversified sampling that will definitely produce better results.

As my study focuses on the boundary between "the private" and "the public", it is adequate to construct a simple linear regression that tested models and examined the motivations behind self-disclosure actions and political expressions. Nevertheless, interactions between independent variables exist and *can* influence the significance of the regression. As such, I recommend that future studies conduct a path analysis to extend the regression model in order to explore the relationship between independent variables.

In this dissertation, I discussed only one circulation of information of the *Mediated Social Communication* model (see Chapter 2.3) from the private to the public space. On the SNSs communication, there may be more than one circulation of information. Therefore, the effect of boundary management might fail. Due to an inadequacy in the design of service and competence of media, and taking into consideration the central business model and the logic of profiles, SNSs users cannot always control the distribution of information that they are sharing on SNSs successfully. In addition to the lack of control function on SNSs, another reason for the loss of boundary management is called the "repercussion" of posting behavior: users may lose control over the personal information and political opinion that they posted because these pieces of information can be reposted without permission by other users, *if* the original poster chooses to make the posts visible to "friends of friends". This way, the visibility of posted information has been extended. As this is a function unique to only Facebook, I left it out of this discussion.

Another obvious limitation of this research is the types of SNSs platforms used in the study. The rapid development of ICTs produces a fast-changing market for SNSs platforms. A researcher's findings on social networking sites today can very well change with the virtual landscape tomorrow. The results of this dissertation are based solely on the survey conducted in the last two months of 2014. Before and after this time period, the SNSs environment in Germany and China was, and may become, totally different (refer to Chapter 4.1 & 4.2). Older SNSs platforms lose users regularly as new platforms emerge and compete with them. The evolution forces each SNS platform to create a niche function in order to remain attractive to the consumers. This accounts for why some platforms (such as Facebook, Renren and Qzone) concentrate on connecting users in a private context while others (like Sina Weibo) facilitate public communication. Based on the rapidly evolving dynamics of SNSs, I doubt that any future studies can remain relevant for a long time. As such, I caution future researchers to take into account the historical specificity of their studies.

Lastly, I must admit that there is a certain degree of challenge in trying to conduct a cross-cultural comparative study on something as evolutional and dynamic as SNSs. This is because each country has its own local media market and SNSs environment. In an effort to simulate comparable online environments, it is essential to compare SNSs platforms of similar characteristics in different countries. This has proven to be a truly daunting task. Cross-cultural research that includes any digital platforms in China is especially difficult because the Chinese Government constructs a digital "Great Wall" to keep out various international digital companies of the likes of Facebook and Twitter. Although Chinese firms developed their own local versions of international digital platforms, the functions and contexts are still different from the originals. In terms of political and media system, as well as digital development, China is a very special case. I encourage future researchers to pay attention to the evolution of Chinese digital products, as the uniquely Chinese characters of these products enhance the dimensions of comparative studies, as well as challenge the limits of global digital commerce.

List of Tables

List of Figures

References

Ahlqvist, Toni, et al.: "Road-mapping The Societal Transformation Potential of Social Media." *foresight* 12(5), 2010, pp. 3–26.

Ajzen, Icek: "The Theory of Planned Behavior." *Organizational Behavior and Human Decision Processes* 50(2), 1991, pp. 179–211.

Almond, Gabriel A.: *The Civic Culture: Political Attitudes and Democracy in Five Nations*. Sage Publications, Inc.: Los Angeles, Washington DC, London, New Delhi and Singapore, 1989.

Altman, Irwin: "Reciprocity of Interpersonal Exchange." *Journal for the Theory of Social Behaviour* 3(2), 1973, pp. 249–261.

Altman, Irwin: *The Environment and Social Behavior*. Brooks: Cole Monterey, 1975.

Altman, Irwin: "Privacy: A Conceptual Analysis." *Environment and behavior* 8(1), 1976, pp. 7–29.

Altman, Irwin / Taylor, Dalmas A.: *Social Penetration: The Development of Interpersonal Relationships*. Holt, Rinehart & Winston: New York, 1973.

Altman, Irwin., et al.: "Dialectic Conceptions in Social Psychology: An Application to Social Penetration and Privacy Regulation." *Advances in Experimental Social Psychology* 14, 1981, pp. 107–160.

ARD / ZDF: *ARD-ZDF Onlinestudie 2014*, retrieved 11.4.2014, from http://www.ard-zdf-onlinestudie.de/index.php?id=421.

Arendt, Hanna: *The Human Condition*. The University of Chicago Press: Chicago, 1958.

Babbie, Earl: *The Practice of Social Research*. Cengage Learning: Boston, 2015.

Baldassare, Mark / Katz, Cheryl: "Measures of Attitude Strength as Predictors of Willingness to Speak to The Media." *Journalism & Mass Communication Quarterly* 73(1), 1996, pp. 147–158.

Bandura, Albert: *Social Foundations of Thought and Action*. NJ Prentice Hall: Englewood Cliffs, 1986.

Bandura, Albert: "Social Cognitive Theory: An Agentic Perspective." *Asian Journal of Social Psychology* 2(1), 1999, pp. 21–41.

Barak, Azy / Gluck-Ofri, Orit: "Degree and Reciprocity of Self-disclosure in Online Forums." *Cyber Psychology & Behavior* 10(3), 2007, pp. 407–417.

Barnes, Susan B.: "A Privacy Paradox: Social Networking in the United States." *First Monday* 11(9), 2006, pp. 11–15.

Barton, Matthew D.: "The Future of Rational-Critical Debate in Online Public Spheres." *Computers and Composition* 22(2), 2005, pp. 177–190.

Baym, Nancy K.: *Personal Connections in The Digital Age*. Polity: Cambridge, 2010.

BBC: *Four in Five Regard Internet Access as a Fundamental Right*, 3.8 2010, retrieved 15.12.2013, from http://news.bbc.co.uk/2/shared/bsp/hi/pdfs/08_03_10_BBC_internet_poll.pdf.

Beck, Klaus: *Computervermittelte Kommunikation im Internet*. Oldenbourg: München und Wien, 2006.

Beck, Klaus: *Kommunikationswissenschaft*. UVK: Konstanz, 2013.

Beebe, Timothy J., et al.: "Computerized School Surveys Design and Development Issues." *Social Science Computer Review* 15(2), 1997, pp. 159–169.

Bellman, Steven, et al.: "International Differences in Information Privacy Concerns: A Global Survey of Consumers." *The Information Society* 20(5), 2004, pp. 313–324.

Ben-Ze'ev, Aaron: *Love Online: Emotions on the Internet*. Cambridge University Press:Cambridge, 2004.

Benhabib, Seyla: "The Public Sphere: Models and Boundaries." In: Calhoun, Craig J. (eds.): *Habermas and the Public Sphere*. MIT Press: Cambridge and London, 1992, pp. 73–98.

Benkler, Yochai: *The Wealth of Networks: How Social Production Transforms Markets and Freedom*. Yale University Press: New Haven, 2006.

Berg, John H. / Valerian J. Derlaga: Themes in The Study of Self-disclosure. In: Derlaga, Valerian J. / John H. Berg (eds.): *Self-disclosure: Theory, Research and Therapy*. Springer Science+Business Media, LLC: New York, 1987, pp. 1–8.

BITKOM: *Soziale Netzwerke 2013: Dritte, Erweiterte Studie Eine Repräsentative Untersuchung zur Nutzung Sozialer Netzwerke im Internet*, Berlin, 2013a, retrieved 15.6.2014, from https://www.bitkom.org/Publikationen/2013/Studien/Soziale-Netzwerke-dritte-erweiterte-Studie/SozialeNetzwerke-2013.pdf.

BITKOM: *Soziale Netzwerke 2013: Eine Repräsentative Untersuchung zur Nutzung Sozialer Netzwerke im Internet*, Berlin, 2013b, retrieved 28.6.2014, from https://www.bitkom.org/Publikationen/2013/Studien/Soziale-Netzwerke-%E2%80%93-dritte-erweiterte-Studie/SozialeNetzwerke_2013.pdf.

Blau, Peter M.: *Exchange and Power in Social Life*. Transaction Publishers: New Brunswick and London, 1964.

Blocker, H. Gene / Starling, Christopher L.: *Japanese Philosophy*. State University of New York Press/ Suny Press: Albany, NY, 2001.

Blumler, Jay G. / Gurevitch, Michael: "The New Media and Our Political Communication Discontents: Democratizing Cyberspace." *Information, Communication & Society* 4(1), 2001, pp. 1–13.

Bode, Leticia, et al.: A New Space for Political Behavior: Political Social Networking and Its Democratic Consequences." *Journal of Computer-Mediated Communication* 19(3), 2013: pp. 414–429.

Boon, Susan D. / Pasveer, Karen A.: "Charting the Topography of Risky Relationship Experiences." *Personal Relationships* 6(3), 1999, pp. 317–336.

Booth, Richard: "Loneliness As a Component of Psychiatric Disorders." *Medscape General Medicine* 2(2), 2000, pp. 1–7.

Boyd, Danah: *Friends, Friendsters, and Myspace Top 8: Writing Community into Being on Social Network Sites*, 2006, retrieved 15.9.2013, from http://www.danah.org/papers/FriendsFriendsterTop8.pdf.

Boyd, Danah: *Taken Out of Context: American Teen Sociality in Networked Publics.* (Doctoral Dissertation) School of Information, University of California-Berkeley, 2008, retrieved 6.3.2014, from www.danah.org/papers/TakenOutOfContext.pdf.

Boyd, Danah: *It's Complicated: The Social Lives of Networked Teens.* New Haven, Yale University Press, 2014.

Brundidge, Jennifer: "Encountering 'Difference' in the Contemporary Public Sphere: The Contribution of the Internet to the Heterogeneity of Political Discussion Networks." *Journal of Communication* 60(4), 2010, pp. 680–700.

Brundidge, Jennifer / Rice, Ronald E.: "Political Engagement Online: Do the Information Rich Get Richer and the Like-minded More Similar." In: Chadwick Andrew / Howard Philip N.: *Routledge Handbook of Internet Politics.* Routledge: New York, 2009, pp. 144–156.

Buchmann, Johannes: *Internet Privacy: Options for Adequate Realisation.* Springer Vieweg: Berlin and Heidelberg, 2013.

Burke, Moria, et al.: *Social Capital on Facebook: Differentiating Uses and Users.* Proceedings of the SIGCHI Conference on Human Factors in Computing Systems, Vancouver, ACM, 2011, retrieved 18.3.2014, from www.cameronmarlow.com/media/burke-2011-social.pdf.

Burkell, Jacquelyn, et al.: "Facebook: Public Space, or Private space?" *Information, Communication & Society* 17(8), 2013, pp. 974–985.

Campbell, Angus, et al. (1954). *The Voter Decides.* Row, Peterson and Co.: Oxford, 1954.

Cao, Jinwei / Everard, Andrea: "User Attitude Towards Instant Messaging: The Effect of Espoused National Cultural Values on Awareness and Privacy." *Journal of Global Information Technology Management* 11(2), 2008, pp. 30–57.

Capurro, Rafael: "Privacy. An Intercultural Perspective." *Ethics and Information Technology* 7(1), 2005, pp. 37–47.

CASS: Survey Report on Internet Use and Impact in Five Chinese Cities., 2005, retrieved 11.2.2015, from http://news.bbc.co.uk/2/shared/bsp/hi/pdfs/10_02_06_china.pdf.

Chan, Darius K-S / Cheng, Grand H-L: "A Comparison of Offline and Online Friendship Qualities at Different Stages of Relationship Development." *Journal of Social and Personal Relationships* 21(3), 2004, pp. 305–320.

Chan, Michael / Guo, Jing: "The Role of Political Efficacy on the Relationship between Facebook Use and Participatory Behaviors: A Comparative Study of Young American and Chinese Adults." *Cyberpsychology, Behavior, and Social Networking* 16(6), 2013, pp. 460–463.

Chan, Michael, et al.: "Microblogging, Online Expression, and Political Efficacy among Young Chinese Citizens: The Moderating Role of Information and Entertainment Needs in the Use of Weibo." *Cyberpsychology, Behavior, and Social Networking* 15(7), 2012, pp. 345–349.

Chen, Guo M.: "Differences in Self-disclosure Patterns among Americans versus Chinese." *Journal of Cross-Cultural Psychology* 26(1), 1995, pp. 84–91.

Cheung, Christy, et al.: "Self-disclosure in Social Networking Sites: The Role of Perceived Cost, Perceived Benefits and Social Influence." *Internet Research* 25(2), 2015, pp. 279–299.

Chibucos, Thomas R., et al.: *Readings in Family Theory*. Sage: Thousand Oaks, London and New Delhi, 2005.

Child, Jeffrey T., et al.: "Blogging Privacy Rule Orientations, Privacy Management, and Content Deletion Practices: The Variability of Online Privacy Management Activity at Different Stages of Social Media Use." *Computers in Human Behavior* 28(5), 2012, pp. 1859–1872.

Cho, Hichang, et al.: "A Multinational Study on Online Privacy: Global Concerns and Local Responses." *New Media & Society* 11(3), 2009, pp. 395–416.

Cialdini, Robert B.: *Influence: Science and Practice*. Allyn & Bacon: Boston, 2001.

Cismaru, Diana. M. (2010). *The Spiral of Silence in the Online Space*, 2010, etrieved 20.3.2012, from https://blogcommunication.wordpress.com/2010/05/05/the-spiral-of-silence-in-the-online-space/.

Clark, Vicki L. P. / Badiee, Manijeh: "Research Questions in Mixed Methods Research." In: Tashakkori, Abbas / Charles, Teddlie (eds.): *Sage Handbook of Mixed Methods in Social & Behavioral Research*. Sage: Thousand Oaks, London, New Delhi and Singapore, 2010, pp. 275–304.

CNNIC: *33rd Statistical Report on Internet Development in China*, 2014, retrieved 12.4.2015, from http://www.cnnic.net.cn/hlwfzyj/hlwxzbg/hlwtjbg/201401/P020140116395418429515.pdf.

CNNIC: *Users' Behavior on Chinese Social Media 2014*, retrieved 12.4. 2015, from https://www.cnnic.net.cn/hlwfzyj/hlwxzbg/201408/P020140822379356612744.pdf.

Collins, Nancy L. / Miller, Lynn C.: "Self-disclosure and Liking: A Meta-analytic Review." *Psychological bulletin* 116(3), 1994, pp. 457–475.

Craig, Stephen C., et al.: "Political Efficacy and Trust: A Report on the NES Pilot Study Items." *Political Behavior* 12(3), 1990, pp. 289–314.

Cropanzano, Russell / Mitchell, Marie S.: "Social Exchange Theory: An Interdisciplinary Review." *Journal of management* 31(6), 2005, pp. 874–900.

Dahlberg, Lincoln: "Computer-mediated Communication and the Public Sphere: A Critical Analysis." *Journal of Computer-Mediated Communication* 7, 2001a, retrieved 11.6.2012, DOI: 10.1111/j.1083-6101.2001.tb00137.x.

Dahlberg, Lincoln: "The Internet and Democratic Discourse: Exploring the Prospects of Online Deliberative Forums Extending the Public Sphere." *Information, Communication & Society* 4(4), 2001b, pp. 615–633.

Dahlberg, Lincoln: "Rethinking the Fragmentation of the Cyberpublic: from Consensus to Contestation." *New Media & Society* 9(5), 2007, pp. 827–847.

Dahlberg, Lincoln: "The Habermasian Public Sphere and Exclusion: An Engagement with Poststructuralist-Influenced Critics." *Communication Theory* 24(1), 2014, pp. 21–41.

Dahlgren, Peter: "The Internet and the Democratization of Civic Culture." *Political Communication* 17(4), 2000, pp. 335–340.

Dahlgren, Peter: "The Internet, Public Spheres, and Political Communication: Dispersion and Deliberation." *Political Communication* 22(2), 2005, pp. 147–162.

Dahlgren, Peter: *Media and Political Engagement*. Cambridge University Press: Cambridge, 2009.

Dean, Jodi: "Why the Net Is Not A Public Sphere." *Constellations* 10(1), 2003, pp. 95–112.

DeCew, Judith W.: *In Pursuit of Privacy: Law, Ethics, and the Rise of Technology*. Cornell University Press, Ithaca, 1997.

Derlega, Valerian J., et al.: "Self-disclosure Reciprocity, Liking and the Deviant." *Journal of Experimental Social Psychology* 9(4), 1973, pp. 277–284.

Derlega, Valerian J., et al.: *Self-disclosure*. Sage: Newbury Park u.a., 1993.

Derlega, Valerian J., et al.: "Self-disclosure and Starting A Close Relationship." In: Sprecher, Susan / Amy Wenzel / John Harvey (eds.): *Handbook of Relationship Beginnings*. Psychology Press: New York, 2008, pp. 153–174.

Deutsch, Morton / Gerard, Harold B.: "A Study of Normative and Informational Social Influences upon Individual Judgment." *The Journal of Abnormal and Social Psychology* 51(3), 1995, pp. 629.

Dienlin, Tobias / Trepte, Sabine: "Is the Privacy Paradox a Relic of the Past? An in-depth Analysis of Privacy Attitudes and Privacy Behaviors." *European Journal of Social Psychology* 45(3), 2014, pp. 285–297.

Dindia, Kathryn: "A Comparison of Several Statistical Tests of Reciprocity of Self-disclosure." *Communication Research* 15(6), 1988, pp. 726–752.

Dindia, Kathryn: "Self-disclosure Research: Knowledge through Meta-analysis." In: Allen, Mike / Raymond W. Preiss / Babara. M. Gayle / Nancy Burrell (eds.): *Interpersonal Communication Research: Advances through Meta-analysis*. Lawrence Erlbaum Associates: Mahwah, 2002, pp. 169–185.

Dindia, Kathryn / Allen, Mike: "Sex Differences in Self-disclosure: A Meta-analysis." *Psychological Bulletin* 112(1), 1992, pp. 106–124.

Dostie-Goulet, Eugénie: "Social Networks and the Development of Political Interest." *Journal of Youth Studies* 12(4), 2009, pp. 405–421.

Dowling, Grahame R. / Staelin, Richard: "A Model of Perceived Risk and Intended Risk-handling Activity." *Journal of Consumer Research* 21(1), 1994, pp. 119–134.

Dutta, Soumitra, et al.: *The New Internet World: A Global Perspective on Freedom of Expression, Privacy, Trust and Security Online. The Global Information Technology Report 2010–2011*. New York, World Economic Forum, 2011. retrieved 8.4.2014, from http://dx.doi.org/10.2139/ssrn.1916005.

Dwyer, Catherine, et al.: *Trust and Privacy Concern within Social Networking Sites: A Comparison of Facebook and MySpace*. AMCIS 2007 Proceedings, 2007, retrieved 1.4.2015, from http://citeseerx.ist.psu.edu/viewdoc/download?doi=10.1.1.148.9388&rep=rep1&type=pdf.

Eggert, Nina / Giugni, Marco: "Does Associational Involvement Spur Political Integration? Political Interest and Participation of Three Immigrant Groups in Zurich." *Swiss Political Science Review* 16(2), 2010, pp. 175–210.

Elias, Nobert: *The Civilizing Process*. Blackwell Publishing: Oxford, 2010.

Ellison, Nicole, et al.: "Managing Impressions Online: Self-presentation Processes in the Online Dating Environment." *Journal of Computer-Mediated Communication* 11(2), 2006, pp. 415–441.

Ellison, Nicole B. / Boyd, Danah (2013). "Sociality through Social Network Sites." In: Dutton, William H. (eds): *The Oxford Handbook of Internet Studies*. Oxford University Press: Oxford, 2013, pp. 151–172.

Ellison, Nicole B., et al.: "The Benefits of Facebook 'Friends': Social Capital and College Students' Use of Online Social Network Sites." *Journal of Computer-Mediated Communication* 12(4), 2007, pp. 1143–1168.

Ellison, Nicole B., et al.: "Connection Strategies: Social Capital Implications of Facebook-enabled Communication Practices." *New Media & Society* 13(6), 2011, pp. 873–892.

Elter, Andreas „,Doch kein Wundermittel'-Wahlkämpfe und das Web 2.0." *Neue Soziale Bewegungen* 23(3), 2010, S. 64–71.

Eveland, William P. / Hively, Myiah H.: "Political Discussion Frequency, Network size, and "Heterogeneity" of Discussion as Predictors of Political Knowledge and Participation." *Journal of Communication* 59(2), 2009, pp. 205–224.

Facebook: *Changing Your Name & Birthday*, 2015, retrieved 15.10.2014, from https://www.facebook.com/help/405674989468892/.

Finkel, Steven E.: "Reciprocal Effects of Participation and Political Efficacy: A Panel Analysis." *American Journal of Political Science* 24(9), 1985, pp. 891–913.

Fisher, Claude S.: *America Calling: A Social History of the Telephone to 1940*. University of California Press: Berkeley, Los Angeles and London, 1992.

Fraser, Nancy: "Rethinking the Public Sphere: A Contribution to the Critique of Actually Existing Democracy." *Social Text* 25/26, 1990, pp. 56–80.

Fraunhofer (2008). *Privatsphärenschutz in Soziale-Netzwerke-Plattformen*. Darmstadt, Fraunhofer-Institut für Sichere Informationstechnologie, 2008, retrieved 13.5.2015, from https://testlab.sit.fraunhofer.de/downloads/Publications/Fraunhofer_SIT_Poller_Privatsphaereschutz_in_Soziale-Netzwerke-Plattformen.pdf.

Fürst, Silke / Schönhagen, Philomen / Bosshart, Stefan: "Mass Communication is More than a One-Way Street: On the Persistent Function and Relevance of Journalism." *Javnost-the Public* 22(4), 2015, pp. 328–344.

Gal, Susan: "A Semiotics of the Public/Private Distinction." *Differences: A Journal of Feminist Cultural Studies* 13(1), 2002, pp. 77–95.

Gerhards, Jürgen / Schäfer, Mike S.: „Demokratische Internet-Öffentlichkeit? Ein Vergleich der öffentlichen Kommunikation im Internet und in den Printmedien am Beispiel der Humangenomforschung." *Publizistik* 52(2), 2007, S. 210–228.

Gerhards, Jürgen / Schäfer, Mike S: "Is the Internet a Better Public Sphere? Comparing Old and New Media in the USA and Germany." *New Media & Society* 12(1), 2010, pp. 143–160.

Gibbs, Jenniger L., et al.: "Self-presentation in Online Personals: The Role of Anticipated Future Interaction, Self-disclosure, and Perceived Success in Internet Dating." *Communication Research* 33(2), 2006, pp. 152–177.

Gibbs, Jenniger L., et al.: "First Comes Love, Then Comes Google: An Investigation of Uncertainty Reduction Strategies and Self-disclosure in Online Dating." *Communication Research* 38(1), 2011, pp. 70–100.

Gil de Zúñiga, Homero, et al.: "Social Media Use for News and Individuals' Social Capital, Civic Engagement and Political Participation." *Journal of Computer-Mediated Communication* 17(3), 2012, pp. 319–336.

Gil de Zúñiga, Homero, et al.: "Social Media, Political Expression, and Political Participation: Panel Analysis of Lagged and Concurrent Relationships." *Journal of Communication* 64(4), 2014, pp. 612–634.

Gilbert, Eric / Karahalios, Karrie: *Predicting Tie Strength with Social Media.* Proceedings of the SIGCHI Conference on Human Factors in Computing Systems, Boston, ACM, 2009, retrieved 12.3.2015, from leonidzhukov.net/hse/2011/seminar/papers/chi09-tie-gilbert.pdf.

Gimmler, Antje: "Deliberative Democracy, the Public Sphere and the Internet." *Philosophy & Social Criticism* 27(4), 2001, pp. 21–39.

Gitter, A. George / Black, Harvey: "Is Self-disclosure Self-revealing?" *Journal of Counseling Psychology* 23(4), 1976, pp. 327.

Gobetti, Daniela. (1997). "Humankind as A System: Private and Public Agency at the Origins of Modern Liberalism." In: Weintraub, Jeff / Krishan Kumar (eds.): *Public and Private in Thought and Practice.* J. Weintraub and K. Kumar. The University of Chicago Press: Chicago, 1997, pp. 103–132.

Goffman, Erving: *The Presentation of Self in Everyday Life.* Doubleday: Garden City, 1959.

Goffman, Erving: *Relations in Public: Microstudies of the Public Order.* Basic Books: New York, 1971.

Gong, Gerrit. W.: *The Standard of Civilization in International Society.* Clarendon Press: Oxford, 1984.

Gordon, Eric, et al. "Why We Engage: How Theories of Human Behavior Contribute to Our Understanding of Civic Engagement in a Digital Era." *Berkman Center Research Publication* 21, 2013, retrieved 28.9.2014, from http://cyber.law.harvard.edu/publications/2013/why_we_engage.

Green, Melanie C. (2007). "Trust and Social Interaction on the Internet." In: Joinson, Adam N. / Katelyn Y. A. McKenna / Tom Postmes/ Ulf-Dietrich Reips (eds.): *The Oxford Handbook of Internet Psychology.* Oxford University Press: Oxford, 2007, pp. 43–51.

Greene, Kathryn, et al.: "Self-disclosure in Personal Relationships." In: Vangelisti, Anita L. / Daniel Perlman (eds.): *The Cambridge Handbook of Personal Relationships*. Cambridge University Press: Cambridge, 2006, pp. 409–428.

Griffin, Em: *A First Look at Communication Theory*. New York, McGraw-Hill, 2012.

Gross, Ralph / Acquisti, Alessandro: *Information Revelation and Privacy in Online Social Networks*. Proceedings of the 2005 ACM Workshop on Privacy in the Electronic Society, Alexandria, VA, USA, ACM, 2005, pp. 71–80.

Gudykunst, William B., et al.: "The Influence of Cultural Individualism-collectivism, Self Construals, and Individual Values on Communication Styles across Cultures." *Human Communication Research* 22(4), 1996, 510–543.

Guillén, Mauro F. / Suárez, Sandra L.: "Explaining the Global Digital Divide: Economic, Political and Sociological Drivers of Cross-national Internet Use." *Social Forces* 84(2), 2005, pp. 681–708.

Habermas, Jürgen: *The Structural Transformation of the Public Sphere: An Inquiry into A Category of Bourgeois Society*. MIT Press: Cambridge, 1991a.

Habermas, Jürgen: "The Public Sphere." In: Mukerji, Chandra / Schudson, Michael (eds.): *Rethinking Popular Culture: Contemporary Perspectives in Cultural Studies*. University of California Press: Berkeley and Los Angeles, 1991b, pp. 398–404.

Habermas, Jürgen: *Public Space and Political Public Sphere–the Biographical Roots of Two Motifs in My Thought*. Commemorative Lecture. Kyoto, 2004, retrieved 15.9.2014, from http://ikesharpless.pbworks.com/f/Kyoto_lecture_Nov_2004,+Jurgen+Habermas.pdf.

Habermas, Jürgen: "Concluding Comments on Empirical Approaches to Deliberative Politics." *Acta Politica* 40(3), 2005, pp. 384–392.

Hacker, Helen M.: "Blabbermouths and Clams: Sex Differences in Self-disclosure in Same-sex and Cross-sex Friendship Dyads." *Psychology of Women Quarterly* 5(3), 1981, pp. 385–401.

Hall, Edward: *The Hidden Dimension*. Doubleday: New York, 1966.

Hallin, Daniel C. / Mancini, Paolo: *Comparing Media Systems: Three Models of Media and Politics*. Cambridge University Press, Cambridge, 2004.

Halpern, Daniel / Gibbs, Jennifer: "Social Media as A Catalyst for Online Deliberation? Exploring the Affordances of Facebook and YouTube for Political Expression." *Computers in Human Behavior* 29(3), 2013, pp. 1159–1168.

Hampton, Keith, et al. (2014). *Social Media and the "Spiral of Silence"*, 2014, retrieved 10.9.2014, from http://www.pewinternet.org/files/2014/08/PI_Social-networks-and-debate_082614.pdf.

Hardy, Bruce W. / Scheufele, Dietram A.: "Examining Differential Gains from Internet Use: Comparing the Moderating Role of Talk and Online Interactions." *Journal of Communication* 55(1), 2006, pp. 71–84.

Hayes, Andrew F.: "Exploring the Forms of Self-Censorship: On the Spiral of Silence and the Use of Opinion Expression Avoidance Strategies." *Journal of Communication* 57(4), 2007, pp. 785–802.

Hayes, Andrew F., et al.: "Willingness to Self-censor: A Construct and Measurement Tool for Public Opinion Research." *International Journal of Public Opinion Research* 17(3), 2005, pp. 298–323.

Hayes, Andrew F., et al.: Stimulating the Quasi-statistical Organ: Fear of Social Isolation Motivates the Quest for Knowledge of the Opinion Climate." *Communication Research*, 2011, retrieved 2.10.2014, from DOI: 10.1177/0093650211428608.

He, Yong: *Totally Exploring on Intenret: Privacy Protection Faces Difficulties, 2011.* retrieved 7.4.2014, from http://sh.eastday.com/qtmt/20110614/u1a891869.html.

Hille, Kathrin: *Renren Plans US Listing This Year, 21.2.2011,* retrieved 15.2.2013, from http://www.ft.com/cms/s/2/c26ed156-3d23-11e0-bbff-00144feabdc0.html#axzz2S8iBfSyy.

Himelboim, Itai: "Civil Society and Online Political Discourse: The Network Structure of Unrestricted Discussions." *Communication Research* 38(5), 2011, pp. 634–659.

Ho, Shirley S. / McLeod, Douglas M.: "Social-psychological Influences on Opinion Expression in Face-to-face and Computer-mediated Communication." *Communication Research* 35(2), 2008, pp. 190–207.

Hofstede, Geert: *Culture's Consequences: International Differences in Work-Related Values*. Sage: Newbury Park, London and New Delhi, 1980.

Hofstede, Geert, et al.: *Cultures and Organizations: Software of the Mind.* McGraw-Hill: New York, 1997.

Hofstede, Geert. H. / Hofstede, Geert: *Culture's Consequences: Comparing Values, Behaviors, Institutions and Organizations across Nations*. Sage: Thousand Oaks, London and New Delhi, 2001.

Hogan, Bernie: "The Presentation of Self in the Age of Social Media: Distinguishing Performances and Exhibitions Online." *Bulletin of Science, Technology & Society* 30(6), 2010, pp. 377–386.

Homans, George C.: "Social Behavior as Exchange." *American Journal of Sociology* 63(6), 1958, pp. 597–606.

Homans, George C.: *Social Behavior: Its Elementary Forms*. Harcourt, Brace & World, Inc.: New York and Burlingame, 1961.

Houghton, David, et al.: *Tagger's Delight? Disclosure and Liking in Facebook: the Effects of Sharing Photographs Amongst Multiple Known Social Circles.* (Disscussion Paper) University of Birmingham, Birminham, 2013, retrieved 11.11.2014, from http://epapers.bham.ac.uk/1723/1/2013-03_D_Houghton.pdf.

Hsu, Chin-Lung / Lin, Judy C-C.: "Acceptance of Blog Usage: The Roles of Technology Acceptance, Social Influence and Knowledge Sharing Motivation." *Information & Management* 45(1), 2008, pp. 65–74.

Huang, Huiping: "A Cross-cultural Test of the Spiral of Silence." *International Journal of Public Opinion Research* 17(3), 2005, pp. 324–345.

Husted, Bryan W. /Allen, David B.: "Toward a Model of Cross-cultural Business Ethics: The Impact of Individualism and Collectivism on the Ethical Decision-making Process." *Journal of Business Ethics* 82(2), 2008, pp. 293–305.

Huth, Nathalie, et al.: *Soziale Netzwerke (2. Auflage): Eine Repräsentative Untersuchung zur Nutzung Sozialer Netzwerke im Internet*, Berlin, Bundesverband Informationswirtschaft, Telekommunikation und Neue Medien e. V., 2011, retrieved 15.11.2014, from https://www.bitkom.org/files/documents/BITKOM_Publikation_Soziale_Netzwerke.pdf.

Iyengar, Shanto / Hahn, Kyu S.: "Red Media, Blue Media: Evidence of Ideological Selectivity in Media Use." *Journal of Communication* 59(1), 2009, pp. 19–39.

Jennings, M. Kent / Zeitner, Vicki: "Internet Use and Civic Engagement: A Longitudinal Analysis." *Public Opinion Quarterly* 67(3), 2003, pp. 311–334.

Jessup, Leonard M., et al.: "The Effects of Anonymity on GDSS Group Process with An Idea-generating Task." *MIS Quarterly* 14(3), 1990, pp. 313–321.

Johnson, Thomas J. / Kaye, Barbara K.: "A Boost or Bust for Democracy? How the Web Influenced Political Attitudes and Behaviors in the 1996 and 2000 Presidential Elections." *The International Journal of Press/Politics* 8(3), 2003, pp. 9–34.

Joinson, Adam. N.: "Self-disclosure in Computer-mediated Communication: The Role of Self-awareness and Visual Anonymity." *European Journal of Social Psychology* 31(2), 2001, pp. 177–192.

Joinson, Adam N.: "Disinhibition and the Internet." *Psychology and the Internet: Intrapersonal, interpersonal, and transpersonal implications* 2, 2007, pp. 75–92.

Joinson, Adam N./ Paine, Carina B.: "Self-disclosure, Privacy and the Internet." In: In: Joinson, Adam N. / Katelyn Y. A. McKenna / Tom Postmes/ Ulf-Dietrich Reips (eds.): *Oxford Handbook of Internet Psychology*. Oxford University Press: Oxford, 2007, pp. 237–252.

Joinson, Adam N., et al.: "Privacy, Trust, and Self-disclosure Online." *Human-Computer Interaction* 25(1), 2010, pp. 1–24.

Jones, Harvey / Soltren, José H.: "Facebook: Threats to Privacy." *Project MAC: MIT Project on Mathematics and Computing* 1, 2005, pp. 1–76.

Jones, W. T.: "Public Roles, Private Roles, and Differential Moral Assessments of Role Performance." *Ethics* 94(4), 1984, pp. 603–620.

Kaczmirek, Lars, et al. (2013). *Social Media Monitoring of the Campaigns for the 2013 German Bundestag Elections on Facebook and Twitter*, 16.12.2013, retrieved 12.12.2014, from http://www.gesis.org/en/publications/gesis-working-papers/.

Kaplan, Andreas M. / Haenlein, Micheal: "Users of the World, Unite! The Challenges and Opportunities of Social Media." *Business Horizons* 53(1), 2010, pp. 59–68.

Karp, Jeffrey. A. / Banducci, Susan A.: How Electoral Systems Shape Political Behaviour." *British Journal of Political Science* 38(2), 2008, pp. 311–334.

Katz, James E. / Rice, Ronald E.: *Social Consequences of Internet Use: Access, Involvement, and Interaction*. MIT Press: Cambridge and London, 2002.

Kaya, Naz / Weber, Margaret J.: Cross-cultural Differences in the Perception of Crowding and Privacy Regulation: American and Turkish Students." *Journal of Environmental Psychology* 23(3), 2003, pp. 301–309.

Kenski, Kate / Stroud, Natalie J.: "Connections between Internet Use and Political Efficacy, Knowledge, and Participation." *Journal of Broadcasting & Electronic Media* 50(2), 2006, pp. 173–192.

Khan, Muhammad Z., et al.: "From Habermas Model to New Public Sphere: A Paradigm Shift." *Global Journal of Human-Social Science Research* 12(5), 2012, pp. 43–51.

Kietzmann, Jan. H., et al.: "Social Media? Get Serious! Understanding the Functional Building Blocks of Social Media." *Business Horizons* 54(3), 2001, pp. 241–251.

Kim, Yonghwan, et al.: "Influence of Social Media Use on Discussion Network Heterogeneity and Civic Engagement: The Moderating Role of Personality Traits." *Journal of Communication* 63(3), 2013, pp. 498–516.

Kiousis, Spiro: "Interactivity: A Concept Explication." *New Media & Society* 4(3), 2002, pp. 355–383.

Kisselburgh, Lorraine G.: *The Social Structure and Discursive Construction of Privacy in Sociotechnological Realms*. (Doctoral Dissertation) Purdue University, West Lafayette, Indiana, 2008, retrieved 12.10.2014, from http://docs.lib.purdue.edu/dissertations/AAI3344076/.

Knoll, Maria / Bronstein, Jenny: "An Examination of the Information Disclosure Behavior of Infertility Bloggers: Patterns of Self-disclosure and Anonymity." *Aslib Journal of Information Management* 66(2), 2014, pp. 175–201.

Ko, Hsiu-Chia / Kuo, Feng-Yang: "Can Blogging Enhance Subjective Well-being Through Self-disclosure?" *Cyber Psychology & Behavior* 12(1), 2009, pp. 75–79.

Kops, Manfred: *The German Broadcasting Order. A Model for China?* 2006, retrieved 11.7.2014, from http://www.rundfunk-institut.uni-koeln.de/sites/rundfunk/Arbeitspapiere/215_06e.pdf.

Krämer, Nicole C. / Haferkamp, Nina: "Online Self-presentation: Balancing Privacy Concerns and Impression Construction on Social Networking Sites." In: Trepte, Sabine / Leonard Reinecke(eds.): *Privacy Online: Perspectives on Privacy and Self-Disclosure in the Social Web*. Heidelberg, Springer: Dordrecht, London and New York, 2011, pp. 127–141.

Kroh, Martin / Neiss, Hannes: "On the Causal Nature of the Relationship between Internet Access and Political Engagement: Evidence from German Panel Data." In: Anduiza, Eva / Michael J. Jensen / Laia Jorba (eds.): *Digital Media and Political Engagement Worlwide: A Comparative Study*. Cambridge University Press: New York, 2013, pp. 160–176.

La Due Lake, Ronald / Huckfeldt, Robert: "Social Capital, Social Networks, and Political Participation." *Political Psychology* 19(3), 1998, pp. 567–584.

Lambe, C. Jay., et al. (2001). "Social Exchange Theory and Research on Business-to-business Relational Exchange." *Journal of Business-to-Business Marketing* 8(3), 2001, pp. 1–36.

Lampe, Cliff, et al.: *Changes in Use and Perception of Facebook*. Proceedings of the 2008 ACM conference on Computer supported cooperative work, San Diego, ACM, 2008, pp. 721–730.

Lampe, Cliff., et al.: *A Familiar Face (book): Profile Elements as Signals in An Online Social Network*. Proceedings of the SIGCHI conference on Human factors in computing systems, San Jose, ACM, 2007, pp. 435–444.

Lasorsa, Dominic L.: "Political Outspokenness: Factors Working against the Spiral of Silence." *Journalism & Mass Communication Quarterly* 68(1–2), 1991, pp. 131–140.

Lea, Martin / Spears, Russell: "Computer-mediated Communication, De-individuation and Group Decision-making." *International Journal of Man-Machine Studies* 34(2), 1991, pp. 283–301.

Lee, Chai. S. /Ma, Long: "News Sharing in Social Media: The Effect of Gratifications and Prior Experience." *Computers in Human Behavior* 28(2), 2012, pp. 331–339.

Lee, Eun-Ju: "Effects of Visual Representation on Social Influence in Computer-Mediated Communication." *Human Communication Research* 30(2), 2004, pp. 234–259.

Lee, Eun-Ju / Nass, Clifford: "Experimental Tests of Normative Group Influence and Representation Effects in Computer-Mediated Communication." *Human Communication Research* 28(3), 2002, pp. 349–381.

Lee, Kwan M.: "Effects of Internet Use on College Students' Political Efficacy." *CyberPsychology & Behavior* 9(4), 2006, pp. 415–422.

Lenhart, Amanda / Madden, Mary: *Social Networking Websites and Teens*, 2007, retrieved 14.9.2014, from http://htlab.psy.unipd.it/uploads/Pdf/lectures/technology_for_young/Social%20Networking%20Websites%20and%20Teens%20text.pdf.

Leung, Louis: "Loneliness, Self-disclosure, and ICQ ("I Seek You") Use." *Cyber Psychology & Behavior* 5(3), 2002, pp. 241–251.

Lewis, Jane / West, Anne: "'Friending': London-based Undergraduates' Experience of Facebook." *New Media & Society* 11(7), 2009, pp. 1209–1229.

Lewis, Kevin, et al.: "The Taste for Privacy: An Analysis of College Student Privacy Settings in An Online Social Network." *Journal of Computer-Mediated Communication* 14(1), 2008, pp. 79–100.

Liu, Xudong / Fahmy, Shahira: "Exploring the Spiral of Silence in the Virtual World: Individuals' Willingness to Express Personal Opinions in Online versus Offline Settings." *Journal of Media and Communication Studies* 3(2), 2011, pp. 45–57.

Livingstone, Sonia: Children's Privacy Online: Experimenting with Boundaries within and Beyond the Family. In: Kraut, Robert / Malcolm Brynin / Sara Kiesle (eds.): *Computers, Phones, and the Internet: Domesticating Information Technology*. Oxford University Press: Oxford, 2006, pp. 128–144.

Livingstone, Sonia: "Taking Risky Opportunities in Youthful Content Creation: Teenagers' Use of Social Networking Sites for Intimacy, Privacy and Self-expression." *New Media & Society* 10(3), 2008, pp. 393–411.

Locke, John: *Two Treatises of Government*. For Whitmore and Fenn, and C. Brown: London, 1821.

Long, William J. / Quek, Marc P.: "Personal Data Privacy Protection in An Age of Globalization: The US-EU Safe Harbor Compromise." *Journal of European Public Policy* 9(3), 2002, pp. 325–344.

Lupia, Arthur / Philpot, Tasha S.: "Views from Inside the Net: How Websites Affect Young Adults' Political Interest." *Journal of Politics* 67(4), 2005, pp. 1122–1142.

Macgowan, John: *Sidelights on Chinese Life*. J.B. Lippincott Company: Philadephia, 1908.

MacKinnon, Rebecca: "Flatter World and Thicker Walls? Blogs, Censorship and Civic Discourse in China." *Public Choice* 134(1–2), 2008, pp. 31–46.

Malhotra, Naresh K., et al.: "Internet Users' Information Privacy Concerns (IUIPC): The Construct, the Scale, and A Causal Model." *Information Systems Research* 15(4), 2004, pp. 336–355.

Malinowski, Bronislaw: *Crime and Custom in Savage Society-An Anthropological Study of Savagery*. Transaction Publishers: New Brunswick and London, 2013.

Markus, Hazel R. / Kitayama, Shinobu: "Culture and the Self: Implications for Cognition, Emotion, and Motivation." *Psychological Review* 98(2), 1991, pp. 224–253.

Marshall, Tara C.: "Cultural Differences in Intimacy: The Influence of Gender-Role Ideology and Individualism—Collectivism." *Journal of Social and Personal Relationships* 25(1), 2008, pp. 143–168.

Marx, Gary: "Identity and Anonymity: Some Conceptual Distinctions and Issues for Research." In: Caplan, Jane / John Torpey (eds.): *Documenting Individual Identity: The Development of State Practices in the Modern World*. Princeton University Press: Princeton and Oxford, 2001, pp. 311–327.

Maslach, Christina, et al.: "Individuation: Conceptual Analysis and Assessment." *Journal of Personality and Social psychology* 49(3), 1985, pp. 729–738.

Matthes, Jörg, et al.: "Exemplifying a Dispositional Approach to Cross-cultural Spiral of Silence Research: Fear of Social Isolation and the Inclination to Self-censor." *International Journal of Public Opinion Research* 24(3), 2012, pp. 287–305.

Mauss, Marcel / Halls, Wilfred D.: *The Gift: Forms and Functions of Exchange in Archaic Societies*. Routledge: London, 1990.

Mayer, Roger C., et al.: "An Integrative Model of Organizational Trust." *Academy of Management Review* 20(3), 1995, pp. 709–734.

McCormick, Barrett L. / Liu, Qing (2003). Globalization and the Chinese Media. In: Lee, Chin-chuan (eds.): *Chinese Media, Global Contexts*. C.-C. Lee. London and New York, RoutledgeCruzon, 2003, pp. 139–158.

McDevitt, Michael, et al.: "Spiral of Moderation: Opinion Expression in Computer-mediated Discussion." *International Journal of Public Opinion Research* 15(4), 2003, pp. 454–470.

McKenna, Katelyn Y. A. / Bargh, John A.: "Plan 9 from Cyberspace: The Implications of the Internet for Personality and Social Psychology." *Personality and Social Psychology Review* 4(1), 2000, pp. 57–75.

McLeod, Jack M.: "Media and Civic Socialization of Youth." *Journal of Adolescent Health* 27(2), 2000, pp. 45–51.

McLuhan, Marshall: *Understanding Media: The Extensions of Man*. MIT Press: Cambridge, 1994.

Mead, George. H.: *The Individual and the Social Self*. University of Chicago Press: Chicago, 1982.

Metzger, Miriam J.: "Privacy, Trust, and Disclosure: Exploring Barriers to Electronic Commerce." *Journal of Computer-Mediated Communication* 9, 2004, retrieved 10.8.2014, from DOI: 10.1111/j.1083-6101.2004.tb00292.x.

Meyrowitz, Joshua: *No Sense of Place: The Impact of Electronic Media on Social Behavior*. Oxford University Press: New York and Oxford, 1985.

Milberg, Sandra J., et al.: "Values, Personal Information Privacy, and Regulatory Approaches." *Communications of the ACM* 38(12), 1995, pp. 65–74.

Milberg, Sandra J., et al.: "Information Privacy: Corporate Management and National Regulation." *Organization science* 11(1), 2000, pp. 35–57.

Mill, John Stuart: *On Liberty and Other Essays*. Oxford University Press: Oxford, 2008.

Miller, Lynn C., et al.: "Openers: Individuals Who Elicit Intimate Self-disclosure." *Journal of Personality and Social psychology* 44(6), 1983, pp. 1234–1244.

Millward, Steven (2013). *The Numbers on China's Top 10 Social Media Sites, 13.3.2013*, retrieved 10.11.2014, from https://www.techinasia.com/2013-china-top-10-social-sites-infographic.

Minkus, Tehila / Memon, Nasir. *On A Scale from 1 to 10, How Private Are You? Scoring Facebook Privacy Settings*. Proceedings of the Workshop on Usable Security (USEC 2014), San Diego, Internet Society, 2014, retrieved 26.9.2015, from http://cse.poly.edu/~tehila/pubs/Usec2014.pdf.

Molm, Linda D., et al.: "Risk and Trust in Social Exchange: An Experimental Test of A Classical Proposition." *American Journal of Sociology* 105(5), 2000, pp. 1396–1427.

Morahan-Martin, Janet / Schumacher, Phyllis: "Loneliness and Social Uses of the Internet." *Computers in Human Behavior* 19(6), 2003, PP. 659–671.

Mou, Yi, et al.: "Predicting Political Discussion in A Censored Virtual Environment." *Political Communication* 28(3), 2011, pp. 341–356.

Neuwirth, Kurt / Frederick, Edward: "Peer and Social Influence on Opinion Expression Combining the Theories of Planned Behavior and the Spiral of Silence." *Communication Research* 31(6), 2004, pp. 669–703.

Nhan, Vi L.: "Media in China: Methods of State Control." *The Orator* 3, 2008, pp. 36–50.

Nielson: *State of the Media: The Social Media Report 2012*, retrieved May 12th, 2013, from http://www.nielsen.com/us/en/reports/2012/state-of-the-media-the-social-media-report-2012.html.

Niemi, Richard G., et al.: "Measuring Internal Political Efficacy in the 1988 National Election Study." *The American Political Science Review* 85(4), 1991, pp. 1407–1413.

Nissenbaum, Helen: "Privacy as Contextual Integrity." *Washington Law Review* 79(1), 2004, pp. 119–158.

Noelle-Neumann, Elisabeth: *The Spiral of Silence: Public Opinion, Our Social Skin*. University of Chicago Press: Chicago and London, 1993.

Norris, Pippa: *Digital Divide: Civic Engagement, Information Poverty, and the Internet Worldwide*. Cambridge University Press: Cambridge, New York, Port Melbourne, Madrid and Cape Town, 2001.

Norris, Pippa: "Preaching to the Converted? Pluralism, Participation and Party Websites." *Party Politics* 9(1), 2003, pp. 21–45.

Norris, Pippa / Inglehart, Ronald: *Cosmopolitan Communications: Cultural Diversity in A Globalized World*. Cambridge University Press: New York, 2009.

Oxford English Dictionary (OED), 2014, retrieved 15.10.2014, from http://www.oed.com/.

Okdie, Bradley M. / Guadagno, Rosanna E.: "Social Influence and Computer Mediated Communication." In: Kelsey, Sigrid / Kirk St. Amant (eds.): *Handbook of Research on Computer Mediated Communication*. Information Science Reference: Hershey and New York, 2008, pp. 477–491.

Oyserman, Daphna., et al.: "Rethinking Individualism and Collectivism: Evaluation of Theoretical Assumptions and Meta-analyses." *Psychological Bulletin* 128(1), 2002, pp. 3–72.

Pan, Yue / Zinkhan, George M.: "Exploring the Impact of Online Privacy Disclosures on Consumer Trust." *Journal of Retailing* 82(4), 2006, pp. 331–338.

Papacharissi, Zizi: "The Virtual Sphere: The Internet as A Public Sphere." *New Media & Society* 4(1), 2002, p. 9–27.

Papacharissi, Zizi: "The Virtual Sphere 2.0: The Internet, the Public Sphere, and Beyond." In: Chadwick, Andrew / Philip Howard (eds.): *Routledge Handbook of Internet Politics*. Routledge: New York, 2009, pp. 230–245.

Papacharissi, Zizi: *A Private Sphere: Democracy in A Digital Age*. Polity: Cambridge, 2010.

Park, Namsu, et al.: "Being Immersed in Social Networking Environment: Facebook Groups, Uses and Gratifications, and Social Outcomes." *Cyber Psychology & Behavior* 12(6), 2009, pp. 729–733.

Pateman, Carole: Feminist Critiques of the Public/Private Dichotomy. In: Grewal, Inderpal / Caren Kaplan (eds.): *An Introduction to Women's Studies:*

Gender in a Transnational World (2nd edition). McGraw-Hill Education: Boston, 2006, pp. 155–160.

Petronio, Sandra: "Communication Boundary Management: A Theoretical Model of Managing Disclosure of Private Information between Marital Couples." *Communication Theory* 1(4), 1999, pp. 311–335.

Petronio, Sandra: *Boundaries of Privacy: Dialectics of Disclosure*. State University of New York Press: Albany, 2002.

Pinkleton, Bruce E. / Austin, Erica W.: "Individual Motivations, Perceived Media Importance, and Political Disaffection." *Political Communication* 18(3), 2001, pp. 321–334.

Pinkleton, Bruce E., et al.: "Relationships of Media Use and Political Disaffection to Political Efficacy and Voting Behavior." *Journal of Broadcasting & Electronic Media* 42(1), 1998, pp. 34–49.

Pistole, M. Carole: "Attachment Relationships: Self-disclosure and Trust." *Journal of Mental Health Counseling* 15(1), 1999, pp. 94–106.

Polat, Rabia K.: "The Internet and Political Participation Exploring the Explanatory Links." *European Journal of Communication* 20(4), 2005, pp. 435–459.

Poor, Nathaniel (2005) "Mechanisms of An Online Public Sphere: The Website Slashdot." *Journal of Computer-Mediated Communication* 10, 2005, retrieved 12.7.2014, from DOI: 10.1111/j.1083-6101.2005.tb00241.x.

Posey, Clay, et al.: "Proposing the Online Community Self-disclosure Model: The Case of Working Professionals in France and the UK Who Use Online Communities." *European Journal of Information Systems* 19(2), 2010, pp. 181–195.

Postmes, Tom, et al.: "Intergroup Differentiation in Computer-mediated Communication: Effects of Depersonalization." *Group Dynamics: Theory, Research, and Practice* 6(1), 2002, pp. 3–16.

Preece, Jenny: "Sociability and Usability: Twenty Years of Chatting Online." *Behavior and Information Technology Journal* 20(5), 2001, pp. 347–356.

Preece, Jenny: Creating Usability and Sociability in Online Social Spaces, 2006, retrieved 2.3.2014, from http://webcast.oii.ox.ac.uk/?view=Webcast&ID=20060608_149.

Prommer, Elizabeth, et al. (2009). *"Real Life Extension" in Web-basierten Sozialen Netzwerken: Studie zur Selbstrepräsentation von Studierenden in StudiVZ*, Berlin, Filmuniversität Babelsberg Konrad Wolf, 2009, retrieved J15.6.2014, from http://opus.kobv.de/hff/volltexte/2009/58/pdf/StudiVZ_Bericht_gesamt_ep_Januar09.pdf.

Punch, Keith F.: *Introduction to Social Research: Quantitative and Qualitative Approaches*. Sage: London, Thousand Oaks, New Delhi and Singapore, 2013.

Putnam, Robert D.: "Bowling Alone: America's Declining Social Capital." *Journal of Democracy* 6(1), 1995, pp. 65–78.

Qian, Hua / Scott, Craig R.: "Anonymity and Self-Disclosure on Weblogs." *Journal of Computer-Mediated Communication* 12(4), 2007, pp. 1428–1451.

Rafaeli, Sheizaf / Ariel, Yaron (2007). Assessing Interactivity in Computer-mediated Research. *Oxford Handbook of Internet Psychology.* A. N. Joinson, K. Y. A. McKenna, T. Postmes and U.-D. Reips. Oxford University Press: Oxford, 2007, pp. 71–88.

Rantanen, Terhi: *The Media and Globalization.* Sage: London, Thousand Oaks, New Delhi, 2005.

Redl, Anke / Simons, Rowan: "Chinese Media- One Channel, Two Systems." In: Donald, Stephanie H. / Yin Hong / Michael Keane (eds.): *Media in China: Consumption, Content and Crisis.* RoutledgeCurzon: New York, 2002, pp. 18–27.

Reinecke, Leonard / Trepte, Sanbine: „Privatsphäre 2.0: Konzepte von Privatheit, Intimsphäre und Werten im Umgang mit ‚user-generated-content'." *Kommunikation, Partizipation und Wirkungen im Social Web* 1, 2008, pp. 205–228.

Robertson, Roland: *Globalization: Social Theory and Global Culture.* Sage: London, Thousand Oaks and New Delhi, 1992.

Robertson, Scott P., et al.: "Off the Wall Political Discourse: Facebook Use in The 2008 US Presidential Election." *Information Polity* 15(1), 2010, pp. 11–31.

Rollman, J. Brian, et al.: "The Chat Room Phenomenon: Reciprocal Communication in Cyberspace." *Cyber Psychology and Behavior* 3(2), 2000, pp. 161–166.

Rollman, J. Brian / Parente, Fredrick: "Relation of Statement Length and Type and Type of Chat Room to Reciprocal Communication on the Internet." *Cyber Psychology & Behavior* 4(5), 2001, pp. 617–622.

Salmon, Charles. T. / Neuwirth, Kurt: "Perceptions of Opinion 'Climates' and Willingness to Discuss the Issue of Abortion." *Journalism & Mass Communication Quarterly* 67(3), 1990, pp. 567–577.

Samuelson, Pamela: "Privacy as Intellectual Property?" *Stanford Law Review* 52(5), 2000, pp. 1125–1173.

Savicki, Victor: "Outcomes of Nonreciprocal Self-disclosure Strategies." *Journal of Personality and Social psychology* 23(2), 1972, pp. 271–276.

Schönhagen, Philomen: *Soziale Kommunikation im Internet: zur Theorie und Systematik computervermittelter Kommunikation vor dem Hintergrund der Kommunikationsgeschichte.* Peter Lang: Bern, 2004.

Scheufele, Dietram A.: "Opinion Climates, Spirals of Silence and Biotechnology: Public Opinion as A Heuristic for Scientific Decision-making." In: Brossard, Dominique / James Shanahan / T. Clint Nesbitt: *The Media, the Public and*

Agricultural Biotechnology. CAB International: Oxon and Cambridge, 2007, pp. 231–244.

Scheufele, Dietram A.: "Examining Differential Gains from Mass Media and Their Implications for Participatory Behavior." *Communication Research* 29(1), 2002, pp. 46–65.

Schiewe, Jürgen: *Öffentlichkeit: Entstehung und Wandel in Deutschland*. Schöningh: Paderborn, München, Wien and Zürich, 2003.

Schildt, Axel / Siegfried, Detlef: *Deutsche Kulturgeschichte: Die Bundesrepublik – 1945 bis zur Gegenwart*. Carl Hanser Verlag: München, 2009.

Schouten, Alexander P.: *Adolescents' Online Self-disclosure and Self-presentation*. (Doctoral Dissertation) Faculty of Social and Behavioural Sciences. Amsterdam, Amsterdam School of Communication Research (ASCoR), 2007, retrieved 15.3.2014, from www.alexanderschouten.nl/thesis_aschouten.pdf.

Schouten, Alexander P., et al.: "An Experimental Test of Processes Underlying Self-disclosure in Computer-mediated Communication." *Cyberpsychology* 3(2), 2009, pp. 1–15.

Schug, Joanna, et al.: "Relational Mobility Explains Between-and Within-Culture Differences in Self-disclosure to Close Friends." *Psychological Science* 21(10), 2010, pp. 1471–1478.

Schulz, Anne / Roessler, Patrick: "The Spiral of Silence and the Internet: Selection of Online Content and the Perception of the Public Opinion Climate in Computer-mediated Communication Environments." *International Journal of Public Opinion Research* 24(3), 2012, pp. 346–367.

Sennet, Richard: *The Fall of Public Man: On the Social Psychology of Capitalism*. Cambridge University Press: Cambridge, London and Melbourne, 1976.

Sheldon, Pavica: ""I'll Poke You. You'll Poke Me!" Self-disclosure, Social Attraction, Predictability and Trust As Important Predictors of Facebook Relationships." *Cyberpsychology: Journal of Psychosocial Research on Cyberspace* 3(2), 2009, fetrieved 2.3.2014, from http://cyberpsychology.eu/view.php?cisloclanku=2009111101&article=1.

Shen, Fei / Liang, Hai: "Cultural Difference, Social Values, or Political Systems? Predicting Willingness to Engage in Online Political Discussion in 75 Societies." *International Journal of Public Opinion Research* 27(1), 2014, pp. 111–124.

Shen, Fei, et al.: "Online Network Size, Efficacy, and Opinion Expression: Assessing the Impacts of Internet Use in China." *International Journal of Public Opinion Research* 21(4), 2009, pp. 451–476.

Shoemaker, Pamela J., et al.: "Fear of Social Isolation: Testing An Assumption from the Spiral of Silence." *Irish Communications Review* 8, 2000, pp. 65–78.

Siri, Jasmin, et al.: „The Political Network: Parteien und politische Kommunikation auf Facebook.“ *kommunikation @ gesellschaft* 6, 2012, retrieved 10.6.2014, from http://www.ssoar.info/ssoar/bitstream/handle/document/28273/B6_2012_Siri_Melchner_Wolff.pdf?sequence=1.

Smith, Aaron W., et al.: *The Internet and Civic Engagement*. Pew Internet & American Life Project. Washington, Pew Research Center, 2009, retrieved 15.5.2014, from http://www.pewinternet.org/files/old-media/Files/Reports/2009/The%20Internet%20and%20Civic%20Engagement.pdf.

Stanton, Jeffrey M.: "An Empirical Assessment of Data Collection Using the Internet." *Personnel Psychology* 51(3), 1998, pp. 709–725.

Suh, Hyungjun, et al.: "Type of Trust and Political Participation in Five Countries: Results of Social Quality Survey." *Development and Society* 42(1), 2013, pp. 1–28.

Sundar, S. Shyam / Nass, Clifford: "Source Orientation in Human-Computer Interaction Programmer, Networker, or Independent Social Actor." *Communication Research* 27(6), 2000, pp. 683–703.

Sunstein, Cass R.: *Republic.com*. Princeton, Princeton University Press, 2001.

Sunstein, Cass R.: *Republic.com 2.0*. Princeton, Princeton University Press, 2009.

Taddicken, Monika: "The 'Privacy Paradox'in the Social Web: the Impact of Privacy Concerns, Individual Characteristics, and the Perceived Social Relevance on Different Forms of Self-Disclosure." *Journal of Computer-Mediated Communication* 19(2), 2014, pp. 248–273.

Taddicken, Monika / Jers, Cornelia: "The Uses of Privacy Online: Trading A Loss of Privacy for Social Web Gratifications." *Privacy Online: Perspectives on Privacy and Self-disclosure in the Social Web*. S. Trepte and L. Reinecke. Heidelberg, Springer, 2011, pp. 143–158.

Tai, Zixue: *The Internet in China: Cyberspace and Civil Society*. Routledge: New York and London, 2013.

Taylor, Dalmas A. / Altman, Irwin: "Self-disclosure as a Function of Reward-Cost Outcomes." *Sociometry* 38(1), 1975, pp. 18–31.

Tesser, Abraham / Shaffer, David R.: "Attitudes and Attitude Change." *Annual Review of Psychology* 41(1): 479–523, 1990.

The World Bank (2015). *Global Purchasing Power Parities and Real Expenditures*, 2015, retrieved 30.5.2015, from http://knoema.de/nwnfkne/world-gdp-ranking-2015-data-and-charts.

Thompson, John B.: *The Media and Modernity: A Social Theory of the Media*. Polity Press: Cambridge, 1995.

Thompson, John B.: "Shifting Boundaries of Public and Private Life." *Theory, Culture & Society* 28(4), 2011, p. 49–70.

Thompson, Lori F., et al.: "From Paper to Pixels: Moving Personnel Surveys to the Web." *Personnel Psychology* 56(1), 2003, pp. 197–227.

Tidwell, Lisa C. / Joseph B. Walther: "Computer-mediated Communication Effects on Disclosure, Impressions, and Interpersonal Evaluations: Getting to Know One Another a Bit at a Time." *Human Communication Research* 28(3), 2002, pp. 317–348.

Trepte, Sabine / Reinecke, Leonard: "The Reciprocal Effects of Social Network Site Use and the Disposition for Self-disclosure: A Longitudinal Study." *Computers in Human Behavior* 29(3), 2012, pp. 1102–1112.

Triandis, Harry C.: "Individualism-Collectivism and Personality." *Journal of Personality* 69(6), 2001, pp. 907–924.

Tufekci, Zeynep: "Grooming, Gossip, Facebook and MySpace: What Can We Learn about These Sites from Those Who Won't Assimilate?" *Information, Communication & Society* 11(4), 2008, pp. 544–564.

Turkle, Sherry: *Life on the Screen: Identity in the Age of the Internet*. New York, Touchstone, 1997.

Tverdek, Edward: "What Makes Information "Public"?" *Public Affairs Quarterly* 22(1), 2008, pp. 63–77.

UN: *International Covenant on Civil and Political Rights*, 1996, retrieved 30.5.2015, from http://www.ohchr.org/en/professionalinterest/pages/ccpr.aspx.

Valenzuela, Sebastián, et al.: "Social Networks That Matter: Exploring the Role of Political Discussion for Online Political Participation." *International Journal of Public Opinion Research* 24(2), 2012, pp. 163–184.

Van Deth, Jan W. / Elff, Martin: "Politicisation, Economic Development, and Political Interest in Europe." *European Journal of Political Research* 43(3), 2004, pp. 477–508.

Van House, Nancy: *Weblogs: Credibility and Collaboration in an Online World.* Computer Supported Cooperative Work Workshop, Chicago, 2004, retrieved 18.5.2015, http://people.ischool.berkeley.edu/~vanhouse/Van%20House%20trust%20workshop.pdf.

VanLear, C. Arthur: "The Formation of Social Relationships: A Longitudinal Study of Social Penetration." *Human Communication Research* 13(3), 1987, pp. 299–322.

Venkatesh, Viswanath, et al.: "User Acceptance of Information Technology: Toward a Unified View." *MIS Quarterly* 27(3), 2003, pp. 425–478.

Verba, Sidney, et al.: "Knowing and Caring about Politics: Gender and Political Engagement." *The Journal of Politics* 59(4), 1997, pp. 1051–1072.

Veyne, Paul: "The Roman Empire." In: Veyne, Paul / Phillippe Aries / Georges Duby (eds.): *A History of Private Life: From Pagan Rome to Byzantium.* The Belknap of Harvard University Press: Cambridge and London, 1987, pp. 5–234.

Vitak, Jessica, et al.: *"Poking" People to Participate: Facebook and Political Participation in the 2008 Election.* Annual Meeting of the International Communication Association. Chicago, 2009, retrieved 30.5.2015, from https://www.academia.edu/attachments/30913693/download_file?st=MTQ4MDIzODMzMCwyMjEuMjIzLjc2Ljc1LDc2MDIxNDE%3D&s=swp-toolbar.

Vitak, Jessica, et al.: "It's Complicated: Facebook Users' Political Participation in the 2008 Election." *Cyberpsychology, Behavior, and Social Networking* 14(3), 2011, pp. 107–114.

Wagner, Hans: „Das Fachstichwort: Massenkommunikation." In: Groth, Otto (hrsg.): *Vermittelte Mitteilung. Ein journalistisches Modell der Massenkommunikation.* Reinhard Fischer: München, 1998, S. 187–240.

Walther, Joseph. B.: "Computer-mediated Communication Impersonal, Interpersonal, and Hyperpersonal Interaction." *Communication Research* 23(1), 1996, pp. 3–43.

Warren, Mark E.: *Democracy and Trust.* Cambridge University Press: Cambridge, 1999.

Waters, Susan / Ackerman, James: "Exploring Privacy Management on Facebook: Motivations and Perceived Consequences of Voluntary Disclosure." *Journal of Computer-Mediated Communication* 17(1), 2011, pp. 101–115.

Weintraub, Jeff: "The Theory and Politics of the Public/Private Distinction." In: Weintraub, Jeff / Krishan Kumar (eds.): *Public and Private in Thought and Practice: Perspectives on a Grand Dichotomy.* The University of Chicago Press: Chicago and London, 1997, pp. 1–42.

West, Anne, et al.: "Facebook 'Friends': Public and Private Spheres." In: Webber, Michelle / Kate Bezanson (eds.): *Rethinking Society in the 21st Century: Critical Readings in Sociology.* Canadian Scholars' Press Inc.: Toronto, 2009, pp. 147–160.

West, Richard L. / Turner, Lynne H. *Introducing Communication Theory: Analysis and Application.* McGraw-Hill Education: New York, 2006.

Wheeless, Lawrence R.: "A Follow-up Study of the Relationships among Trust, Disclosure, and Interpersonal Solidarity." *Human Communication Research* 4(2), 1978, pp. 143–157.

Wheeless, Lawrence R. / Grotz, Jams: "Conceptualization and Measurement of Reported Self-disclosure." *Human Communication Research* 2(4), 1976, pp. 338–346.

Wheeless, Lawrence R. / Grotz, Jams: "The Measurement of Trust and Its Relationship to Self-disclosure." *Human Communication Research* 3(3), 1977, pp. 250–257.

Won-Doornink, Myong J.: "Self-disclosure and Reciprocity in Conversation: A Cross-national Study." *Social Psychology Quarterly* 48(2), 1985, pp. 97–107.

Woong Yun, Gi / Park, Sung-Yeon: "Selective Posting: Willingness to Post a Message Online." *Journal of Computer-Mediated Communication* 16(2), 2011, pp. 201–227.

Worthy, Mogan, et al.: "Self-disclosure as an Exchange Process." *Journal of Personality and Social Psychology* 13(1), 1969, pp. 59–63.

Wright, Kevin B.: "Researching Internet-based Populations: Advantages and Disadvantages of Online Survey Research, Online Questionnaire Authoring Software Packages, and Web Survey Services." *Journal of Computer-Mediated Communication* 10, 2005, retrieved 12.6.2014, from DOI: 10.1111/j.1083-6101.2005.tb00259.x.

Wu, Jingwei: *Communication Technology and Willingness to Speak Out: The Impact of Social Media in China*. World Association for Public Opinion Research 66th annual conference. Boston, US, 2013, retrieved 26.5.2015, from https://www.academia.edu/attachments/50565185/download_file?st=MTQ4MDIxODQ0MiwyMjEuMjIzLjc2Ljc1LDc2MDIxNDE%3D&s=profile.

Wu, Jingwei / Lu, Heng: "Cultural and Gender Differences in Self-Disclosure on Social Networking Sites." In: Petley, Julian (eds.): *Media and Public Shaming: Drawing the Boundaries of Disclosure*. I B Tauris: London, 2013, pp. 97–114.

Wu, Yanfang, et al.: "A Comparative Study of Online Privacy Regulations in the US and China." *Telecommunications Policy* 35(7), 2011, pp. 603–616.

Wynn, Eleanor / Katz, James E.: "Hyperbole over Cyberspace: Self-presentation and Social Boundaries in Internet Home Pages and Discourse." *The Information Society* 13(4), 1997, pp. 297–327.

Yan, Yunxiang: *The Individualization of Chinese Society*. Berg: Oxford and New York, 2009.

Yang, Guobin / Calhoun, Craig: "Media, Civil Society, and the Rise of a Green Public Sphere in China." *China Information* 21(2), 2007, pp. 211–236.

Young, Alyson L. / Quan-Haase, Anabel: *Information Revelation and Internet Privacy Concerns on Social Network Sites: A Case Study of Facebook*. Proceedings of the fourth international conference on Communities and technologies, Philadelphia, ACM, 2009.

Yuan, Elaine J., et al.: ""Privacy" in Semantic Networks on Chinese Social Media: The Case of Sina Weibo." *Journal of Communication* 63(6), 2013, pp. 1011–1031.

Zhang, Weiwu, et al. (2010). "The Revolution Will be Networked: The Influence of Social Networking Sites on Political Attitudes and Behavior." *Social Science Computer Review* 28(1), 2010, pp. 75–92.

Zhao, C., et al. (2012). *How and to Whom People Share: The Role of Culture in Self-disclosure in Online Communities*. Proceedings of the ACM 2012 conference on Computer Supported Cooperative Work, Seattle, ACM, 2012, retrieved 6.6.2014, from DOI: 10.1145/2145204.2145219.

Zhou, Xiang, et al.: "Deliberativeness of Online Political Discussion: A Content Analysis of the Guangzhou Daily Website." *Journalism Studies* 9(5), 2008, pp. 759–770.

Zittrain, Jonathan L.: "What the Publisher Can Teach the Patient: Intellectual Property and Privacy in an Era of Trusted Privication." *Stanford Law Review* 52: 2000, pp. 1201–1250.

沟口雄三: *中国的公与私* (*Public and Private in China*).生活.读书.新知三联书店: 北京, 2011.

Appendixes

A. Questionnaire

Thank you for joining our survey!

This survey queries the ways in which you share personal information and political opinions on social network sites (SNSs), and the audience to whom this information is visible. If you are a student between 18–35 years old and you use Facebook, I would like to invite you to fill out the questionnaire. Your participation in the study is very vital, so please take 10 minutes to complete the survey.

Your information will confidential and anonymous for the purpose of this academic research.

Thank you very much!

Jingwei Wu, Institut für Publizistik- und Kommunikationswissenschaft, FU Berlin

---

Q1. Which one of the following SNSs do you use most?
German users: [1] Facebook [2] Google+ [3] None of them
Chinese users: [4] Renren [5]Qzone [6]Sina Weibo

Q2. What kind of name do you use on your online profile of SNSs currently?
[1] Obvious pseudonym (e.g., Katzenliebhaber 134)
[2] Non-obvious pseudonym (e.g., Hans Müller, which sounds like a real name but is not your real name)
[3] Partial real name (like your real first name, or last name, nick name, or initials only)
[4] Full real name
[5] Others (please describe your name) ______________________

Q3. What type of photo do you use as your current profile picture?
[1] I do not use any photo
[2] A borrowed picture, e.g. a celebrity, landscape or other image, like cartoons or animals
[3] A photo of my family members or friends, excluding myself (e.g., my son's photo)
[4] A partially obscured picture (e.g., my real picture but with my face doctored or hidden in the shadow)
[5] An actual photo with my family or friends

[6] A real picture of me alone
[7] Others (please describe your profile photo)________________________

Q4. Here are some statements about SNSs. Please tell us how strongly you agree or disagree with them. 1=*strongly disagree* → 5=*strongly agree*
[1] SNSs is part of my daily activity
[2] I use SNSs several times a day
[3] I feel out of touch when I haven't logged onto SNSs for a while
[4] I don't feel that I belong to the SNSs community

Q5. Here are some statements about privacy on SNSs. Can you tell us how strongly you agree or disagree with each? Please read out and code one answer for each statement.
1=strongly disagree → 5=strongly agree
[1] I don't think any stranger can see my personal information
[2] I don't care that any stranger may see my personal information
[3] I'm concerned about my privacy, but it doesn't affect my use of SNSs
[4] I'm trying to keep strangers away from my profile through the privacy settings of SNSs
[5] I'm worried about my privacy and I'm thinking of quitting SNSs

Q6. Do you fill the following information on your SNSs profile? If "Yes", who can see this information? (If you have forgotten, you can double-check with your profile)

* *Also includes friends of friends*
** *"Public" also includes the situation that "you open your information to all on SNSs but not for family".*

Items	**Yes, who can see it?**						**No**
	Only me	**Family**	**Friend**	**Colleague / Classmate**	***Friend on SNSs**	****Public**	
Gender							
Birthday							
Local residence							
Employer							
School/University							
Relationships							
Contact Info. (e.g. Email)							

Items	Yes, who can see it?						No
	Only me	**Family**	**Friend**	**Colleague / Classmate**	***Friend on SNSs**	****Public**	
Photos of oneself alone							
Photos with family							
Photos with friend							
Photos with colleague/ classmate							

* *Also includes friends of friends*
** *"Public" also includes the situation that "you open your information to all on SNSs but not for family".*

Q7. How many "friends" in total do you have in your SNSs friend list currently?

____

(If you have forgotten, you can double-check with your profile)

Q8. Can you estimate the number of users in each of the following categories? (Please fill a number for each blank. Note: the sum of the following shouldn't exceed the number that you've provided in Q7)

Family Members ____________
Close/best friends (incl. a romantic partner) ____________
Colleagues /Classmates ____________
Acquaintances ____________
Strangers (incl. people who you met on SNSs and have never met offline) ____________

Q9. How often do you update or post the following information on SNSs? From the categories of family, friend, colleagues/classmates, acquaintances and public, who can see this information?

How often do you update or post?	Who can see this information
0 Never	0 Never update or post
1 Rarely	1 Only me
2 Several days a month	2 Family
3 Several days a week	3 Friend
4 Once a day	4 Colleague/Classmate
5 Many times a day	5 *Friend on SNSs
	6 **Public

* *Also includes friends of friends*
** *"Public" also includes the situation that "you open your information to all on SNSs but not for family".*

[1] My personal habits
[2] Things I have done which I feel guilty about
[3] Things I would not do in public
[4] My deepest feelings
[5] What I like and dislike about myself
[6] What is important to me in life
[7] What makes me the person I am
[8] My worst fears things
[9] I have done which I am proud of
[10] Close relationships with other people

Q10. For the following statements, can you tell me how strongly you agree or disagree with each? Please read out and code one answer for each statement.
1=strongly disagree → 5=strongly agree
[1] When I see others posting personal information on SNSs, I believe that they expect me to do the same
[2] Other SNSs users trust me to return the favor of sharing personal information
[3] I know that other users post information about themselves on SNSs, so it is only fair to do the same
[4] People who are important to me think that I should participate on SNSs
[5] People who influence my behavior encourage me to participate on SNSs
[6] I use SNSs because a lot of my friends use it

[7] Overall, the people in my friend list of SNSs are NOT trustworthy
[8] People on my SNSs friend-list are usually considerate of other's feelings
[9] Generally, people in my friend list of SNSs are friendly
[10] I can rely on those to whom I disclose personal information in my SNSs

Continued with last page, please read out and code how strongly you agree or disagree with the following statements.

[1] In general, it is risky to post my personal information in SNSs
[2] There is a high potential for loss associated with posting my personal information in SNSs
[3] Some uncertainties may arise when posting my personal information in SNSs
[4] Providing others with my personal information in SNSs involves many unexpected problems
[5] I feel safe giving my personal information to others in SNSs (RE)
[6] While participating in SNSs, I experienced pleasure
[7] The process of participating in SNSs is enjoyable
[8] I have fun using SNSs

Q11. To what extent do you think you are anonymous on SNSs?

Totally anonymous---→Totally identifiable				
1	2	3	4	5

Q12. How often do you share political information or sentiments on SNSs? From the categories of family members, friends, colleagues/classmates, acquaintances and public, who can see this information?

How often do you post or share?	**Who can see this information**
0 Never	0 Never update or post
1 Rarely	1 Only me
2 Several days a month	2 Family
3 Several days a week	3 Friend
4 Once a day	4 Colleague /Classmate
5 Many times a day	5 *Friend on SNSs
	6 **Public

* *Also includes friends of friends.*
** *"Public" also includes the situation that "you publish your information to everyone on SNSs except for family".*

[1] Posting personal experiences related to politics or campaigning
[2] Sharing a public profile of political news, political advocate or politician
[3] Posting or sharing thoughts about politics
[4] Posting or sharing photos, videos, or audio files about politics
[5] Forwarding political commentaries of others to somebody else

Q13. For the following statements, can you tell me how strongly you agree or disagree with each? Please select one answer for each statement.
1=strongly disagree → 5=strongly agree
[1] It's difficult for me to express my opinion if I think others won't agree with what I say
[2] There have been many times when I have thought others around me were wrong but I didn't let them know
[3] When I disagree with others, I'd rather go along with them than argue about it
[4] It's easy for me to express my opinion around others who I think will disagree with me
[5] I'd feel uncomfortable if someone asked my opinion and I knew that he or she wouldn't agree with me
[6] I tend speak my opinion only around friends or other people I trust
[7] It's safer to keep quiet than publicly speaking an opinion that you know most others don't share
[8] If I disagree with others, I have no problem letting them know it

Continued with last page, please select how strongly you agree or disagree with the following statements.
1=strongly disagree → 5=strongly agree
[1] SNSs can help people have a say about politics
[2] Political discussion in SNSs can NOT influence the government
[3] SNSs can help people be better informed about political affairs
[4] People like me don't have any say about what the government does
[5] Sometimes politics and government seem so complicated that a person like me can't really understand what's going on

Continued with last page, please select how strongly you agree or disagree with the following statements.
1=strongly disagree → 5=strongly agree
[1] I trust the information from the press
[2] I DON'T trust the information from public TV (RE)
[3] I trust the information from private TV
[4] I trust the information posted on SNSs

[5] I believe that the news from the press is reliable
[6] I believe that the news from public TV is reliable
[7] I believe that the news from private TV is NOT reliable (RE)
[8] I believe that the news posted in SNSs is NOT reliable (RE)
[9] I believe that the news from press is skewed in general (RE)
[10] I believe that the news from public TV is skewed in general (RE)
[11] I believe that the news from private TV is skewed in general (RE)
[12] I believe that the news posted in SNSs is NOT skewed in general

Q14. How interested would you say you are in politics?

Not at all interested--→Very interested				
1	2	3	4	5

Q15. Please indicate your gender: [1] Male [2] Female

Q16. Your age: ________

Q17. You are a:
[1] Bachelor-Student, 1st Semester
[2] Bachelor-Student/in, more than 1st Semester
[3] Master-Student, 1st Semester
[4] Master-Student, more than 1st Semester
[5] Ph.D. student, 1st Semester
[6] Ph.D. student, more than 1st Semester
[7] Diplom-Student, 1st Semester (for German student)
[8] Diplom-Student, more than 1st Semester (for German student)

Q18. After finishing the online questionnaire, we would like to invite some you to join us for an interview. It is an online chat session that will last approximately 40 minutes. You will be asked about your understanding of SNSs as a private or a private space, how you post personal information and public opinions to family, friends, colleagues or even strangers and how you control the visibility of your information and opinions.
Could you please leave your contact information (Email, Skype, Telephone…) here? Your information will be confidential. To thank you for your participation in the interview, an Amazon coupon will be given as a token of appreciation.

____

End of questionnaire.

Thank you very much for your support. If you have any questions about the questionnaire or interview, please contact: wu.jingwei@fu-berlin.de.

B. Question for Semi-Structured Interview

**Interviewees are selected from the pool of respondents who use Facebook, Renren, Qzone and Sina Weibo*

SNSs Use

When and why did you begin using SNSs?

You have been using SNSs for several years now. During this period, do you find a change in your user behavior, such as sharing more or less things on SNSs as compared to before?

When you first began using SNSs, who can see the personal information on your profile and the personal posts on your status? What about now? Did you change the privacy setting after that?

Profile:

Why do you provide a partially/ fully real name on SNSs (most of users)?

–DE users: why did you use a full real name on SNSs?
–CN users: why did you use an obvious pseudonym on SNSs?

Why did you use a borrowed picture/ real photograph on your SNSs profile?

–DE users: why did you post "a real picture in my real life, alone" in your profile?
–CN users: why did you post "a borrowed picture" in your profile?

Why do you share the following information in your profile? And why not? (Refer to the table of profile on the questionnaire for details. Each user is asked about different information.)

Friend list:

Generally, how do you add friend on SNSs (meet offline at first, and then connect online? search the name on SNSs? add according to the suggestion of SNSs)?

What kind of person are they (classmates, colleagues, acquaintance: met once before, or strangers)

Are your family members/parents on your friend-list? Do you have any concern over them seeing your personal information on SNSs?

Why do you (not) add strangers in your friend list?

Privacy concern:

Do you have a target audience or communication partner on your mind before you post something on your status? Who are they?

Do you think strangers can see your personal information on SNSs?

If a stranger wants to add you as an online friend, will you accept his or her request?

Are you concerned about your privacy? What kinds of solution do you undertake to deal with this problem?

Did you change your privacy setting after having used SNSs for a while? Since when did you start having concerns about privacy?

Do you trust the people on your SNSs? Why?

The boundary between *private* and *public*:

Is SNSs a private or a public space for you? Why?

Do you feel happy and positive when using SNSs?

Generally, who can see your political discussion on SNSs? Why?

Comparing the offline and online situations, do you face any pressure from others on SNSs when you express a different opinion from the majority?

Why do (don't) you think SNSs can help you to have a say about politics?

DE: public TV vs. private TV, which do you trust more? Why?
CN: state TV and private TV, which do you trust more? Why?

Do you think the use of SNSs increases your political expression (both online and offline)?

Do you express more political opinion offline or online? Why?

C. Interviewed SNSs users' Demographics

German SNSs Users

- Anna, female, 21, Bachelor student, Facebook user. Facebook message: Jan. 13th, 2015, 19:00–20:00.
- Iwo, female, 27, Ph.D. student, Facebook user. Facebook message: Jan. 3rd, 2015, 20:00–21:10
- Nell, female, 18, Bachelor student, Facebook user. Skype chat: Jan. 15th, 2015, 14:50–16:00
- Denny, male, 28, Ph.D. student, Facebook user. Skype chat: Jan. 15th, 2015, 17:50–19:00
- Kai, male, 25, Master student, Facebook user. Facebook message, Jan. 22nd, 2015, 19:00–20:15
- Julchen, female, 21, Bachelor student, Facebook users. Facebook message: Jan. 23rd, 2015, 15:00–16:00
- John, male, 24, Master student, Facebook user. Facebook message: Jan. 25th, 2015, 18:00–19:00
- Ansgarb, male, 25, Master student, Facebook user. Skype chat, Feb. 5th, 2015, 19:00–20:00
- Eramthgin, male, 22, Bachelor student, Facebook user. Email Interview: Feb. 3rd, 2015
- Fabian, male, 22, Bachelor student, Facebook user. Facebook message, Feb. 7th, 2015, 11:30–12:30

Chinese SNSs Users

- Juan, female, 23, Master student, Q-Zone user. Wechat chat: Jan. 11th, 2015, 13:00–14:00
- Mickey, female, 22, Master student, Renren user. Telephone Interview: Jan. 11th, 2015, 14:00–15:00
- Tang, female, 24, Master student, QQ-Zone user. QQ Chat, Jan. 14th, 2015, 12:00–13:00
- Potter, female, 23, Master student, Sina Weibo users. QQ chat: Jan. 16th, 2015, 14:00–15:30
- Lulu, female, 23, Master student, Sina Weibo user. QQ chat: Jan. 20th, 2015, 14:00–15:00
- Alice, female, 24, Master student, Sina Weibo user. QQ chat: Jan. 22rd, 2015, 16:00–17:00

- InD, male, 22, Master student, Sina Weibo user. QQ chat: Jan. 23rd, 2015, 13:00–14:00
- Tao, male, 25, Master student, Renren users. QQ chat, Feb. 2nd, 2015, 16:00–17:00
- Xu, male, 23, Master student, Sina Weibo user. QQ Chat, Feb. 3rd, 2015, 14:00–15:00
- Ting, female, 22, Master student, Sina Weibo user, QQ Chat, Feb. 6th, 2015, 14:00–15:00

www.ingramcontent.com/pod-product-compliance
Ingram Content Group UK Ltd.
Pitfield, Milton Keynes, MK11 3LW, UK
UKHW021842100926
8556IPUK00019B/1007

9 783631 681039